TABLE OF CONTE

Top 20 Test Taking Tips

1. Carefully follow all the test registration procedures
2. Know the test directions, duration, topics, question types, how many questions
3. Setup a flexible study schedule at least 3-4 weeks before test day
4. Study during the time of day you are most alert, relaxed, and stress free
5. Maximize your learning style; visual learner use visual study aids, auditory learner use auditory study aids
6. Focus on your weakest knowledge base
7. Find a study partner to review with and help clarify questions
8. Practice, practice, practice
9. Get a good night's sleep; don't try to cram the night before the test
10. Eat a well balanced meal
11. Know the exact physical location of the testing site; drive the route to the site prior to test day
12. Bring a set of ear plugs; the testing center could be noisy
13. Wear comfortable, loose fitting, layered clothing to the testing center; prepare for it to be either cold or hot during the test
14. Bring at least 2 current forms of ID to the testing center
15. Arrive to the test early; be prepared to wait and be patient
16. Eliminate the obviously wrong answer choices, then guess the first remaining choice
17. Pace yourself; don't rush, but keep working and move on if you get stuck
18. Maintain a positive attitude even if the test is going poorly
19. Keep your first answer unless you are positive it is wrong
20. Check your work, don't make a careless mistake

Foundations of Linguistics and Language Learning

Stages of first-language acquisition

Children go through five recognizable stages in the development of their primary language skills. The first stage occurs when the child is between six and eight months old, and is known as the babbling stage. During this period, the child begins making repetitive patterns of sound with his mouth. During the one-word (also known as one-morpheme, one-unit, or holophrastic) stage, which extends from nine to eighteen months of age, the child begins to make basic word stems and single open-class words. During the two-word stage, which extends from eighteen to twenty-four months, the child begins making miniature sentences with simple semantic relations. During the telegraphic stage (also known as the early multiword or multimorpheme stage), which extends from twenty-four to thirty months, the child begins to express sentence structures with lexical rather than functional or grammatical morphemes. Finally, during the later multiword stage, which typically occurs after thirty months, the characteristic grammatical or functional structures of the primary language emerge and are incorporated.

Behaviorist model

The behaviorist view of language acquisition, developed by B.F. Skinner, asserts that individuals learn language as a direct response to stimuli. Certain words or patterns of language produce certain activities or events in the external world, and then the individual over time develops a mental response to those stimuli. Correct responses to stimuli are reinforced and therefore perpetuated. There are a few problems with this theory as it applies to language acquisition. For one thing, the creation of language is a somewhat improvisatory act and is therefore difficult to see as a response to stimuli in many cases. Also, many scientists feel that the behaviorist interpretation of language acquisition is overly simplistic and does not take into account the extreme complexity of language. Finally, linguistic response does not always elicit clear and recognizable rewards or punishments, which suggests that it would be difficult for a child to have his responses reinforced.

Nativist model

The nativist model of language acquisition, pioneered by Noam Chomsky, is an attempt to explain how people are able to understand and produce a seemingly infinite number of linguistic expressions. According to this model, individuals are born with a universal grammar wired into their brains, which they use as a template for language acquisition. According to this theory, all a child needs to learn is the specific ways in which his native language utilizes the rules of universal grammar. In other words, the principles of language are innate, and the specific parameters of each language are acquired in the first few years of life. The human mind has a "language acquisition device" that enables the acquisition of the linguistic principles of other languages. This theory remains present in much contemporary thought, though researchers continue to explore the relationship between an innate capacity for language and environmental factors.

Vygotsky and Bronfenbrenner

Vygotsky's sociocultural theory states that learning begins as a result of interpersonal communication and is then internalized as intrapersonal. Vygotsky studied incremental gains in learning and came up with the phrase "zone of proximal development" to describe the difference between what a person knows and what he could know if given a bit of assistance from someone else. The process of giving temporary aid to facilitate learning is called scaffolding, and includes modeling, providing cues, and encouraging the person. Bronfenbrenner's ecological model described development in terms of four nested levels: microsystem (child's immediate environment); mesosystem (interactions between components of the microsystem); exosystem (more general elements of the child's environment); and macrosystem (overarching environmental influences, like cultural beliefs).

Steven Pinker and Jim Cummins

Steven Pinker and Jim Cummins are two of the most prominent living theorists on human language acquisition. Steven Pinker agreed with Noam Chomsky that human beings are born with an innate capacity for learning and understanding language. However, he added the idea that this capacity is the result of millions of years of evolution. According to Pinker, people developed a predisposition towards language because communication increased their odds of survival. Jim Cummins, meanwhile, coined the terms Basic Interpersonal Communicative Skills (BICS) and Cognitive Academic Language Proficiency (CALP), which are distinct types of fluency. In general, BICS is the use of language in informal and social settings, and CALP is the use of language in the classroom. The use of these terms has made it easier for educators to assess linguistic ability.

Social interactionist model

The social interactionist interpretation of language acquisition emphasizes the relationship of the newborn with his caregivers. According to this model, the child will learn to speak in the manner and syntax of those people who speak to him. The child's ever-expanding knowledge of the world and linguistic context will give him tools for understanding language. According to the social interactionists, the child will begin to establish goals in the world and will need to devise linguistic strategies for achieving them. The child will draw on the linguistic and nonlinguistic utterances that he has heard, and will use this information in combination with other knowledge to achieve his ends. The social interactionist model is useful but, like the nativist approach, it does not provide an explanation for the startling ability to improvise language exhibited by even very young children.

Cognitive model

The cognitive model of language acquisition, developed by Piaget, asserts that individuals develop linguistic skills in order to control their environment. Piaget outlined four basic stages of cognitive development: sensorimotor intelligence (zero to two years of age), in which the child learns to physically handle the objects of the external world; preoperational thought (two to seven years), in which the child improves physically and begins to think conceptually; concrete operations (seven to eleven years), in which the child develops logical thinking skills; and formal operations (eleven to fifteen years), in which the child begins to think abstractly and can develop mental hypotheses. As the child moves through these stages, he will work through various strategies of language use. In the assimilation phase, the child uses a known word to describe a new object or concept until he is corrected. In the accommodation phase, the child learns to correct his own errors of linguistic identification. In the equilibrium phase, the child uses the right word to describe the object.

Acquisition-learning model

One model of second-language learning, known as the acquisition-learning hypothesis, posits two ways in which an individual develops proficiency in a second language. The first way is called acquisition, and is the subconscious process by which vocabulary and the basic rules of grammar are slowly and steadily absorbed. Acquisition is the way that small children learn their native language. The second way in which people develop language is called learning: a conscious study and knowledge of vocabulary and the rules of grammar. In general, this theory emphasizes the superiority of acquisition as a means of acquiring fluency. Although learning can be helpful in speeding the process of acquisition, it is ultimately long-term exposure to a language that allows the individual to develop an unconscious sense of its rules and idiom.

Input hypothesis

The input hypothesis is one of Stephen Krashen's models of second-language acquisition. According to this model, individuals need to be given information slightly above their ability level in a given language. As the individual acquires the ability to understand the given material, the level should be raised. In order for acquisition to be possible at all, the learner needs to understand the majority of what he is hearing. However, the addition of a small amount of incomprehensible information will encourage the listener to continue expanding his vocabulary and overall sense of grammatical structures. The input hypothesis can be difficult to apply in a classroom setting, because it is very difficult to set the instruction level at the appropriate point for each child. It is for this reason that self-instruction techniques like reciprocal teaching and scaffolding are essential parts of practice as an ESL teacher.

Monitor hypothesis

The monitor hypothesis explains how learning grammatical rules affects language acquisition. According to this hypothesis, when an individual learns rules of grammar, he is able to monitor consciously the discourse he hears in the future. Over time, learning these rules of grammar encourages the individual to refine and polish his speech. Individuals will use grammatical rules to monitor their speech to a greater or lesser degree depending on temperament. Krashen found that extroverted individuals tend to ignore the rules of grammar and simply plunge ahead, while introverted individuals strive for perfection in their speech. Most language experts agree that the basic rules of grammar will be unconsciously acquired over time regardless of whether they are ever explicitly learned. However, the monitor hypothesis indicates that it can be helpful to learn these rules as a part of second-language training.

Sociocognitive approach

According to the sociocognitive approach to language development, true competence is demonstrated in the ability to express oneself in different social contexts. Unlike the other approaches to language development, the sociocognitive approach emphasizes conversation in social contexts. The sociocognitive school admits that certain semantic, cognitive, and syntactical achievements must be made before language can be produced, but nevertheless asserts that social necessity is the primary motivator of language development. In other words, according to the sociocognitivists, children develop their linguistic ability by engaging with different people. A student must learn to converse with teachers, parents, siblings, other students, and strangers. True language development is evident when a student can modify his expression in these different contexts.

Natural order hypothesis

The natural order hypothesis asserts that the acquisition of a second language will follow predictable patterns. For any given language, certain grammatical structures will almost always be acquired before others, regardless of the age of the learner. This supports the idea that bilingual programs should follow a specific order of instruction. There are occasional exceptions to the natural order of language acquisition, but they are so few as to not merit consideration. Interestingly, Krashen felt that the appropriate specific order of instruction will not be exactly the same as the natural order. He felt that in order to achieve the most rapid and comprehensive acquisition of a second language, a rigid sequence of grammatical instruction should be avoided in favor of immersion and interactive performance.

Affective filter hypothesis

According to the affective filter hypothesis, a number of emotional factors contribute to the acquisition of a second language. Specifically, self-confidence, anxiety, and motivation exert a significant influence on the ability to internalize vocabulary and grammatical rules. The presence of significant anxiety or low self-esteem can make it almost impossible for a student to incorporate comprehensible input in the formation of a new language. This is known as raising the affective filter. It should be noted that the presence of relaxation and high self-esteem does not in and of itself guarantee success in language acquisition; these qualities merely make it possible for the individual to succeed with hard work and aptitude. This hypothesis has been used to stress the importance of establishing a positive and welcoming environment in the bilingual classroom.

BICS

In their consideration of second-language acquisition, experts distinguish between social and academic discourse. The language skills required in social situations are known as Basic Interpersonal Communication Skills (BICS). These are the basic expressions and linguistic formations that an individual will need to conduct himself in normal situations. Students will be using these skills in interactions with their fellow students in the cafeteria, on the playground, and on the school bus. While these interactions are not necessarily demanding in a cognitive sense, they do require a subtle understanding of context. Most students are able to acquire BICS within six to twenty-four months of beginning language study. Teachers are often mistaken when they declare that a student has achieved fluency because the student has developed excellent social language skills. Until a student has also acquired a mastery of formal discourse, he cannot be said to have achieved total fluency.

CALP

The ability to participate in formal and grammatically correct discourse is known as Cognitive Academic Language Proficiency (CALP). Students with adequate CALP are able to listen, speak, read, and write about content material at their grade level. Students are not considered to have achieved total language proficiency until they can do so. Some recent research indicates that achieving CALP takes between five and seven years. This is because academic language acquisition requires not only learning new vocabulary, but also developing academic skills such as comparing, synthesizing, summarizing, and inferring. There is also much less context in academic language than there is in social interaction, so students are constantly forced to utilize their own contextualization skills to understand new information. There is some evidence to suggest that students can use what is known as a common underlying proficiency (CUP) to incorporate ideas and skills learned in their first language.

Relationship between primary language academic success and English

Research suggests that for ESL students, the development of high proficiency in cognitive academic language in the primary language is often the basis for a similar proficiency in English. Once a student has achieved a high level of cognitive academic language proficiency in the primary language, he should be able to make normal academic progress. This is because such a student can receive content information in his primary language even when it is impossible to deliver it in English. The increase in cognitive academic language proficiency in the primary language allows the student to acquire similar skills in English by increasing the range of comprehensible input. Indeed, research suggests that for language minority students, the development of high cognitive academic language proficiency in the primary language directly contributes to a positive adjustment to both minority and majority cultures.

Verbal/linguistic and logical/mathematical students

Beginning teachers will need to develop instructional strategies that are appropriate for students of every learning type. Students who are predominantly verbal/linguistic will enjoy reading, learning about language, speaking, writing, and manipulating words in puzzles. These students are often best served by a "traditional" approach to language instruction. They will enjoy reading stories in the new language, writing letters, and participating in role-play exercises. Logical/mathematical students, on the other hand, will enjoy solving problems with numbers, performing experiments and calculations, and coming up with hypothetical questions. These students will enjoy collecting and evaluating data about the new language and culture.

Kinesthetic and visual/spatial students

Beginning teachers will need to develop instructional strategies that are appropriate for students of every learning type. Kinesthetic students are often poorly served by a traditional instructional approach. They typically enjoy exercise and need to move around the classroom frequently in order to maintain concentration and absorb new material. These students should manipulate new objects whose names they are learning, and they should participate in activities in which they are required to follow directions in English. Visual/spatial students, meanwhile, learn best with their eyes, and will enjoy making maps, charts, drawings, and illustrations of new material.

Musical and interpersonal students

Beginning teachers will need to develop instructional strategies that are appropriate for students of every learning type. Musical students have a knack for singing and playing instruments, and they also enjoy rhythmic games and listening to music. Helping these students acquire English might be ameliorated by teaching them songs and musical mnemonics. Interpersonal students thrive in a group, are able to mediate disputes between other students, and are excellent judges of the moods of others. These students will perform best in activities that allow them to communicate with their peers and interpret the social cues and gestures of English speakers.

Intrapersonal and naturalistic students

Beginning teachers will need to develop instructional strategies that are appropriate for students of every learning type. Intrapersonal students are introverted; they prefer to work by themselves and set their own goals. These students are often capable of thinking deeply on a particular subject, but may not be as good at thinking on their feet. Students of this type often enjoy pen-pal relationships with students from other schools. Naturalistic students, on the other hand, enjoy the outdoors and are sensitive to small differences and details among living things. These students will especially enjoy exploration of the language for natural phenomena, and would benefit from being encouraged to maintain a journal in English.

Language variation

Many people who study language assume that there is a standard, correct version of a language that can serve as a reference point for other versions. This is only partially correct. While there are general rules that can be used to systematize the currently accepted version of a language, there is no such thing as a permanent, infallible standard language. Instead, every language undergoes constant variation, as denotations, connotations, phonology, and pragmatics vary. Many critics suggest that standard language is simply the version of language preferred by the group in power. They cite examples from history in which a dominant religious or ethnic group attempted to formalize the language used by the people. It should be noted that all of these attempts met with failure. At this point, most scholars agree that languages are constantly evolving to meet the needs of the speakers.

Dialect

A dialect is the version of a language that is used by a particular group of people. This may be a group of people of a certain region, socioeconomic background, or ethnicity. Dialects are usually indicated by idiosyncratic vocabulary. Dialects that are common to individuals of a certain social class are occasionally referred to as sociolects. Many social critics suggest that upward mobility in many countries is hindered by the stigmatization of certain dialects. The particular speech of an individual may be referred to as an idiolect. Each person's idiolect is created from the influence of regional and class dialects. As a teacher, one must be careful not to prejudge students based on their dialects.

Register

The register of a language is the form of that language that is appropriate to a given situation. The register appropriate to the situation may vary depending on setting, the relationship between the two parties, and the intention of the linguistic interaction. Attaining the proper register is often one of the most difficult lessons for an individual learning a new language. Teachers need to keep the concept of register in mind when instructing students in a second language and assessing language proficiency. Often,

- 10 -

students will learn a "classroom" form of a language and will be unable to speak the language in an informal setting. Comprehensive language instruction should include opportunities for both formal and informal communication.

Slang

Slang is a general term used to describe any nonstandard form of a language. Slang is typically used in a derogative sense, to indicate words and phrases that are not considered proper for social interaction. Slang is also known for being ephemeral, meaning it does not last for very long. Particular socioeconomic and ethnic groups often have their own slang, which gives them a sense of community and excludes nonmembers from participating in discourse. The distinction between what is standard and what is lacking is increasingly being seen as an arbitrary one made by whichever group happens to be in power. Often, slang terms obtain a more universal usage and enter the lexicon.

Development of phonics knowledge

Logographic phase
There are three phases in the development of phonics knowledge: the logographic phase, the analytic phase, and the orthographic phase. In the logographic (literally, "word-picture") phase, the child will be able to identify familiar words by sight. Interestingly, most children can identify common words before they can name the individual component letters in those words. They see words as shapes. Many pre-literate children can recognize their own names and the names of their friends, and almost all children will be familiar with the fonts and color schemes of well-known logos and product names. People may bemoan the ubiquity of advertising in our culture, but one advantage is that it establishes an early

link between the shapes of words and the way they sound. Teachers often augment this process by labeling classroom objects such as plants, doors, windows, etc. This is an excellent method of passive instruction: simply being around the labeled objects will encourage children to make the connection between printed words and the names of things.

Analytic phase
In the analytic phase of phonics knowledge, children begin to take a closer look at the components of words. They begin to notice that words that sound alike often have a similar appearance as well. For instance, students may see the resemblance between the words *boy* and *toy*. In this phase, children are receptive to instruction about the reasons for the differences between sounds; for instance, why *boy* sounds different than *toy* because of the initial letter. Many teachers exploit this curiosity by creating "word families," or collections of printed words that resemble one another. Students should be asked to brainstorm possible additions to these families. The analytic phase of phonics development is also a good time to focus on rhyming words, which will be almost identical except for the beginning letter. The analytic phase is the most intense period of phonics development.

Orthographic phase
The third phase of phonics knowledge is called the orthographic phase. In the orthographic phase, students have acquired almost all of the tools required to sound out familiar and unfamiliar words. They know all of the sounds of the letters and read most common words automatically. Indeed, the development of a large sight vocabulary indicates the shift into the orthographic phase. A word is in sight vocabulary when the student no longer has to break it down or sound it out one syllable at a time. In large part, sight vocabulary emerges from frequent

and prolonged exposure to simple texts. However, many teachers take extra effort to help students memorize common words and words with irregular spellings. Once students have a sufficient sight vocabulary, they can begin to understand unfamiliar words from context and thus move on to more sophisticated texts. Most education experts believe that it is only in the orthographic phase of phonics knowledge that students can truly begin to obtain knowledge and pleasure from reading.

Spelling development

There are four stages in the development of spelling. In order, they are the pre-phonetic, phonetic, transitional, and conventional stages. The pre-phonetic stage of spelling is characterized by incomplete understanding of the relationship between sounds and letters. At this stage, children will not understand that every sound in a word must be represented by at least one letter. So, children will often leave out syllables in their attempts at spelling. Also, children in the pre-phonetic stage may still be in the logographic stage of phonics development, meaning that they may identify words simply as pictures and not as sequences of individual letters. In other words, pre-phonetic children may not yet have acquired the alphabetic principle. Students may attempt to spell words with a jumble of letter-like forms rather than with a series of discrete letters. Such students are sometimes referred to as pre-communicative spellers, because their work does not yet demonstrate understanding of the correspondence between sounds and symbols.

Pre-phonetic to phonetic
The transition out of the pre-phonetic stage is marked by steady progress rather than sudden enlightenment. Gradually, students will begin to use the appropriate letters for the sounds of a word, and over time students will attempt, however imperfectly, to represent all of the sounds in a word. Indeed, once students demonstrate these skills, they are considered to be in the phonetic stage of spelling development. In this stage, students are likely to use one letter to represent a complex sound that requires two or more letters. Students in the phonetic stage understand how to write all of the letters, though occasionally they will write letters upside down or backwards. By this stage, it should be possible to make out what the student intends to communicate with his writing. However, students will have a limited sight vocabulary at this point, and therefore will always misspell words with silent vowels or unusual consonant patterns.

Transitional stage
Once the student has developed a small sight vocabulary and a solid understanding of the correspondence between English letters and sounds, he is in the transitional stage of spelling development. In this stage, it should be easy to understand a written message composed by the student. Indeed, students may be capable of writing short sentences with no spelling mistakes at all. The development of a basic sight vocabulary means that the student will spell some difficult words correctly, but is still likely to misspell words with long vowel sounds, which in English tend to be represented in different ways.

Conventional stage
The final stage of spelling development, known as the conventional stage, is characterized by near-perfect spelling and a massive sight vocabulary. Students in the conventional stage of spelling will spell irregularly written but common words correctly almost all of the time. Spelling errors will mainly be confined to especially large and unusual words. Also,

students in the conventional stage will have developed an intuitive sense of spelling, such that they will often detect a spelling error even before precisely locating it in the sentence. Of course, in order to attain this degree of spelling competence, a student will have to be a fluent reader with excellent comprehension skills as well. In the conventional stage of spelling development, students are ready to learn content-specific words. In particular, spelling instruction should focus on words from the sciences and mathematics. Also, spelling instruction should focus on words with extremely unusual spellings. It can be assumed by this stage that students will be able to improvise the correct spelling of a regular but unfamiliar word.

Phonology

The way a language sounds is known as its phonological system. The smallest distinguishable unit of sound that can hold meaning in a given language is known as a phoneme. Each human language has a different set of phonemes. Each of these sets is relatively small compared to the entire set of possible sounds that can be made by the human voice. For instance, many languages do not distinguish between the plosive *p* and *b*, as we do in English. Individuals who speak these languages are incapable of telling the word *pan* from the word *ban* because they are not used to differentiating the voiced *b* from the unvoiced *p*.

Morphology

The morphology of a language is the system by which words are constructed out of letters. The smallest meaningful unit of a morphological system is known as a morpheme. Morphemes may appear by themselves as coherent words, but also may be combined with other morphemes to form words that are more complex. For instance, the morpheme *boy* can stand by itself, but it can also be combined with the morpheme –*s* to form *boys*. Every language has a distinct morphology, but there may be many exceptions to the basic rules of the system. English in particular is notorious for its morphological exceptions. Students of language should be aware that words are constructed in a systematic way, just as sentences and paragraphs are.

Syntax

The syntax of a language is the basic structure of the sentences. Syntax is distinguished from grammar by the fact that grammar offers recommendations for proper syntax, whereas syntax is the entire collection of proper and improper formulations. Utterances that appear crude and ungrammatical will still be understandable if they are placed into a standard acceptable syntax. Syntax, then, is the basic set of linguistic rules that must be followed in order for linguistic expressions to be understood. Grammar, on the other hand, is the set of rules that must be followed in order to attain a certain, somewhat arbitrary standard of acceptable expression. The concept of a standard of language has been frequently debated in education.

Phonetics

Phonetics is the study of sounds made during human speech. These sounds, known in the discipline as "phones," have distinct properties with respect to their production, audition, and perception. Phonetics is distinct from phonology in that it deals with real, measurable sounds, rather than abstract or arbitrary sound units like phonemes. In other words, phonetics focuses on specific sounds and does not concern itself with the context in which these sounds are used. There is no consideration of semantics in the field of phonetics. There are three main areas of research in phonetics. Articulatory phonetics focuses on the precise positions and movements of the speech organs. Acoustic phonetics focuses on the properties of sound waves and their reception by the inner ear. Auditory phonetics focuses on the process by which the brain forms a perceptual representation of phonetic input.

Semantics

The semantics of a language are the meanings of its words. Basic semantics studies explore the denotations and connotations of words. The denotation of a word is the thing or set of things to which it refers. The word *table*, for instance, denotes a four-legged, flat-topped piece of furniture. Of course, this word may have other denotations, such as a chart of data or an underground collection of water. The connotation of a word is the set of judgments and references that accompany it. For example, the word *idealist* denotes someone loyal to a particular idea, but it connotes a person out of touch with mundane matters. Every language is a mass of ambiguous denotations and connotations.

Pragmatics

The pragmatics of a language is the system by which it is used in social interactions. The ways in which people use language with one another are determined by the type of expression required as well as by the relationship of the speaker with his audience. Similar linguistic utterances can have vastly different pragmatic utility depending on their context. For example, the words *will you go out with me* have a different meaning when they are uttered by a young man to a young woman than when they are uttered by someone wanting to

go outside to throw the Frisbee! People who speak a given language fluently will have an intuitive understanding of the pragmatics systems in that language. Indeed, this type of understanding often only comes with long experience.

Phonemic awareness

Perhaps the most basic prerequisite for literacy is phonemic awareness: that is, the understanding that words are made up of individual speech sounds. Phonemes are any speech sounds that can be distinguished from one another. For instance, if a teacher said the words *ball* and *fall*, the class would be able to distinguish the words because they would hear a difference between the /b/ and /f/ sounds. These sounds, then, are phonemes, though of course they are not the only phonemes in the words *ball* and *fall*. Phonemic awareness does not require written language, because it is entirely based on speech. At its core, phonemic awareness is the understanding that language is made up of sounds.

Phonemic awareness vs. phonics

Phonemic awareness should not be confused with phonics, which is the direct correspondence between letters and sounds (and which therefore requires the presence of print). Phonemic awareness precedes phonics instruction. Phonics depends on the alphabetic principle, which is that letters or other characters represent sounds. Phonemic awareness is much more basic. It has been said that literacy cannot develop without phonemic awareness and phonemic awareness cannot grow without the advance of literacy. In any case, it is recommended that all kindergartners develop phonemic awareness as part of their preparation for learning to read.

Phonemes and graphemes

As mentioned above, the core of phonemic awareness is the perception of distinguishing sounds, otherwise known as phonemes. Phonemes can be represented in two different ways. Some teachers use a phonetic alphabet, in which each phoneme is always represented with the same symbol. A hard *c* or *k* sound, for instance, is represented by /k/. Another way to represent phonemes is with an illustrative series of letters called graphemes. According to this method, the hard *c* or *k* could be represented as the *c* in *cold* or the *k* in *kilogram*. The vowel sounds permit a number of grapheme depictions: for example, a long *i* could be represented as the *y* in *fly* or the *igh* in *sigh*. Both the phonetic alphabet and the grapheme are acceptable modes of depicting phonemes.

Consonants and vowels

Phonemes can be either consonants or vowels, depending on how they are formed by the mouth. Consonants are formed by a motion that somehow blocks the flow of air. This is one reason why it is hard to hold a consonant sound while singing. Vowels, on the other hand, are formed by the vibration of air moving through the voice box and mouth. The English vowels are *a*, *e*, *i*, *o*, and *u*. The letter *y* is considered a vowel in words like *fly* and *rhythm*, and the letter *w* is considered a vowel in words like *now* and *brown*. All of the other letters in the English language are consonants exclusively.

Consonant blends, diphthongs, and digraphs

A consonant blend is a combination of two or more consonants into a single sound. Some examples of consonant blends are the initial sounds in *stay*, *drive*,

and *gloat*. A diphthong is a single but shifting sound made by the combination of two or more vowels. Developing an ear for diphthongs takes a little work. One example is the word *boil*, in which the *oi* combination is pronounced first as *oy*, and then as a short *u*, such that the pronunciation is essentially *boy-ull*. This gliding vowel sound is characteristic of the diphthong. Finally, a digraph is a group of two or more letters that create a sound different from the individual sounds of the letters. Some common English digraphs are *sh*, *ph*, and *ch*, respectively. Note that none of these combinations produces a sound like the component sounds of the letters.

Onsets and rimes

English phonemes may be distinguished by their placement in a syllable or a word. The sound that initiates a syllable is known as the onset, while the vowel and any consonants after the vowel are referred to as the rime. For instance, in the one-syllable word *boy*, *b* is the onset and *oy* is the rime. It is not necessary for a syllable to have an onset, but every syllable has a rime. *I*, *of*, and *at* are all examples of words without an onset. Every syllable has a rime because every syllable has some sort of vowel sound.

Beginning, end, and medial phonemes

Another way in which phonemes are distinguished is by their placement in a word. The initial phoneme in a word is called the beginning phoneme, the final phoneme in a word is called the end phoneme, and all of the phonemes in between the beginning and end are called the medial phonemes. In the word bully, then, /b/ is the beginning phoneme, /u/ and /l/ are the medial phonemes, and /e/ is the end phoneme. Of course, a word may have numerous medial phonemes, though there may only be one initial and end phoneme. It is not necessary for students to understand the distinctions between these phoneme positions.

Skills associated with phonemic awareness

As a concept, phonemic awareness seems almost too vague and abstract to teach. For this reason, education experts have invented a program for testing and improving phonemic awareness. Phonemic awareness is demonstrated by the performance of six tasks. A student is not considered to have phonemic awareness unless he can perform all six. The tasks are sound matching, sound isolation, sound blending, sound substitution, sound deletion, and sound segmentation. Of these, sound segmentation is considered the most difficult and is therefore the last to be taught. There are specific exercises and assessments for each of the six components of phonemic awareness.

Transfer of literacy competence

According to the most current research, students are able to make positive transfers of knowledge between a first language and English in several areas: phonemic awareness, reading phonics, word recognition strategies, and cognates. In particular, the research has suggested that there are reading strategies common to English and languages like Spanish. However, there are some aspects of the graphic and phonetic systems particular to each of languages. In these areas, teachers will need to provide explicit instruction. For most students, the biggest obstacle to the transfer of literacy is the lack of vocabulary in English. Also, students need to possess a certain amount of background knowledge in order to understand specific texts. After students have developed adequate translation skills and acquired a satisfactory set of cognates, their ability to transfer literacy

skills from their first language to English will be greatly improved.

Research focusing on the transfer of literacy from a first language to English has emphasized that transitions will occur at different points of English development for different students. Teachers should be aware of the potential for rapid gains and long plateaus in this development. A transition point is loosely defined as a shift in the relationship of the two languages to one another. It is a point at which the teacher will shift his expectations for the student. The first point of transition in literacy instruction occurs when students who have received formal instruction in their first language begin formal reading and content-area instruction in English. A second point of transition, known as redesignation, occurs when students receive all their instruction in English, without language support in their first language. In order to accurately ascertain that a student has reached one of these transition points, a teacher needs to be skilled in language assessment and evaluation of test data. Students will need to demonstrate competence in phonemic awareness, structural analysis, word recognition, comprehension skills, writing skills, and overall reading fluency in order to be considered literate.

Microprocesses

The most basic reading functions in English as a second language are called microprocesses. At this level, students are working to group the words and ideas within sentences into units of meaning. Essentially, the student will be unconsciously deciding what is important about the sentence and storing that information in short-term memory. For English language learners, lack of proficiency in grammar and syntax may force them to read word by word and miss the overall concept described by the sentence. The students may also be confused by idiomatic expressions and unfamiliar grammatical constructions. Some activities that can be useful at improving microprocesses are choral reading (in which students read aloud) and marking sentences to identify units of meaning. Students may also write sentences out on paper and cut them into meaningful units. In order to accelerate microprocesses, teachers may need to describe explicitly unfamiliar grammatical and syntactic forms. Also, teachers will need to explain the meaning of common idiomatic expressions.

Integrative processes

In order to be successful in learning English as a second language, students will need to improve their integrative processes: that is, their ability to identify relationships between clauses and sentences at the multiple-sentence and paragraph level of complexity. In order to do this, readers will have to notice pronoun substitutions, infer cause and effect, identify synonym substitutions, and recognize conjunctions. English language learners will probably have more difficulty with complex and compound sentences. They are more likely to lose the meaning of references when there is a frequent use of pronouns. The use of pronouns often varies from language to language. One way to improve integrative processes is to perform a close reading of sentences and paragraphs. Students may also perform sentence transformation activities to gain a better understanding of the construction of complex sentences. One helpful activity can be to go through a sample of text and replace antecedents and referents with nouns. Teachers can isolate a paragraph and have students diagram or draw relationships using circles and arrows.

Macroprocesses

The macroprocesses of learning English as a second language are relating small chunks of text to the whole text and organizing sections of text. In order to develop these skills, students will need to understand elements of story structure, expository text structure, poetic formulas, and the various literary genres. Often, English language learners have a hard time varying their reading strategy to align with the intent of the author. Students may not be familiar with the particular structures of genres in another language. One way to improve macroprocesses is by outlining and summarizing paragraphs, with an emphasis on the ways in which the main idea is supported by details. Students might be asked to identify the problem and solution in an expository text. Through the use of guided questions, teachers can encourage students to think critically about the structure and content of the text. Finally, more advanced students can benefit from going through a text paragraph by paragraph and identifying the function of each section.

Elaborative processes

The elaborative process of reading is extending literal comprehension to an understanding of the author's intent and themes. In order to exercise this skill, readers need to make personal connections with what they read, using prior knowledge and making predictions. Readers also need to identify with characters and understand their emotional responses. Sometimes, English language learners have a hard time identifying themes within a literary work if those themes are particular to the culture. Differing expectations and cultural norms may cause students to miss the intent of a literary work. The chains of cause and effect may be unfamiliar to students from another

- 17 -

culture, and therefore the consequences or emotional reactions in the story may be incomprehensible. In order to develop the elaborative processes of English language learners, teachers can provide background knowledge and encourage students to connect literary material to their own lives. Teachers can use graphic organizers, maps, and other visual representations to familiarize students with characters, setting, and plot. Whenever necessary, teachers must explicitly describe the cultural values and beliefs that inform a piece of literature.

Metacognitive processes

The metacognitive process of reading is the ability to self-critique comprehension and analysis. In order to develop metacognitive processes, students need to be able to predict, organize, and relate the information in a text to their own lives. Students who achieve excellent fluency in English will be able to recognize cognates and translate/paraphrase ideas from a literary text in English into their primary language. However, one of the obstacles to metacognitive development is the tendency to apply the grammatical and syntactic patterns of the native language to English. Unfamiliar vocabulary can hinder metacognitive development, especially when students lack the strategies to discover meaning from context. In order to develop metacognitive skill, teachers can model self-monitoring through read-and-retell lessons, in which students read independently and then report on what they have learned. Also, students may be able to improve their metacognitive skills by working with a partner or in a small group.

William Labov and Joshua Fishman

William Labov and Joshua Fishman are sociolinguists responsible for popularizing and providing academic backing for marginalized dialects and languages. William Labov is responsible for establishing African-American Vernacular English as a legitimate dialect. He did this by demonstrating that AAVE has its own internal grammatical and syntactical rules. One result of Labov's research is that speakers of AAVE are now instructed in a manner similar to English language learners. Joshua Fishman, meanwhile, concentrated on the evolution of languages. Fishman's work concentrated on Gaelic, Yiddish, and Welsh, but it has been used to describe the societal forces that cause all languages to thrive or disappear. Fishman is a strong advocate for the survival of obscure languages, which he describes as the most important artifacts of a culture.

Dell Hymes and Basil Bernstein

Dell Hymes was a sociolinguist primarily concerned with the interactions between language, society, and cultural context. He came up with the SPEAKING mnemonic for the essential characteristics of discourse: Setting and Scene; Participants; Ends (as in goals or intentions); Act sequence (that is, the structure of the linguistic interaction); Key (gestures or inflections that influence tone and mood); Instrumentalities (methods or conventions of speech); Norms; and Genre. Basil Bernstein, meanwhile, is famous for distinguishing between the restricted code, which is used by people who have a similar cultural background or know each other well, and the elaborated code, which is used by people who are unfamiliar with one another or with one another's culture. Expression in the elaborated code requires more explicit context and verbiage.

Sheltered English approach

The sheltered English approach to content-area instruction is similar to language immersion. Sheltered English instruction is characterized by comprehensible input, meaning that all the information disseminated in the class should be understandable to the students. The teacher will strive to encourage student interaction, including frequent small-group and cooperative learning. There will be more hands-on activities in a sheltered English classroom, with students encouraged to become active participants in the lesson. In order for sheltered instruction to work, a teacher should engage in careful and comprehensive planning, and should develop a warm environment for students. Teachers should use student background knowledge and experience to determine activities. Teachers should also incorporate a variety of instructional strategies and frequent formal and informal assessment. Teachers should always explicitly state the lesson objectives.

Components

A sheltered English instructor will have to use a variety of instructional strategies and materials to be effective. Specifically, sheltered English instruction requires frequent hands-on activities. Modeling and demonstrations are common activities in the classroom. The teacher will also want to incorporate maps and globes for social studies or geography lessons. Many teachers find computers with interactive software to be especially helpful in sheltered English instruction. Teachers will also want to use other graphical displays, such as timelines, bulletin boards, pictures, and graphs. In order to ensure that all content in the classroom is comprehensible to students (as mandated by the terms of sheltered English instruction), the teacher will want to incorporate objects with which the students are already familiar.

Language and conceptual development

In order to provide effective sheltered English instruction, a teacher will need to understand certain theoretical principles. Specifically, teachers will need to understand the relationship between language development and conceptual development. Language gives us the labels and categories for certain familiar concepts. It also provides a means of describing or expressing insights about concepts that have already been learned. In other words, a student's mastery of language must increase along with his mastery of concepts. Teachers need to take into account both the linguistic and conceptual complexity of content-area instruction. It is essential that all input be comprehensible to students and that students receive adequate linguistic support. So, when a teacher is describing an unknown concept, he should use known language; when the teacher is describing linguistic principles that are unknown to students, he should use known concepts as illustration.

Making input comprehensible

In order to help students remain at grade level in their conceptual understanding, a teacher needs to ensure that all content-area instruction is comprehensible. To that end, the teacher should explicitly define any tricky vocabulary associated with the lesson. Manipulatives and graphical depictions can be especially useful in making some material comprehensible. The teacher should create a context in which students can solve problems, and should design activities that can be performed cooperatively to foster group understanding. If necessary, the teacher should provide content-area instruction in the primary language of students. In order to provide this kind of instruction, teachers need to receive explicit training in sheltered English and SDAIE (specially designed academic instruction in English) methods and strategies.

Mathematics instruction

Of all the content areas, mathematics is the one that ESL teachers often have the most trouble determining how to teach. This is due in part to the large amount of vocabulary unique to the discipline. The essential accomplishment that a teacher needs to make is to help develop a conceptual understanding of mathematics, and to help the student make connections between concrete, semi-concrete, and abstract expressions of new concepts. In mathematics, a single symbol can often represent several different words or an entire conceptual relationship. Often, a word may have a different meaning in mathematics than it does when used in ordinary conversation. In order to surmount the challenges of mathematics instruction, a teacher needs to pay special attention to issues of terminology. Manipulatives and group work can be especially helpful for students whose first language is not English. Above all, teachers and students need to remain patient as students work to achieve the linguistic understanding that will enable conceptual mastery in mathematics.

Sheltered instruction vs. ESL

In sheltered instruction, the focus of instruction is mastery of the content area, whereas in ESL, the focus is on development of English skills. So, a sheltered instruction program will follow the mainstream scope and sequence, whereas an ESL program may follow some other prescription. In order to provide sheltered instruction, a teacher should be certified in the content area and must have some ESL training, whereas an ESL teacher need only be endorsed in ESL. Both sheltered instruction and ESL focus on the terminology of content areas. Finally, both sheltered English instruction and ESL instruction emphasize the need to teach metacognitive strategies; that is, both sheltered English and ESL instruction encourage students to self-monitor and think about their performance.

Submersion programs

One of the more extreme versions of an ESL program is known as a submersion program. The image conjured up by this name, of a student literally drowning in new information, is supported by the motto of this kind of program: sink or swim. Submersion programs provide very little structured support for the acquisition of English, with students being thrust directly into content-area instruction at their grade level. The advocates of submersion programs usually insist that most students in them will fall hopelessly behind unless they learn English almost immediately. Instruction is given almost exclusively in English, and students are not provided with very much opportunity to ask questions and receive scaffolding. As one might suspect, submersion programs have a high rate of failure. Unfortunately, however, it is very common for school administrations to blame the students for their failure to acquire English rapidly. In general, submersion programs are currently thought to be inappropriate.

Transitional ESL education

One of the more common models of ESL education is known as transitional education. In this model of instruction, the methodology of teaching a second language is incorporated. Students will receive content-area instruction in both their primary and secondary language according to their proficiency. Over time, the teacher will attempt to raise the level of English use in the classroom. To begin with, however, students will be assessed in their first language and will be given direct instruction to help them master the cognitive academic language required for each content area. Transitional education is considered one of the more beneficial forms of education for non-English-speaking students. It also aligns nicely with Krashen's input hypothesis, which declares that students should receive gradually increasing levels of difficulty in language.

Primary language instruction

In some ESL programs, a great deal of the content-area material is covered in the native language of the students. This is especially common in classes where the overwhelming majority of the students are native Spanish speakers. The goal of this method of instruction is to prevent students from falling far behind their grade level during the process of English acquisition. Over time, the teacher will gradually increase the amount of English used in content-area instruction. A classroom that incorporates primary language instruction will typically have a slightly expanded amount of time every day devoted to mastering the fundamentals of cognitive academic language in English, with the ultimate goal being instruction in every content area in English.

English language development

One of the more common methods used in ESL programs is English language development, which simply means a graduated program of improvement in English language proficiency. This model of education requires summative assessment at its beginning, so that the teacher can differentiate levels of proficiency among students. One of the things that separate English language development programs from other programs is the focus on incorporating a wide variety of methods and approaches to address various learning styles. English language development programs also endeavor to provide a large amount of practice time and ungraded opportunities for students to apply their burgeoning knowledge of English to specific content areas. In order to adequately provide an English language development program, all teachers must be fluent in both languages and well versed in the full spectrum of instructional methods in all content areas.

SDAIE

One of the methods used for teaching academic content to non-English-speaking students is called specially designed academic instruction in English, or SDAIE. In order for this method to be used, the student must have at least intermediate fluency in English. The student is given all course material in his native language, but is provided with access to English language versions of all content as well. Students are encouraged to use the English language versions of the content material as much as possible. This approach puts great demands for motivation on each student, and is therefore not appropriate for students who are not prepared to work. The teacher will set out goals for both content and language acquisition for each student. In the best SDAIE classes, students acquire language skills almost involuntarily as they are going through the normal process of learning course content. Of course, in order to be successful at this method, a teacher will need to be well organized and fluent in both languages.

Characteristics of an ESL program

In an ESL program, content is taught in the students' primary language and separate instruction is provided in English language skills. The methodology used to teach English does not necessarily involve making connections with other content areas. ESL programs work best when they are intensive, taking up the majority of the school day. One of the dangers of these programs, of course, is that they can prevent students from learning other content material. Also, students who participate in ESL programs may have a difficult time transferring their knowledge of English language skills to the core curriculum. For this reason, many schools at present avoid ESL courses except in those cases where students need intense English training in order to survive in other areas.

Dual immersion programs

One of the newer models of ESL program is known as dual immersion. In this kind of program, groups of students with different first languages are placed together and encouraged to learn each other's native tongue. Research has suggested a number of excellent benefits to this instruction model. In many cases, it has been found to promote true bilingualism and a healthy respect for another culture. Many students have seen their skills in their native language improve as a result of explaining themselves to their peers. In other words, dual immersion programs force students to consider and analyze their original language, which improves their skill in that language as well as their ability to learn English. Also, of course, schools that feature dual immersion programs typically have fewer problems integrating non-English speakers into the student body. At present, dual immersion programs are uncommon but increasing in number.

Basic orientations for teaching ESL

There are four basic orientations to teaching English as a second language: structural/linguistic; cognitive; affective/motivational; and functional/communicative. The structural/linguistic approach is based on comparisons between the structures of different languages. Teachers who use this method isolate grammatical and syntactic elements in each language and teach their students in a prescribed sequence. A cognitive approach entails objectives that enable the student to make generalizations about the rules of English. There is an emphasis on individual learning style with this approach. The affective/motivational approach emphasizes the predispositions of the student that can enhance or inhibit learning. Teachers who use this approach try to diminish the anxiety associated with learning by increasing identification with native English speakers. The functional/communicative approach involves selecting language structures on the basis of their utility in achieving a communicative purpose. The focus of this instruction is on transmission and reception of speech.

Audiolingual method
The audiolingual method of teaching English as a second language relies on repetition of structural patterns. Material is supposed to be overlearned, so students can easily incorporate it in future lessons. Instruction tries to prevent student errors and immediately reinforces correct expression. Grammar is typically taught inductively, meaning that students are informed of the rules of grammar after they have intuitively learned proper expression. New material is typically presented in a dialogue format and essential linguistic structures and skills are placed in a set sequence. Exposure to new vocabulary is rigidly controlled and linguistic patterns are taught using rote memorization and repetitive drills. The audiolingual method has somewhat fallen out of favor in recent years, though it is still a major component of traditional programs.

Total physical response approach
The total physical response method of teaching English as a second language incorporates psychomotor systems to inculcate vocabulary and syntactic forms.

Students are not required to produce language, either orally or in written form, until they are ready. Command forms are typically used to convey information, and the teacher must gradually increase the complexity of his linguistic expressions in English. This type of instruction is especially suited to students with a kinesthetic learning style. The sequence of instruction in total physical response is as follows: the teacher gives the command and performs the accompanying action; the teacher then says the command and both the teacher and the students perform the action; the teacher then says the command as students perform the action; the teacher tells one student to perform the action; and finally the students give one another commands or command the teacher to perform the action.

Communicative strategy

The communicative approach to teaching English as a second language assumes the comprehension of linguistic principles always comes before production of speech or writing. The overarching goal of this approach is for students to create meaningful communication. Because this method relies heavily on goodwill among the students, it is important for the teacher to create a positive learning environment to lower the affective filters of the students. When this method is used, the language is gradually acquired through interaction with fellow students at the same time that it is being learned from the teacher. In order to create a successful lesson, the teacher will need to ensure that students have the specific vocabulary and expressions they will need in order to accomplish the communicative intent. In some cases, it may be useful to prepare dialogue before practicing an actual verbal exchange. Teachers may also use graphs and displays.

Grammar-translation approach

For most of American history, second languages were taught according to the grammar-translation approach. This method of instruction still persists in some ESL classrooms. In this format, lessons are taught almost exclusively in the primary language of the students. There is very little active use of English. Vocabulary is taught in list format, and students are provided with detailed explanation of grammatical rules. From close to the beginning of a course of study, students will be required to read complex and advanced texts. These texts, however, are primarily studied for their grammatical structures rather than for their specific content. There is very little attention given to spoken forms of the language, and almost no instruction in pronunciation is given. Almost all work in the class involves translating sentences from one language to the other.

Direct approach

The direct approach to teaching English as a second language came after the grammar-translation approach and attempted to incorporate the secondary language in instruction a bit more. When this approach is used, lessons begin with a dialogue incorporating a modern conversational style in English. There is a translation at this point, as students are given a series of questions in English based on the dialogue that was just presented. Students learn the rules of grammar through induction; that is, they generalize rules from practice and experience with English. Students will not read advanced literature until they are well along in their mastery of cognitive academic language. When they do read literature in English, they will consider it in terms of its own content rather than its grammatical structures. There is some attempt to teach the English-speaking culture in the direct approach method.

Reading approach

The reading approach to teaching English as a second language has both practical and academic benefits, but is only appropriate for certain individuals. Specifically, the reading approach is appropriate for those individuals who will not be living in an English-speaking community and for whom reading is the most important skill to master. The two primary emphases of the reading approach are improving reading ability and establishing current events and historical knowledge of English-speaking countries. Grammar instruction is limited to what is necessary for reading comprehension and fluency. There is almost no attention paid to pronunciation or the development of conversational skills. As one would expect, the majority of time is spent on reading passages. There is a constant emphasis on the acquisition of vocabulary. Teachers who use this approach will rely almost exclusively on translation from English into the native language of the student.

Community language learning approach

According to the community language learning approach, the most important thing is to lower the affective filter of the student and gradually introduce him to a linguistic community in English. The student is considered more as a client, and the teacher is trained in counseling skills. At first, the teacher/counselor tries to make the student comfortable by getting a sense of his anxieties about language acquisition. The student and teacher work closely to develop linguistic independence for the student. There are five basic stages of language acquisition in community language learning. At first, the student is completely dependent on the teacher. In the second stage, the student begins to have contact with other members of the target linguistic group (i.e., English speakers). In the third stage, the student begins to speak directly to the members of the target linguistic group. In the fourth stage, the client can speak freely and assume that the members of the target linguistic group understand him. In the final stage, the student refines his linguistic skills.

Functional-notional approach

Among the communicative approaches to teaching English as a second language is the functional-notional approach, which emphasizes a strictly organized syllabus of language. Teachers who take the functional-notional approach divide a language into discrete units of analysis, usually by social context. In other words, the specific units of instruction are situations in which the student will be forced to express himself in English. The term *notion* refers to meaningful expressions of language. The intent of the functional-notional approach is to equip students with appropriate notions for every common social situation. This may involve variations of dialect, formality, and mode of expression. A special set of terminology is used in this approach to ESL instruction. An *exponent* is the statement that is appropriate to a given function, situation, and topic. A *code* is the shared language of a community of speakers. *Code-switching* is the process by which individuals shift the tone or formality of their speech in order to convey hierarchy, bonding, or some other interpersonal relation.

Categories of discourse

The functional-notional approach to teaching English as a second language asserts that there are five major functional categories of discourse: personal, interpersonal, directive, referential, and imaginative. The personal function involves expressing and elaborating one's own thoughts, ideas, or feelings. The interpersonal function is used to establish and maintain positive social and professional relationships, whether by exchanging basic pleasantries

- 24 -

or organizing social relations. Examples of speech used in an interpersonal function are apologies or invitations. Language that is used in a directive function attempts to change the actions of others. This may include giving instructions, requesting permission, or asking for directions. Language that is used in a referential function describes things, actions, events, or people. Referential language can also be used to discuss abstract concepts. Finally, imaginative language expresses creativity and artistic expression. The most obvious example of imaginative language is fictional dialogue, but this category can also include creative solutions to concrete problems.

Marie M. Clay, Sharon Taberski, Priscilla Vail, and Marilyn Jager Adams

Marie M. Clay is credited as the originator of the Reading Recovery movement, which is an effective method of accelerating the progress of struggling readers. The foundation of the program is continuous and specific assessment, which enables teachers to diagnose reading problems early on. The program usually lasts twelve to twenty weeks, after which the student ought to be ready to rejoin the class. Sharon Taberski has written a number of popular books about the personal relationships between teachers and new readers. Priscilla Vail is an expert on dyslexia, and in particular on the assessment of dyslexic children. She advocates a whole-language approach to teaching dyslexics and other students with special needs. Marilyn Jager Adams established basic criteria for early reading success and helped to create voice recognition software for developing readers.

Planning, Implementing, and Managing Instruction

Recommended sequence for phonics skills instruction

Having outlined the three phases of phonics knowledge, let us now examine the instructional techniques for nurturing this development. There is a prescribed sequence for the teaching of phonics skills. Teachers should begin by naming the letters, both uppercase and lowercase. Once students have mastered the names of all twenty-six letters, the teacher should move on to the sounds of the letters. It is not necessary at this point to explore the various sounds a letter can make, such as long and short vowel sounds. It is at this point that many teachers discuss the differences between consonants and vowels. One easy way of doing so is to show how vowels can be spoken indefinitely, while consonants can only be spoken in staccato bursts.

Three-letter words, basic digraphs, and consonant blends

Having covered the letters and their sounds, the teacher can begin to discuss very short words. The simplest words for young students to understand are three-letter words with a consonant-vowel-consonant (known as CVC) structure: for example, *cat*, *dog*, and *hat*. To begin with, the teacher should only discuss CVC words with short vowel sounds. Next, the teacher can introduce simple words that have initial digraphs: that is, two consonants that produce a sound unlike either of the component letters (e.g., *sh*, *ch*, and *th*). The discussion of these words will show students some of the flexibility and ambiguity related to English pronunciation. Also, of course, it will familiarize them with some of the more common sounds in the language. After covering some basic digraphs, the teacher can move on to short-vowel words beginning with consonant blends like *bl*, *sl*, and *st*. These blends require students to remember the individual sounds of the consonants, but also to combine them into a slightly new form. Work with consonant blends helps accelerate pronunciation for many students, as they begin to combine several letters into a single sound.

Long vowel sounds and multisyllabic words

After addressing short vowel sounds, the teacher can move on to words featuring the long vowel sounds. As much as possible, the teacher should focus on one-syllable words, like *row* and *mate*. Instruction can then move on to a look at diphthongs and other irregular vowel formations. Some vowels sound different when they precede an *r* or an *l*: they are called r- and l- controlled vowels. Some examples of these words are *car*, *walk*, and *bird*. Such words should be discussed, though it is not necessary to give students an entire explanation of the linguistic phenomenon. Finally, once all of the above topics have been covered, the teacher can conclude by exploring some common multisyllabic words. For the most part, multisyllabic words are read just like combinations of one-syllable words. However, students should receive some guided practice before being asked to sound out these words on their own.

Synthetic and analytic phonics instruction

The specific techniques of phonics instruction can be divided into two categories: those that build words out of sounds (synthesis) and those that break words down into their component sounds (analysis). These are reciprocal skills; the presence of one reinforces the development of the other. Activities that require students to make words out of disparate sounds are called synthetic phonics activities. In perhaps the most common synthetic phonics activity, the teacher writes an initial letter on the board and asks the students to pronounce it. Once students have mastered the sound of the letter or letters, the teacher should ask students to think of words that begin with that sound. This is an excellent way to demonstrate how the same sound can begin any number of words.

Initial consonant, digraph, and blend cards

Another synthetic phonics activity is for the teacher to distribute cards printed with initial consonants, digraphs, and blends. The teacher then writes a number of common rimes on the board and asks students to tape their cards where they combine with a rime to form a complete word. So, for instance, the teacher could write the rime *at* on the board, and students holding *b*, *c*, *s*, and *f* could tape up their cards to form a complete word. Students should be encouraged to attach their onsets to a number of different rimes, as this will reinforce the idea that many common words share an initial sound.

Digraph, letter, and blend cards

In sophisticated synthetic phonics activity, students are given cards printed with letters, digraphs, and blends, and are asked to cooperate with one another to create short words. Every student should be given several cards, and there should be plenty of vowels. Once students have formed some short words, the teacher should ask them to attempt multisyllabic words. Of course, this activity is best suited to students who are well into the analytic phase of phonics knowledge. An advantage of it, though, is that it requires students to consider not only the onset or initial sound in the word, but also the medial and end sounds. In another activity, a teacher combines letter recognition with synthetic phonics instruction by writing a letter on the board and asking students to name objects in the class that begin with that letter. So long as this activity is conducted orally, it will be a good exercise for phonics skills. Any activity that requires students to consider the initial sound of a vocabulary word is a reinforcement of phonic skills.

Underlining

Whereas synthetic phonics instruction encourages students to build words out of sounds, analytic phonics instruction requires them to break words apart into discrete sounds. One easy introductory activity is to present students with a short text and ask them to underline all of the appearances of a given letter or digraph. For example, students might be asked to underline all the instances of the letter *p*. The teacher will then reread the text aloud, pointing at the words as they are pronounced, so that students can see how the *p* is used in each different case. This activity helps to build understanding of how letters function in words.

Repeated consonant sound

One advanced phonics exercise begins when the teacher writes several sentences on the board, each of which contains the same consonant sound. The words that contain the consonant sound should be underlined. Students will be asked to read the underlined words, and then to identify the sound these words have in common. (The activity is more effective if the words only have one sound in common.) Once the sound has been identified, the teacher writes the consonant, digraph, or blend next to the list of sentences. This activity moves the students' attention from the entire sentence to the individual words and finally to the recurrent sound. In essence, it helps students "zoom in" on phonics as it occurs in real language.

Word sort

One method of analytic phonics instruction is a word sort, in which students are given cards on which short words have been printed. Students are then asked to organize the cards according to some criterion: for instance, they may be asked to put all of the cards beginning with a *sh* sound together. Later, the teacher might ask the students to group words that have a *sh* sound in any position. If the teacher prefers students to work by themselves on a word sort, the activity can be recreated on paper: the teacher simply passes out a list of words and asks the students to underline those that meet the criterion.

Decoding and encoding

Phonics assessments are typically categorized depending on whether the student is putting sounds together to make a written word or converting written words into sounds. The former is called encoding and the latter is called decoding. In an encoding exercise, the student writes down words as the teacher says them. The traditional spelling test, in which the word is read aloud by the teacher several times and the student must attempt to spell it on paper, is a classic encoding assessment. This type of assessment is excellent for spelling, of course, but it is also good at pinpointing basic phonics problems.

Encoding assessments

With more advanced students, it is useful to require encoding assessments that place words in context. In a typical exercise, students are asked to transcribe a few sentences spoken by the teacher. A longer writing sample helps the teacher spot recurrent errors that may be based on faulty correspondences between sound and symbol. For instance, a student may consistently use a *d* when he means to use a *t*. This sort of error can be spotted rapidly when encoding is performed in context. Encoding in context tends to work better with older students, who are capable of generating a text long enough to be analyzed.

Decoding assessments

Whereas encoding assessments require students to write down words as they are spoken, a decoding assessment requires them to pronounce the words they read. For obvious reasons, it is more difficult to administer a formal decoding assessment to a large class, so teachers tend to perform most of their decoding assessments informally, by having students read words aloud or name the letters written on the board. In a more defined decoding assessment, however, the teacher should be given a list of simple, similar words and asked to read them aloud. The list of words should systematically isolate different letters, for instance by including several words with the same ending but different initial letters. This will allow the teacher to pinpoint problems related to particular letters.

One common feature of formal decoding assessments is a series of nonsense words, like *gop*, *bam*, and *rud*. These words are included because, since they could not be a part of the student's sight vocabulary, they provide a clearer look at phonics skills. The value of including

- 28 -

such words is debated among educators: some feel that the words serve a useful purpose, while others feel that phonics assessments should focus on words that actually appear in the English language. When they are used, the teacher should note any disparity between performance on real and made-up words, as a large drop-off related to fake words may indicate serious problems with phonics.

Reading aloud

While beginning students will only be able to decode words in isolation, more advanced readers should be asked to read sentences, short passages, and even complete stories. Once a student has mastered the fundamentals of phonics, any residual problems will only become evident during prolonged sessions of reading aloud. For this reason, teachers tend to perform this assessment piecemeal by calling on various students to read aloud during the course of a content-area lesson. Of course, this technique is counterproductive when students have not obtained sufficient fluency, because listening to a peer stumble through a long paragraph about science is a bad way for the rest of the class to learn. In a more formal version of this exercise, often included as part of an Informal Reading Inventory, the student and teacher are separated from the rest of the class, and the student is asked to read a long section of text out loud. The teacher should keep careful notes of any mispronunciations made by the student. Specifically, the teacher should take note of how words are mispronounced, as repetition of the same mispronunciation will indicate the problem to be resolved.

Reliability and validity

For assessments to be effective, they need to be reliable and valid. In testing, reliability is the consistency between scores from different administrations of

the assessment. If you use the same assessment on the same student twice and get wildly different results, the assessment is unreliable. Validity, on the other hand, is the degree to which a test measures what it was intended to measure. A test with questions about reading comprehension, for example, is an invalid assessment of phonemic awareness. It is essential that an assessment target the specific knowledge and skills the teacher is trying to identify.

Formal assessment

There are a few important terms related to the scoring of formal assessments. When an assessment is norm-referenced, the student's score is compared with those of his peers. Scores from norm-referenced tests are often presented as a percentile. A percentile indicates the percentage of students who scored worse than the student in question. So, if a student scores in the 78th percentile, she has performed better than 78 percent of the other students in her grade. Percentile scores are a good way of seeing how students compare to their classmates; they help identify trends in performance. Another way of presenting formal assessment results is as a grade-equivalent score. In this case, the score is translated into a grade level. A high-achieving third grader might be assigned a grade-equivalent score of 5.2, meaning that his level of knowledge and skill is the same as that of an average fifth grader in the second month of school. Grade-equivalent scores are a handy way of expressing scores in academic terms. Finally, some formal assessments use stanine scores. Stanine, short for standard nine, is a nine-point scale, with one lowest and nine highest. The stanine system provides a general look at performance.

Informal assessment

Whereas formal assessments generate objective results, informal assessments contribute more generally to the teacher's understanding of the student's strengths and weaknesses. Informal assessment is an extremely broad concept: it includes any observation made by the teacher that does not generate a concrete score. For instance, when a teacher asks her class questions about a story they have read together, she is performing an informal assessment of the class. She may not be grading the class' answers, but she is surely taking note of the students who understood the story and those who did not. When a teacher asks students to read aloud, she is collecting information about their ability. Informal assessment can also include assignments completed during class, homework, class presentations, and student conferences. Any interaction between student and teacher that helps the teacher gauge the student's progress can be considered informal assessment.

Theoretical orientation

In the promotion of biliteracy in the ESL classroom, teachers have to juggle a number of competing interests. They want to maintain and develop reading skills in the primary language, but they also want to improve academic language proficiency in English. They may also be constricted by the elements of the ESL program design. In order to organize their efforts, many teachers subscribe to a specific theoretical orientation to reading instruction. The theoretical orientation is simply a set of assumptions and beliefs that prescribe goals and expectations for students. Many teachers use a specific theoretical orientation as a guide to choosing instructional procedures and materials. Teachers will select a theoretical orientation that creates the type of environment they believe is most conducive to expansion of reading skills. There are three main types of theoretical orientation in reading instruction: the phonics approach; the skills or balanced approach; and the whole language approach.

Phonics approach

The phonics approach to ESL reading instruction emphasizes the importance of the relationship between sound and comprehension. A teacher who uses this approach starts out with the basic units of spoken language, phonemes, and gradually increases complexity to include word units, phrases, and sentences. A teacher using this approach goes to a great deal of trouble to outline and make explicit the correspondences between sounds and letters. Instruction on recognizing specific words by sight is only used for words that cannot be decoded by phonics. English is notorious for having a large number of exceptions to the rules of phonics. The phonics approach emphasizes language units smaller than word level, so students typically do not begin reading out loud until they have developed a strong foundation.

Skills/balanced approach

The skills/balanced approach to reading instruction in a secondary language focuses on giving students a set of tools with which to make sense of simple texts. Students in a class that uses this approach will find themselves reading authentic texts in English much faster than will students in a classroom using the phonics approach. The skills approach emphasizes building a large vocabulary of words that can be recognized on sight, with less priority placed on the systematic teaching of phonics. The teacher will try to give students the ability to recognize words by root, prefix, suffix, or configuration. Over time, students will be given the tools to

Copyright © Mometrix Media. You have been licensed one copy of this document for personal use only. Any other reproduction or redistribution is strictly prohibited. All rights reserved.

recognize a word by context. At first, however, the teacher will concentrate on introducing vocabulary words with a concentration on the first and last consonant sounds. Teachers need to perform constant assessment when using this approach to ensure that students are not overwhelmed by the plunge into texts in English.

Whole language approach

Teachers who use the whole language approach to ESL reading instruction concentrate on the specific functions of language. From almost the very beginning of instruction, students are provided with quality children's literature. There is a strong emphasis on communication skills in the whole language approach, with students encouraged to participate in dialogues and role-plays in the English. Students are often encouraged to generate their own stories, and one of the priorities of instruction is to develop an overarching sense of narrative structure before teaching smaller units of language. To the extent that they are used at all, phonics and word attack skills are incorporated in the general reading experience. They are typically mentioned only when they have a direct correlation to a part of the assignment. This approach is especially popular for teaching older students and adults.

Graphophonemic cueing systems

Teachers will often have to use what are known as cueing systems in their interactions with students. There are three basic kinds of cueing system. In the graphophonemic system, the teacher concentrates on explicating grapho-phoneme-morpheme relationships to speed word recognition. In other words, students are encouraged to declare the similarities and differences between written and spoken forms of a sound.

Over time, the teacher seeks to extend phonemic awareness based on sounds in the student's primary language that are different from sounds in English. In general, it is a good idea to conduct this kind of cueing after students have developed a small sight vocabulary. Cueing should follow a logical sequence, and should be sure to inculcate rules thoroughly before presenting any exceptions. Students should be encouraged to apply what they learn about phonics to their independent work.

Semantic/syntactic cueing

The second kind of cueing system that many teachers will need to use is known as the semantic/syntactic cueing system. This involves asking the student to predict the meaning of a word based on syntax and grammar clues. Obviously, this kind of cueing can only work with students who have achieved a moderate level of linguistic knowledge. It is especially valuable with students who need a little practice in discovering context clues and solidifying their understanding of the structure of English syntax. The final kind of cueing system is referred to as discourse or deep structure cueing. In this process, students are encouraged to associate relevant background knowledge with the words that are being discussed. Through creating these associations, it has been found that students improve their chances of memorizing new vocabulary. The discourse method of cueing also enables students to discover underlying patterns of exposition and discourse; that is, it familiarizes them with the ways in which arguments are made in different languages.

Yopp-Singer Test of Phonemic Segmentation

Because sound segmentation is considered the most difficult test of phonemic awareness, many teachers use the Yopp-Singer Test of Phonemic Segmentation as a general measure. In this oral test, the teacher reads 22 words aloud and the student states the component sounds in order. The test should be composed of simple, one-syllable words that the student is likely to know already. The Yopp-Singer Test is a good yardstick for general progress in phonemic awareness, but in order to get a comprehensive look, a teacher needs to assess each of the six phonemic awareness skills. This can be done in similar fashion to the Yopp-Singer, by providing the student with a list of about twenty words and asking him to perform the phonemic task. Of course, the words are to be read aloud to the student.

Sound blending, deletion, isolation, matching, and substitution

To test sound blending the teacher might read words slowly, one phoneme at a time, and ask the student to say the word at regular speed. In the assessment of sound deletion, sound isolation, sound matching, and sound substitution, separate examinations need to be given for beginning, medial, and end phonemes. A sound matching test, for instance, must include twenty cases in which the phonemes are at the beginning of the words, twenty in which the phonemes are in the middle, and twenty in which the phonemes are at the end. Also, it is important to use different phonemes in the exercises. For example, there should not be a long /a/ sound at the beginning of all the words used in a sound matching exercise. Students need to demonstrate that they can perform these phonemic awareness tests with all of the phonemes in the English language.

Emergent literacy model

Three of the most common approaches to providing balanced instruction are the emergent literacy, language acquisition, and reading readiness models. The emergent literacy model suggests that children have a natural tendency towards language learning. In other words, children are constantly exposed to the concepts of print, reading, and oral language, and therefore do not need a great deal of explicit instruction on these subjects. According to the proponents of emergent literacy, students do not need a great deal of external motivation to acquire literacy. Instead, adults and other teachers should create a good environment for learning and then stay out of the way.

Language acquisition model

The language acquisition model is slightly different from the emergent literacy model. Proponents of this model agree that students have a predisposition to become literate, but disagree about the influence of direct instruction. The language acquisition model emphasizes the role of educators in solidifying students' natural understanding of language and literacy. A teacher who subscribes to the language acquisition model would use a greater mix of explicit teaching strategies, so that students can examine their assumptions about language. The language acquisition model, then, includes a great deal of metacognition, or thinking about thinking. Students are encouraged to self-correct their learning processes.

Reading readiness model

The reading readiness model for balanced teaching is opposite to the emergent literacy model. It places a great deal of emphasis on the direct instruction of reading skills, going so far as to suggest that some students will remain illiterate unless they are given explicit instruction in the basics of reading. The proponents of reading readiness deny that literacy can spontaneously emerge from long exposure to texts and language; on the contrary, they claim that certain reading skills are prerequisite to literacy. That is, students must be ready to learn how to read. This model is somewhat undermined by instances of self-teaching, but for most students, it is true that explicit attention must be paid to concepts of literacy.

Basic concepts of print

According to the influential researcher Marie M. Clay, there are four basic print concepts: the meaning of print; the direction of text; letter, word, and sentence representation; and book orientation. The fundamental concept of print is that it has meaning. Some students will arrive in the classroom with this understanding, but others, especially those who do not come from a print-rich home, will not. It is possible to understand that print has meaning without being able to read. Indeed, many students who have not yet obtained literacy demonstrate print awareness by improvising words and narratives for illustrated books. The child cannot read the text, but is aware that it is telling a story related to the illustrations. Such a child has mastered the fundamental concept of print. There are innumerable teaching activities that reinforce this concept: writing on the board, reading a book aloud, and pointing out the words on common traffic signs, for instance. It is important for students to understand that print appears in many places besides books and magazines. Billboards, signs, and product labels all contain meaningful print.

English print orientation

Once a child has mastered the concept that print carries meaning, he can begin to appreciate the style in which English print is written. Specifically, the child can begin to see that English is read from left to right, and that lines of print are read in descending order. The movement from the right end of one line to the left end of the line beneath is known as a return sweep. When a student can perform the return sweep, he has mastered the directionality and tracking of printed English. This concept can be assessed rather easily by following the student's eyes as print is read.

Recognition of letters and sentences

Having obtained some basic orientating principles, students can discover the units of printed English: letters, words, and sentences. Before they can learn to read, students must understand that letters make up words, and that words make up sentences. Students must be able to identify how many letters are in a word, as well as how spaces indicate the boundaries of a word. Provided they have sufficient counting ability, students should be able to enumerate the letters in the word and the words in a sentence. Students should be able to identify the marks of punctuation that indicate the end of a sentence (namely the period, question mark, and exclamation point). Moreover, students should be able to recognize how these rules of print exist in different formats, such as on books, signs, and labels. Of course, students do not need to be literate to demonstrate all of these skills. On the contrary, most students acquire a basic knowledge of print units long before they can read, much less identify specific letters and words.

Features of a book

The last of the basic print concepts outlined by Clay is the features of a book. Students need to be able to identify the various book parts, like the cover, the pages, and the back cover. Students should know how a book is held and how it is stored. Eventually, students should be able to distinguish between the name of the book and the name of the author on the front cover. The student should know that a book is read from the front to the back and from the left page to the right page. Picture books are especially good at demonstrating these concepts, because the sequence of the pictures corresponding to the action is the same as the sequence of print locations. In other words, the illustrations can be followed throughout the book in the same way as the print. Almost all students will have a basic idea of how a book is handled while it is being read. A teacher, though, needs to ensure that students understand the steps in reading a book, as well as the parts of a book.

Letter recognition

Along with these four concepts, many educators include letter recognition as a fundamental part of early print awareness. Letter recognition is simply the identification of the letter in both uppercase and lowercase forms. Accurate and rapid uppercase and lowercase letter recognition is an essential component of reading development. Letter recognition does not entail writing the letter or even knowing the sound produced by the letter. All it entails is seeing the letter and being able to give its name. Some teachers do combine letter recognition with basic letter production, though it is not necessary to do so. Letter recognition develops along with the alphabetic principle: that is, the idea that English words are made up of individual letters, each of which has an identity of its own.

Alphabetic principle

The alphabet in a language is the set of letters that make up all the words. One of the first things that most students learn in their linguistic studies is the alphabet. For one thing, students need to be familiar with all the letterforms before they can begin producing written expressions. As students are learning their letters, the teacher needs to ensure that they make the connection between the way a letter is written and the way it sounds. Even when this connection is primitive, it paves the way for a more sophisticated understanding of language in the future. At this point, teachers are attempting to promote the so-called alphabetical principle: specific sounds are consistently associated with specific letters.

One of the problems with implementing the alphabetic principle in English is that English does not always do a very good job of following the alphabetic principle. There are innumerable examples of letters that have multiple sounds or words in which particular letters make no sound at all. To avoid burdening students with these exceptions to the basic alphabetic rules, a teacher needs to be good at selecting solid examples for early class instruction. As students progress, it may become appropriate to begin discussing the complexity of the English language as it relates to the alphabet. The only way to determine when it is appropriate is to have a solid mastery of informal and formal assessment.

For some students, establishing the alphabetic principle is quite difficult. For this reason, teachers need to have on hand a broad spectrum of instructional materials, including books, drawings, and manipulatives. Furthermore, teachers need to be able to use all of these materials appropriately. Some students learn more effectively through the use of touch, and should be given manipulatives in the shapes of the letters. The ability to effectively implement a wide variety of instructional strategies obviously depends on accurate assessment. Other good sources of information about instructional methodology are coworkers and research journals.

Reading aloud

The easiest way to solidify print concepts is to read aloud to the class. Reading aloud demonstrates how books are held, how pages are turned, and, most important, how those mysterious symbols on the page become spoken words with meaning. Of course, the students will not be thinking such dry thoughts as the story is being read. Nevertheless, simply reading an interesting storybook to a group of students is a great way to indicate the basic concepts of print. This process is strengthened when the teacher points at the words as they are read and moves slowly through each line of text. Even when students have little letter recognition, they will quickly figure out that the hand movements of the teacher correspond to the words coming out of her mouth. Also, before beginning the book, the teacher can show students the cover and point to the title and the name of the author.

Sometimes, reading aloud is undermined by the size of the class. If there are too many students, the ones farthest away from the teacher may not be able to see her point to each word as it is read. Thus, some of the value of the exercise is lost. Some ingenious publishers have surmounted this problem by creating enormous books with extra-large type, so that even students in the very back row can see the layout clearly. When these books are not available, however, teachers should be ready to use some alternate strategies. For instance, many teachers just divide the class into groups and read the story to the groups in turn. One advantage of this strategy is that the teacher has more opportunity to observe each of the students. Also, students in a small group are more likely to pay attention to the book. (Of course, this presumes that the remaining students will stay on task!) Reading aloud to small groups is a great job to give teaching assistants and parent volunteers. The reader should move slowly through the book, pointing at every word as it is read.

Developing sound matching skills

Sound matching is the identification of identical phonemes. In other words, sound matching requires the student to discern when two words contain the same sound. This is not the same as rhyming, because the identical sounds can appear in different parts of the words and need not appear at the end. For instance, a teacher might ask students to name the sound the words *apple*, *pear*, and *peach* have in common. If the students can see that the /p/ sound is present in all three of these words, then they are adept at sound matching. Another way to teach sound matching is to have students identify classroom objects that begin with a certain sound. For instance, a teacher might make the /p/ sounds and see if students can point out the posters, plants, picture frames, and other items that begin with a *p*. To work on sound matching with phonemes in the medial or end positions, the teacher could pronounce a phoneme and then three words, only one of which contains the given phoneme. This word should have the phoneme in the medial or end position. The teacher can then ask the students to identify the word containing the given phoneme.

Sound isolation skills

Sound isolation is the identification of the component sounds in a word. Even one-syllable words can have multiple phonemes. Students with no training in syllabification or word analysis may nevertheless be able to identify the series of discrete sounds that make up a word. To begin with, sound isolation can be taught by asking students to identify the sound at the beginning of a number of words with the same initial letter. For example, the teacher might determine whether students can identify that *girl*, *gift*, and *gear* all start with the /g/ sound. A teacher might ask her class to isolate the sounds in the word *flag*. This word contains four separate sounds, one for each of its letters. To be competent at sound isolation, students must be able to identify the beginning, medial, and end phonemes. Of course, some phonemes (like diphthongs) are more difficult to identify. So long as students are capable of identifying simple phonemes in all the possible positions within a word, they are judged to have phonemic awareness. It is a good idea to show students how the same phoneme can appear in different words, so that students do not too closely associate a phoneme with a particular word.

Sound blending skills

Sound blending is the combination of disparate phonemes to create a word. When teachers slowly pronounce a word, one sound at a time, they are essentially modeling sound blending for their students. Students demonstrate sound blending by speeding up this slow pronunciation and using the word as it is normally spoken. For instance, a teacher could model the word *ball* by saying *b*, then *aw*, then *ll*. Students should be able to combine these sounds to form the entire word. One common technique when modeling this pronunciation is to include a drawing or photograph of the object being pronounced. Also, sound blending often occurs as part of a phonics lesson, in which students pronounce the parts of the word as the teacher points at the various letters. However, for the purposes of phonemic awareness, it is not necessary to have the written version of the word. All that matters is that the students can identify how the constituent phonemes join to create a word.

Sound substitution skills

Sound substitution is the transfer of different phonemes into a given position in a word. For example, a student with phonemic awareness could hear the word *boy* and would know that if a /k/ sound were used instead, the resulting word would sound like *coy*. Once again, a student does not need to have any understanding of print or written language in order to master sound substitution. Also, it is perfectly acceptable for the class to create nonsense words when practicing sound substitution. One common method of reinforcing this skill is with the song, "I Like to Eat Apples and Bananas." This song has very simple lyrics, but in each verse all of the vowel sounds are replaced with a single sound. So, after the initial verse of "I like to eat apples and bananas," the song proceeds to "A lake tay ate apples and bananas," with all of the *a* sounds being long. The song then moves on to *e*, *i*, *o*, and *u*. Of course, the lyrics of the song become gibberish when all of the vowel sounds are the same, but students will soon find it easy to substitute phonemes.

Sound deletion skills

Sound deletion is the identification of what results when a phoneme is removed from a given word. This task is a little bit more difficult, because it requires students not only to understand that words are composed of individual sounds, but that sounds can be taken away from words. As an example, a teacher might ask the class to pronounce the word *boy*, and then to pronounce what is left when the /b/ sound is removed. It is a good idea to begin by removing initial phonemes, but students should eventually be able to delete medial and end phonemes as well. Many teachers have found that sound deletion is best introduced with consonant blends (such

- 36 -

as in the words *spray* and *glade*), perhaps because the removal of the initial consonant does not drastically change the structure of the word.

Sound segmentation skills

Sound segmentation is the identification of all the component phonemes in a word. This is considered by most education experts to be the most difficult task in phonemic awareness. Most students can easily identify the beginning phonemes but have a harder time with the medial and end phonemes. It is best to start with simple words. For instance, a teacher might pronounce the word *tub* and see if students can identify the /t/, /u/, and /b/ sounds. In order for sound segmentation to be complete, the student must identify all three of the sounds. It is not a good idea to begin sound segmentation with multisyllable words or words with diphthongs. Also, sound segmentation should not be confused with syllabification, in which words are divided into their component syllables.

Promoting phonemic awareness

Several activities promote phonemic awareness. Even children in the early stages of literacy will have an intuitive understanding of rhyme, so a teacher could ask students to come up with rhymes for a simple word like *cat*. Similarly, a teacher can use simple songs to illustrate rhyming and promote phonemic awareness. Many books for children are written in verse or feature alliteration (the repetition of initial sounds), both of which can be used to introduce phonemic concepts. Assonance, which is the repetition of a vowel sound, can also be used to demonstrate phonemic awareness.

Identification of the main idea

Literal comprehension is an understanding of the explicit elements of the text. In other words, it is the comprehension of the author's direct message. There are four component skills in literal comprehension. To begin with, a student must be able to identify an explicit main idea. Of course, in many texts (for instance, in stories), there will be no main idea as such or the main idea will not be stated directly. When reading an expository or informational text, however, students must be able to ascertain the author's central message. Even when a main idea is not explicit, a reader should be able to describe the tone of the message.

Identification of details, sequence of events, and causal relationships

The second literal comprehension skill is the ability to identify important details in the text. As with the main idea, some texts will not permit ready identification of important details. Nevertheless, a student should be able to identify some important supporting elements in the text and be able to articulate why they are important. The third skill is identifying the sequence of events in a story or the sequence of argument in an expository text. If the student has mastered the identification of main idea and supporting details, recognizing the sequence should not pose any problems. Finally, literal comprehension requires the identification of cause-and-effect relationships. This is similar to identifying the sequence of events, though it forces the student to look for specific and explicit reasons for the events.

Inferential comprehension

Inferential comprehension, meanwhile, is the understanding of the implicit elements of the text. Everything that is not written by the author but can be guessed by the reader is in the realm of inferential comprehension. Inferential comprehension skills are essentially the same as literal comprehension skills, except they rely on the perception of implied ideas and events. The two components of inferential comprehension are inferring an implicit main idea and inferring details, sequence of events, and cause-and-effect relationships. For most students, inferential comprehension lags behind literal comprehension. This is to be expected: students who are still solidifying the mechanics of reading have no thought to spare for implied messages. Nevertheless, even at a young age, students can be encouraged to begin thinking of the implications of what they read, so that once their basic skills have evolved, they will be primed to think about texts in a more sophisticated manner.

Evaluative comprehension

The third set of reading comprehension skills, those of evaluative comprehension, is probably the most advanced. Evaluative comprehension is the ability to consider the text as a whole and to make judgments about it. Students must achieve fluency in all areas of reading before they can evaluate a text effectively. Three specific skills combine in evaluative comprehension. To begin with, a student must be able to recognize an author's bias. This is similar perhaps to inferential comprehension, insofar as it requires the reader to look beyond the explicit message in the text. When making an ostensibly objective argument, an author will often reveal his personal inclination through details, passing comments, and subtle characterizations. It takes a great deal of perception on the part of the reader to detect bias.

Detecting propaganda

A significant component of evaluative comprehension is the detection of propaganda. Propaganda is argument or information communicated for the sole purpose of helping or harming a particular group. Although the word has acquired a negative connotation in English, not all propaganda is destructive. A leaflet outlining the reasons to help the poor, for instance, might be propaganda on behalf of a charity organization, but not many people would criticize it. Often, however, propaganda is not explicitly declared as such. When this is the case, students need to be able to identify it.

Fact and opinion

The final component of evaluative comprehension is distinguishing between fact and opinion. In the first few years of reading instruction, a student is unlikely to encounter texts in which the boundary between fact and opinion is ambiguous. As students grow up and begin reading texts of greater complexity, however, it will sometimes be difficult to tell when an author is stating an established truth and when he is simply giving an opinion. It is essential for students to recognize the difference, so that they can make informed decisions about what is being said. As with propaganda, it should be noted that subtle or implied opinion is not necessarily a bad thing. In many cases, students will agree wholeheartedly with the opinion of the author. The important thing is to recognize when an opinion is being given. Students need to cultivate this skill so that they can think critically about advertising, editorial messages, and other opinionated communications.

Syntax and comprehension

Syntax (the order of the words in a sentence) can facilitate or impede reading comprehension. English is an uninflected language, which means that the grammatical use of words is not denoted by their ending. Unlike inflected languages like Latin, then, the words in an English sentence must be in a particular order to make sense. As students begin to encounter texts of greater sophistication, however, they will see increasingly complex sentence structures. Some of these may be inscrutable to developing readers. It is very important for students to understand complex grammatical structures. This understanding can be aided by sentence diagramming, though oral presentation of complex sentences can also have a positive effect. If a teacher reads a complex sentence with appropriate prosodic emphasis, the student receives a model for comprehension.

Independent reading

Independent reading can be a great help in the reinforcement of comprehension skills and strategies. Students who read by themselves become self-reliant with respect to comprehension. To this end, teachers should provide frequent opportunities for sustained silent reading in class. As students grow older, these sessions may increase in duration. Students should be encouraged to select books related to their interests or books that they will enjoy. Independent reading texts should always be at grade level. Education experts agree that the promotion of purposeful independent reading is the foundation of healthy reading habits for life.

Self-monitoring and reading comprehension

A teacher needs to have some explicit instruction strategies for improving comprehension and helping students monitor their own comprehension. Reading is not as simple as moving the eyes across the page and following the word-for-word meaning of the message. It also includes relating sentences, paragraphs, and chapters to one another, weighing the argument or style of the author, and evaluating the message in its totality. This is a tall order, and students need to become accustomed to self-monitoring their performance in order to ensure optimal comprehension. Students should get into the habit of continually asking themselves, "Do I understand this?" If the answer is no, the student needs to reread and possibly ask for assistance. Students should be taught that there is no shame in not understanding a text, but that failing to recognize this and respond is unacceptable.

Self-monitoring

There are a number of activities that students can use to self-monitor. If a student truly understands a text, he should be able to paraphrase its message. This means that the student should be able to articulate the main ideas without direct reference to the text. Also, the student should be able to put these ideas in his own words. This can be done orally or in writing. When the student's self-monitoring indicates that comprehension is suboptimal, the student should know to slow down. Sometimes, students feel pressure to finish a reading assignment quickly, and so they short-change comprehension. When this is the case, the teacher should relax any time constraints and allow the student to take as much time as necessary with the text. There is no benefit to reading unless there is comprehension, so simply skimming a text that needs to be learned is a waste of time. Students would be better off reading a short passage closely than merely glancing over the entire text.

Taking notes

One way to ensure comprehension during the reading process is to take notes. In many cases, it will not be appropriate for students to write directly in the book, but they may write key ideas and questions on their own paper. Simply writing out the ideas from a text can be a major spur to comprehension. Students should be encouraged to write down any questions they develop while reading. It is a good habit to read with a pen and paper handy, since even the best readers cannot achieve total recall. At the very least, students should mark sections that ought to be reread, either because of their significance or their obscurity.

Class discussion

After reading is complete, the teacher should use different instructional strategies to reinforce and cultivate comprehension. As much as possible, the teacher should lead class discussions of texts immediately after they are read and while they are still fresh in the minds of the class. Articulating the ideas of the text and listening to the reactions of classmates is a great way for students to solidify their understanding. In particular, the teacher should encourage students to make text-to-self, text-to-text, and text-to-world connections; that is, students should be encouraged to relate the ideas and events of the text to themselves, to other texts, and to the world in general. Comprehension requires critical as well as creative thinking.

Pictures, semantic maps, and Venn diagrams

One of the most popular methods for increasing creative thinking about texts is to lead students in the creation of pictures, semantic maps, and Venn diagrams. Works of fiction often lend themselves to interpretation through drawing or painting. Students might be asked to draw a main character based on the description in the text, or perhaps to depict a major scene from the story. A semantic map is more appropriate for an expository or informational text, in which ideas and new vocabulary are presented in a network of relationships. A Venn diagram, finally, is composed of overlapping circles. For instance, an article about Congress might inspire a Venn diagram with two circles: one representing the Senate, and one representing the House of Representatives. These circles should partially overlap. The functions that are exclusive to each body would be written in the non-overlapping part, and the functions that are shared or performed by both bodies would be placed in the overlapping part.

SQ3R

SQ3R stands for survey, question, read, recite, and review. This formula for in-depth reading has been around since 1946. It breaks the process down into five simple steps, in part as a way to demystify the experience of deep reading. The student begins by surveying the entire passage to be read, noting the title and section headings, any key words in bold, and any pulled quotes. Next, the student writes down a few questions that he expects will be answered by the text. This helps the student to structure his thinking about the text. The student then reads the text, all the while considering the questions he has posed. After reading, the student recites the material in the text, and in particular seeks to answer the questions posed earlier. Finally, the student reviews the material a few times in the future.

KWL charts

KWL charts are used to improve reading comprehension and textual analysis. The chart is divided into three parts: what students already **know** about the subject, what they **want** the text to teach them about the subject, and, after they finish reading, what they have **learned** about the subject. The titles of the three sections (**K**now, **W**ant to know, and **L**earned) give the chart its name. A KWL chart helps students approach a text in such a way that they will obtain maximum benefit from reading. These charts are a simple way to organize one's thoughts about a text.

QAR system

The QAR (question-answer relationships) system is an easy way for teachers to guarantee that they are asking a healthy range of reading comprehension questions. The QAR system distinguishes four types of question: right there; think and search; author and you; and on my own. A "right there" question probes literal comprehension by asking student to identify explicit details from the text. A "think and search" question requires the student to draw information from different parts of the text. Such a question might require the student to support his answer with examples from all over the text. An "author and you" question assesses inferential comprehension by asking the students to draw on their own knowledge and experience to answer a question about the text. This is distinct from an "on my own" question, which encourages the students to think about their own lives in the context of issues raised by the text. An "on my own" question takes the text as a starting point and asks the student to consider examples from his own life.

CLOZE tests

CLOZE (short for "closure") tests are used to determine whether students will be able to understand a given text. Teachers often use them before beginning work with a particular textbook in a content area like science or social studies. The teacher takes a passage from the beginning of any chapter besides the first. He then enters the passage into a word processor and deletes every fifth word. The teacher hands out copies of the modified passage to the students and asks them to read the passage in its entirety, and then go back and attempt to fill in the blanks. If the student gets at least 40 percent of the answers correct (the only correct answer is the word in the original text), then the teacher should be able to use the text successfully. The passage must be at least 275 words so that there will be sufficient blanks.

Read-alouds

Listening comprehension is the foundation of reading comprehension development. To this end, teachers need to incorporate oral language activities in the development of comprehension skills. For example, teachers can lead strategic, purposeful read-alouds. A read-aloud is the guided oral presentation of a story, with pauses at key points for questioning and discussion. As the class proceeds through the text, the teacher might pause to ask them to evaluate what has happened or predict what is about to happen. The teacher might also pause just to ask students to identify some main ideas or details from the text.

Methods of text-based discussion

Text-based discussions, such as instructional conversations, questions for the author, and think-pair-share exercises, can enhance reading comprehension. In an instructional conversation, the teacher helps the student develop an approach to comprehension by asking questions about the main idea and details. This is a sort of

Socratic dialogue, in which the teacher probes the student's knowledge and tries to make the student evaluate his assumptions and judgments. Another method is to have students come up with questions for the author. This exercise is good for demonstrating that texts do not just provide answers, they also generate questions. In a think-pair-share exercise, the teacher asks the entire class a question about the text they have just read. Students then arrange themselves into pairs, where they discuss their answers to the question. The student pairs then share their answers with the class at large. This progressive activity gives students a chance to refine their insights.

Letter recognition

Letter recognition can be reinforced through reading aloud, but it will probably require some more direct instruction at first. The tried and true method of developing letter recognition is to lead children slowly through the alphabet song while pointing to each letter as it is sung. Research has indicated that students learn unfamiliar material much more quickly when they are given a mnemonic, or memory aid. In this case, the alphabet song is such a mnemonic. Of course, the song only primes the students' brains for more specific training in letter recognition. A teacher should also lead the class in activities that require more sophisticated letter recognition. For instance, a teacher might ask the students to identify individual letters in a storybook.

Alphabet books

There are a number of books that proceed through the alphabet in order, exemplifying each letter with a couple of objects ("A is for apple," etc.). Another way to build letter recognition is to hand out index cards printed with a letter and

then write a message in large print on the chalkboard. Students will then be asked to tape their index card over the letter where it appears in the chalkboard message. The cards can be shuffled and distributed several times, so that students get to perform the exercise with different letters. It is important for students to recognize letters both in and out of the alphabetic sequence. In other words, if a student can only identify a *J* by saying to himself "H, I, J, K," then this student needs to improve his letter recognition.

Concepts About Print

One simple formal assessment for print concepts is the Concepts About Print test, developed by Marie M. Clay. This test requires special books, which are available from educational publishers or can be made easily by teachers. A CAP test book contains at least ten pages, some of which are upside down and on some of which the print is jumbled and oriented incorrectly. For instance, the print on one page might run from right to left or vertically up the page. However, the majority of the pages in the book should be laid out in the traditional manner. The book should be a simple story and should only include basic vocabulary. The cover and title pages should be positioned correctly.

To perform a CAP test, the teacher gives the book to the student and asks her to identify the cover, the title, and the author's name. The teacher then asks the child to open the book to the first page. Once there, the student should be asked to identify the starting word of the book. The teacher should read through the book slowly. At various times, the student should be asked where the teacher is to read next. Also, the student should be asked to count the letters in a word and the words in a sentence. If the student is advanced enough to have developed some sight vocabulary, he should be asked to identify some elementary words. If possible, the student should hold the book and turn the pages throughout the test. As the test continues, the student should be asked to identify common punctuation marks and in particular those that end a sentence. When the student comes to later sections in which text has been jumbled or laid out improperly, the student should be asked how to resolve the situation.

Print concept instruction

Students whose first language is not English may require extra help with print concepts. In particular, students whose native language is fundamentally different from English should receive special attention. Differentiated instruction for English language learners should recognize that not all languages are alphabetic. Alphabetic languages are those in which words are composed of letters. The letters in an alphabetic language remain the same, but are arranged into thousands of words. Alphabetic languages are distinguished by how regular the correspondence is between symbol and sound. Spanish, for example, is described as a transparent language because the sound of each letter is very predictable. English, on the other hand, is called an opaque language because many letters can make a variety of different sounds. If a child has experience only with transparent alphabetic languages, he may need some help in understanding that English letters are capable of producing a range of sounds.

Problems with print concepts

Native English speakers are often surprised to learn that only some languages adhere to the alphabetic principle. Many languages, such as Chinese, are not alphabetic at all. Chinese is a logographic language, which means that it is composed of pictures that represent entire words. A Chinese character is not a sequence of letters; it is an entire entity representing one word alone. Children who have grown up in a logographic linguistic culture will need more instruction with regard to print concepts in English. In many of these languages, the direction of print is different as well, so this too may necessitate instruction.

Fluency and reading

Fluency plays an important role in all stages of reading development. Indeed, fluency, word analysis skills, vocabulary, academic language, background knowledge, and comprehension are all related. For instance, fluency helps connect word analysis skills and comprehension. Once a child is fluent enough to decode words automatically, he will also be able to comprehend text much more quickly. According to the automaticity theory, fluency is directly responsible for reading comprehension improvement. In particular, students seem to demonstrate rapid advances in comprehension once they are fluent enough to read at a rate similar to that at which words are spoken. Once it is possible for a student to read at this normal rate, it becomes much easier to concentrate on the message of the text. Indeed, many authorities state that prosody and comprehension have a reciprocal relationship; that is, the improvement of prosody will contribute to the development of reading comprehension skills. The addition of the dramatic phrasing and intonation of prosody makes basic comprehension much easier. Indeed, phrasing and intonation communicate information as surely as words do: by spacing out blocks of words and placing emphasis on certain parts of a sentence, these prosodic elements tell the listener or reader what is important and what is not.

Accuracy, rate, and prosody

There are three interrelated indicators of reading fluency: accuracy, rate, and prosody. Accuracy is the correct decoding and recognition of words. Rate is the speed at which words are recognized correctly. Automaticity, then, is a combination of exceptional accuracy and a rapid rate of reading. Prosody, meanwhile, is the dramatic and artful reading style that improves the attention and understanding of the listener. Prosody may include applying the appropriate stresses or emphases, varying pitch and intonation, and pausing at appropriate times. All of the devices that an experienced speaker can use to present a text artfully fall under the heading of prosody. To do this, a speaker must have mastered the basics of written language. In order to phrase well, for instance, one must have a good knowledge of syntax and mechanics.

Fluency disruption

Unfortunately, a number of factors can disrupt fluency. They include a lack of familiarity with vocabulary, weak word analysis skills, a lack of background knowledge, a lack of familiarity with complicated syntactic structures, and an encounter with a text that has a number of seldom-used, multisyllabic content words. Fluency cannot be developed by repeated exposure to sophisticated texts. Instead, it must be cultivated gradually by repeated exposure to texts of ever-increasing sophistication. It is very important to give students decodable texts in order to promote fluent reading, especially while students are developing basic phonics skills. Over time, students should be shifted to texts of greater sophistication.

Repeated reading and choral reading

As with other elements of reading instruction, systematic and explicit instruction is very important in promoting fluency development. A number of activities promote fluency. One is repeated reading, in which the teacher or students read the same text aloud two or more times in a row. Repeated reading allows students to anticipate words and phrases, which means they are more likely to improve their accuracy and rate and incorporate elements of prosody. Another way to improve fluency is through choral reading, in which the class reads a text aloud in unison. Choral reading will be dominated by the most advanced students in the class; however, as long as they are not discouraged, other students will improve their fluency in their effort to keep up. Choral reading should be performed slowly and should be led by the teacher.

Dramatic reading and reading with a recording

In dramatic reading exercises, students are encouraged to act out the narrative described in the text. Students will need to be familiar with the text before they can provide a decent dramatic reading, but once they do so, they may gain appreciation for the ways that reading can resemble performance. Encouraging students to think of a text as a message with emotional and dramatic content is a great way to develop fluency. Dramatic reading works well for developing fluency, but it requires a great deal of class participation. In some cases, it may be better to have students work individually. A great individual activity to improve fluency is to have students follow along with a recorded reading of a book. Students can read silently while listening to the recorded version on headphones. It is essential that the

- 44 -

recorded book be easily decodable for the student.

Reading silently vs. reading aloud

In the past, many education authorities recommended independent reading for improving fluency. However, independent, silent reading can only create so much in the way of automaticity. Students tend to skip over words they do not understand without spending any time trying to decode structure or context. Before students acquire automaticity, they need to work on reading aloud, even if only to themselves. The act of reading aloud forces students to confront every word in the text and to try pronouncing it at least. Repeated attempts in this manner will eventually result in automaticity.

Improving fluency

Developing the fluency of English language learners creates some unique challenges. For English learners and speakers of nonstandard English, it may be necessary to give extra instruction with English patterns of intonation, phrasing, syntax, and punctuation. In particular, students who come from logographic linguistic communities may need assistance with these uniquely English elements of written and spoken language. One easy way to provide such an opportunity is to show these students movies in English. In many cases, students live with non-English speakers and have had much less incidental exposure to the rhythms and conventions of spoken English.

Informal reading inventory

One of the most common versions of informal assessment is called the informal reading inventory, or IRI. The precise contents of an informal reading inventory vary by student ability, but the following tests are frequently included: word recognition list; graded reading passage; reading interest survey; print concepts test; phonemic awareness test; phonics test; structural analysis test; CLOZE test for content-area reading; vocabulary test; and spelling test. These assessments make up a comprehensive assessment of reading. Informal reading inventories are typically administered individually, so that the teacher can observe the student's performance. In some cases, the informal reading inventories administered to two students in the same class will be different. There is more flexibility in informal assessment; the teacher has more freedom to select the precise array of assessments that will be most helpful.

The purpose of the informal reading inventory is to establish the student's independent, instructional, and frustration reading levels. At the independent reading level, the student understands and can pronounce 95 percent of the words in the text and answers 90 percent of grade-level reading comprehension questions correctly. Students reading at this level do not need any help from the teacher or from their classmates. This is a good level for pleasure and research reading. At the instructional reading level, the student understands and can pronounce 90 percent of the words in the text and answers at least 60 percent of grade-level reading comprehension questions. A student reading at the instructional level will need some help, though he ultimately will be capable of reading the text. A textbook or basal reader should be at the student's instructional reading level, so that he will be challenged but not overwhelmed.

The protocol for performing an informal reading inventory with an ESL student is only slightly different. Because these students may have comprehension skills that far surpass their vocabulary, they

- 45 -

should be given an opportunity to demonstrate understanding in ways other than language. For instance, ESL students might be asked to draw a picture or short comic strip depicting the events of a story. Indeed, illustrated stories can be a particular help with ESL students, because the connections between illustration and text reinforce fluency. ESL students may also benefit from hearing a story read aloud, since otherwise they may develop bad pronunciation habits based on their native language.

Frustration reading level

At the frustration reading level, the student cannot understand or pronounce at least 90 percent of the words in the text and cannot answer at least 60 percent of grade-level reading comprehension questions. Children should not be made to read at their frustration level without assistance. It should be noted that children are perfectly able to listen to and obtain meaning from texts they themselves would read at the frustration level. However, children will not obtain any benefit from reading such advanced texts on their own or aloud. On the contrary, prolonged exposure to frustration-level texts can be damaging to self-esteem and the development of literacy.

Assessing the components of fluency

The assessment of fluency is generally holistic, since fluency itself is an integration of disparate language skills. There are unique assessments for the components of fluency, however. A teacher needs to be able to use all types of assessments with respect to all three components of fluency. Accuracy and rate can be easily assessed by having the student read a grade-level text aloud. The accuracy of reading can be determined by calculating the number of words read

correctly as a portion of the total words read. The rate of reading can be calculated on a per-minute basis by timing the student as he reads. Students should not be encouraged to read quickly, but rather to read with as much expression as they can. Prosody is a little more difficult to measure directly. Students may be asked to read a narrative aloud with as much expression as possible. Various generic rubrics are available that allow teachers to grade all areas of prosody: intonation, phrasing, etc. Many teachers audiotape these readings so that they can assess in more depth.

Holistic methods

The holistic assessment of fluency can be accomplished many different ways. Teachers often use dramatic or choral readings as informal assessments of fluency. Fluency should be assessed with regard to both unfamiliar and familiar texts. When students are being assessed on their reading of a text with which they are unfamiliar, the text must be at grade level. If a text is too difficult for the student to read fluently, the results of assessment will be useless. This is because a student's performance on a text that is just a little too hard is liable to be indistinguishable from his performance on a text that is way too hard. It is also worthwhile to assess students as they read texts that they have read a few times. Students who have a concept of prosody but do not yet have enough accuracy or speed to make use of this knowledge will demonstrate much more fluency when they are working with a familiar text.

Phonemic instruction for ELL

There are not many changes in phonemic instruction for English language learners. It is likely that most of the English phonemes will be present in the student's native language. The teacher should consult a reference to determine which phonemes the student is unlikely to know already. These phonemes should receive extra attention during instruction. Other than that, the instructional methods for English language learners are the same as for native English speakers. If necessary, the teacher may begin activities by working in the student's first language, though the transition to English should be made as soon as possible.

Problems learning phonics

Students for whom English is a second language may have some initial trouble with phonics. Long exposure to their native language will have created certain "habits of listening," which may make it difficult for the students to identify subtle variations in the way English letters (in particular vowels) are pronounced. These students may be well served by extra exposure to English rhymes and word families, though simply receiving greater exposure to English as it is spoken will inevitably bring them up to speed. Indeed, most experts assert that English language learners ought to acquire basic oral fluency before turning to written language. In large part, this is because the habits of speech contribute to an intuitive understanding of orthography and spelling. In addition, however, the comfort and confidence derived from oral fluency will be important during what is often a difficult transition. Some languages, including Spanish, use a similar alphabet and have significant overlap with English phonics. Teachers should reinforce these similarities while spending more time going over the differences. It should be assumed that advanced English language learners already have competence in phonics in their first language, so instruction in English can focus on specific problem areas.

Sight vocabulary

The assessment of sight vocabulary is fairly simple and can be conducted either formally or informally. The student should be presented with the word and asked to read it aloud. If the word is in sight vocabulary, the student should be able to read the word without hesitation and without sounding it out. If the word has more than one phoneme or syllable, there should be no gaps or pauses during pronunciation. Sight vocabulary should be assessed both in and out of context. In other words, the teacher should observe the student reading sight vocabulary words as part of a sentence as well as on their own. Sometimes, students automatically pronounce isolated words that they might stumble over in the midst of a complex sentence. For a word truly to be in sight vocabulary, it must be read almost reflexively, no matter how it is presented.

Teaching multisyllabic words

Instruction must begin by covering multisyllabic words that are formed by the addition of a common prefix or suffix to a base word. One of the most common strategies for improving word identification is to teach students the common morphemes and affixes (prefixes and suffixes). This strategy is especially useful with words derived from Latin, because they have a more regular structure. Structural analysis can be taught through a phonics-centered method or through the balanced literary approach. Either way, the teacher should be familiar with the basic word parts: root words, prefixes, suffixes, inflectional endings, and contractions.

Root words, affixes, and contractions

Root words are the bases from which complex words are developed. In the word *working*, for instance, the root word

- 47 -

is *work*. The other part of this word, *–ing*, is both a suffix and an inflectional ending. A suffix is any ending attached to a root word, while an inflectional ending is a suffix that alters the meaning of the word. In this case, the addition of the suffix *–ing* changes the tense of *work*. A prefix, meanwhile, is attached to the beginning of a word. Adding the prefix *re-* to the start of *working*, for instance, would make the word mean "working again." Prefixes have regular meanings and can be taught easily. Contractions are abbreviated combinations of two words, like *don't* for *do not* or *would've* for *would have*. In a contraction, the deleted letters are replaced by an apostrophe.

Teaching affixes

There is a recommended sequence for the instruction of affixes. The teacher should begin by focusing on the correspondence between letters and sounds. Once this has been established, the teacher should introduce the affixes in isolation. Some of the most common prefixes are *pre-*, *re-*, *un-*; some of the most common suffixes are *–ing*, *-tion*, and *–ment*. Students should become familiar with these affixes by themselves at first. Then, the teacher can give examples of how they are used in specific words. Once students have learned some examples of these common affixes, the words can be taught as they appear in context. One way to expand on discussion of common word structures is to guide students in the creation of word webs. A word web has at its center a common root, like *port*. Students can then draw lines out from this hub to other words that share that root, like *deport*, *important*, *import*, and *portable*. Many students benefit from this kind of depiction of the relationships between words.

Syllabic analysis

Structural analysis will be useful with many types of words, but students also need to have syllabic analysis skills. Instruction should cover multisyllabic words with the common syllable patterns. In particular, students should receive special instruction related to compound words. Compound words comprise two or more base words. Some common compound words are *mailbox*, *bookmark*, and *butterfly*. Some students will benefit here from special instruction on syllabification. Although students may have developed solid phonemic awareness, they may not yet understand the division of a large word into syllables. There are many ways to teach this lesson, but perhaps the easiest is through song. In a song, notes are correspondent not to words but to syllables. By singing along with a simple song, children can learn to appreciate how words are divided. In addition, the teacher might ask students to pronounce multisyllabic words one syllable at a time, clapping on each syllable. Creating a rhythm of syllables helps many students understand the structural characteristics of words.

Natural order hypothesis

In developing the secondary language writing skills of students, teachers should keep in mind the natural order hypothesis introduced by Krashen. This hypothesis suggests that there is a typical order of linguistic acquisition. In general, the ability to write will lag one or two levels behind oral proficiency level. Students will take a bit longer to develop a sense of form in their writing, and it may take them even longer to describe events and things accurately in their writing. Students will begin by learning to write words and simple phrases; with time, they will be able to compose sentences and eventually simple narratives. Bilingual students will often exhibit a strong reliance on their primary language proficiency in their English compositions. Some of the syntax errors that the individual makes in oral speech are likely to appear in writing as well. It is also common for bilingual students to spell words according to the letter-sound correspondence common to their primary language.

Development of written communication

The ability to create thoughtful and meaningful written communication is one of the last elements of literacy to develop. Teachers need to be patient with students as they develop these skills. Although the development of written communication skills may lag behind the development of reading and speaking skills, teachers should not ignore the many connections between these aspects of literacy. For instance, through reading, students can develop an appreciation for the various letterforms. Speaking and listening to language can help students develop a feel for the rhythms and intonations of English sentences, so that when they begin to compose their own written work, they will intuitively mimic these qualities.

Writing activities that improve reading comprehension

Writing activities can help to support and reinforce comprehension. For example, summarizing, outlining, and responding are all very useful. Summarizing is the brief recapitulation of the main points or events in a text. It can be performed orally or in writing. Outlining is the organization of main points or events in a text, typically according to a system of Roman numerals, numbers, and letters. In an outline, the main points are distinguished from supporting details. Responding is an immediate description of how the story or text made the reader feel. A student response might include

questions generated by the text or experiences from the student's own life that can be related to the text.

Importance of writing

Throughout instruction, the teacher should include activities that require students to write. Research has confirmed that there is a strong relationship between orthographic knowledge and word analysis. In other words, students who have ample practice writing out long words are more likely to learn the basics of structural and syllabic analysis. This stands to reason, as the process of writing forces students to consider the way in which words are constructed. After a time, students should be able to apply orthographic generalizations to unfamiliar words. One example of an orthographic rule is a change from –y in the singular to –ies in the plural. Many of these changes in written English occur according to regular patterns, so that students may be able to guess correctly when they encounter an unfamiliar pattern.

Dialogue, double-entry, reader response, and personal

In a dialogue journal, the student makes an entry and receives a written response from another student or the teacher. A dialogue journal will take on the character of a conversation, in which the student and his interlocutor ask questions, compare experiences, and trade information. In a double-entry journal, students divide the page in half and write down different types of information on either side. For instance, on one side of the page the student might make a list of characters, and on the other side, he might detail the statements and actions of each character. In a reader response journal, students describe their emotional and intellectual reactions to a text. In a personal journal, students record their personal feelings and thoughts. The entries in a personal journal should only be read by the teacher, so that students feel comfortable recording ideas they may be embarrassed to share with their classmates.

Stages of composition

Many teachers break the composition process down into four stages. Pre-writing is the first stage. It includes the selection and narrowing of a topic, the determination of the audience, and, in some cases, the creation of an outline. During the pre-writing stage, students will narrow their topic and determine their target audience. In the second stage, drafting, the student composes a first version of the text. In the third stage, revising/editing, the student looks over the first draft and makes changes. Sometimes, it is useful to bring in another person, like a teacher or classmate, to make suggestions. This stage can also be called the proofreading stage. In the fourth stage, final draft, the student makes all necessary revisions and polishes the final version of the text.

Pre-phonetic stage spelling development

Pre-phonetic students may understand the alphabetic principle and yet not have developed letter recognition: such students will use any letter that comes to mind in their attempts at spelling. Students at this level are sometimes called semi-phonetic. Semi-phonetic spellers are also prone to omitting syllables, so their writing may be virtually unreadable. The instruction of students in the pre-phonetic stage largely focuses on the alphabetic principle. At this point, spelling cannot be addressed directly; to the contrary, spelling instruction should be a byproduct of instruction in the alphabet, phonics, and phonemic awareness. This makes sense: students

cannot begin to arrange letters correctly (i.e., spell) until they have learned the alphabet and the correspondence between sounds and symbols. So, there is no need to develop or implement spelling lessons while students are in the pre-phonetic stage.

Phonetic stage spelling development

A student in the phonetic stage will have basic letter recognition skills and some basic knowledge about the common sounds made by the letters. During the phonetic stage, spelling instruction may become more direct. Students in the phonetic stage will be learning about the correspondences between letters and sounds, and so they will naturally be receptive to spelling-centered lessons. Spelling instruction should be limited to words with common consonant patterns and short vowel sounds. In addition, students can begin to learn common prefixes, suffixes, and rimes. Much of this information will also be a part of phonics and phonemic awareness instruction.

Transitional stage spelling development

During the transitional stage, spelling instruction becomes more variable. Some students may respond well to lessons about etymology or morphology, while others will improve their spelling simply by reading and writing as much as possible. Teachers have a great deal of freedom when working with students in the transitional stage, and so informal assessment should guide the development and implementation of lesson plans. This is a great time for lessons that cater to tactile or kinesthetic learners. For instance, students could be asked to mold letters out of clay or to chant the letters in a word while bouncing a ball. Some students respond very well to odd lessons like this. At the same time, transitional spellers are more receptive to detailed information about spelling. Indeed, many teachers wait until the transitional stage of spelling development to begin discussing homophones (words that sound the same despite having different spellings, like *bare* and *bear*).

Word walls

One common instructional method for students in the phonetic stage of spelling development is the creation of a word wall. A word wall is a large sheet of paper, taped to the wall, at the top of which is written a common word. The word at the top of the word wall should feature a common pattern of vowels or consonants. Students should then be encouraged to write on the paper other words with the same spelling pattern. As an example, a teacher might write the word *chair* at the top of the word wall. This word features the unique but commonplace rime *–air*. Underneath *chair*, students could write words like *air*, *pair*, *stair*, and so on. Teachers will often leave a word wall posted for days or weeks at a time, so that students can continue to find new words for inclusion. Word walls are a great way to encourage students to think about common spelling patterns and thereby promote strategic spelling.

Word banks

One task that teachers often assign conventional spellers is the creation of a word bank. Students are asked to keep an ongoing list of words they spell incorrectly or find confusing. For even the best conventional spellers, a few words cause consistent trouble. Students can use their word bank as a quick reference when they come upon one of their problem words, or they can spend some time consciously committing these words to memory. In one easy system for memorizing a difficult word, the student begins by saying the word aloud. Then, the student silently mouths each letter in the word. The student then shuts his eyes and attempts to spell the word aloud. Next, the student writes the word down and checks his spelling. If the spelling is incorrect, the student starts over. If the spelling is correct, the student writes the word one more time and then moves on to the next one. This memorization method perhaps seems laborious, but it involves a number of the senses and forces the student to become an active learner.

Spelling test

The traditional mode of assessment for spelling is the written test, in which the teacher reads a list of words aloud and students attempt to spell them. This is an acceptable method of assessing spelling, but it should be supplemented by assessment that is more rooted in everyday language use. Too often, spelling lessons consist of a word list handed out on Monday, studied on Thursday, tested on Friday, and forgotten by Saturday. Increasingly, education experts are asserting the importance of context for spelling instruction. Spelling books now organize word lists by letter pattern or theme: for instance, a list may be devoted to words associated with geology. Spelling lists should also include words that the student is likely to encounter in his reading, since this subsequent meeting will help to reinforce what has been learned. In general, early spelling tests conducted in the traditional style should only include words with common orthographic patterns; that is, words with regular roots, affixes, rimes, blends, diphthongs, and digraphs.

Spelling assessments

Despite the utility of the traditional spelling test, it is necessary for spelling assessment to encompass other methods as well. In particular, spelling assessment should focus on language as it is used in context. Students' writing should be evaluated not only for its diction, syntax, and content, but also for its spelling. It is while looking at a student's spelling in context that a teacher can develop a full appreciation for the student's competence. For instance, it should become clear when a student has not entirely mastered the correspondence between a particular sound and symbol. Also, some students (especially those with dyslexia) will invert the order of letters in common words. It is not enough to note that a word has been spelled incorrectly: the teacher needs to determine *how* it was spelled incorrectly. Spelling amounts to a series of choices, and a poor choice made in one instance is likely to be duplicated in similar situations unless there is an intervention. In other words, simply correcting a student's mistake is not effective. A teacher must demonstrate the applicable rule of spelling, or, if the student has erred with regard to a word that is an exception to the rule, must indicate this to be the case. Just as the context in which the error was made informs the assessment, so must the intervention provide context to the student.

Structural and syllabic analysis vs. word analysis and spelling

Regardless of whether these skills are explicitly taught, structural analysis and syllabic analysis are essential to accurate word analysis and the successful spelling of multisyllabic words. Students who develop excellent spelling will have obtained these skills, though they may not be able to articulate their principles. Structural analysis is the decoding of multisyllabic words that have a prefix or suffix attached to a root. Syllabic analysis, on the other hand, is the decoding of a multisyllabic word that follows one of the common syllable patterns, such as open and closed syllables. An open syllable

ends with a vowel, typically a long vowel. A closed syllable has a vowel but ends with a consonant. In a closed syllable, the vowel is much more likely to be short. By learning this trick of syllabic structure, students can improve their spelling skills and word recognition.

Contextual redefinition, semantic mapping, and semantic feature analysis

In contextual redefinition, the teacher writes out the sentence in which the new word first appears and then asks the students to use the context to guess the meaning of the new word. In some cases, it may be necessary to include a couple of surrounding sentences. In semantic mapping, the teacher guides the students in the creation of a diagram demonstrating the relationships between the new word and other known words. Semantic feature analysis is a common method for teaching a group of related words. The teacher makes a grid, with the new words along the left side and a series of questions along the top. The students then answer the questions for each new word.

Cognitive academic language learning

One of the common approaches to helping students understand content-area instruction in their second language is known as the cognitive academic language learning approach. This approach relies on explicit teaching of learning strategies and endeavors to involve students in all aspects of their education. Advocates of this method believe that learning academic strategies in one area will translate into success in other areas. This method assumes that learning is an active and dynamic process in which information is selected and retained when it is made important to the learner. This method also emphasizes the need to make clear associations in content material. This approach is sometimes referred to as a metacognitive learning strategy, because it requires students to "think about thinking." Students are told explicitly the learning objectives, and help to develop the structure of the lesson to meet these objectives. Students are encouraged to relate learning processes to linguistic demands in the domains of listening, speaking, reading, and writing.

Cognitive approaches

Many teachers endorse cognitive approaches to teaching a second language because they feel that making students as active as possible in their own education is advantageous. In order to do this, teachers need to be constantly making associations with students between current and prior instruction. Students may be asked to group words or concepts according to their attributes, or may be asked to elaborate how new ideas and concepts connect to their own lives. Teachers who use the cognitive approach often refer students to textbooks, dictionaries, and encyclopedias. Students will frequently be asked to make mental, oral, or written summaries of information. Teachers should frequently ask students to make inferences from the instructional material they have learned. Cognitive approaches do a good job of engaging advanced and motivated students, but they run the risk of alienating less-active types.

Scaffolding

One of the instructional techniques frequently utilized by successful instructors is scaffolding, in which students receive occasional but timely support from the teacher, with the eventual goal being student independence. Scaffolding can be either verbal or procedural. In verbal scaffolding, teachers outline a subject,

model it, and then allow students to practice until they achieve mastery. As the students get better, the teacher should provide less instruction. Procedural scaffolding, on the other hand, is the process whereby students are placed into different grouping configurations as they gain greater proficiency. Students will begin work as part of the whole class and then will be broken into small groups. Once a reasonable level of proficiency is achieved, students will work with a partner, with the eventual goal being proficient work as an individual.

Tying curriculum to universals

When providing content-area instruction in English, the ESL teacher must be sure to maintain the connections between subjects. It is especially important for students working in their second language to get an explicit account of the associations between various subjects, as this tends to increase engagement and motivation. Whenever possible, teachers should illustrate the connections between disparate content areas and use overlapping vocabulary. Teachers should endeavor to connect specific content with overarching questions that pertain to all areas of study, and should encourage students to discuss these issues in class. By making connections between seemingly disconnected content areas, teachers can naturally foster fluency in English.

Reciprocal teaching

Reciprocal teaching is an instructional strategy wherein teacher and students alternate leading a discussion about a piece of text. In other words, the teacher will lead the discussion for a while, and then students will take over. There are four basic steps in reciprocal teaching: summarizing, questioning, clarifying, and predicting. During the summarizing period, students will identify and discuss the most important parts of the text. At first, students will probably only be able to discuss and integrate themes on the sentence and paragraph levels. As they become more adept at summarizing, however, they should be able to evaluate and integrate information at the paragraph and passage levels. The teacher will guide students through this summarizing process at first, and then will allow students to take over.

There are quite a few advantages to reciprocal teaching. For one thing, it gives students the tools they will need to read independently with comprehension and insight. Also, the interactive nature of the instruction forces all the students in the class to participate. Many teachers find that reciprocal teaching encourages the formation of new relationships between low- and high-functioning students. Reciprocal teaching is especially effective for students who are good at decoding but have poor comprehension skills. Reciprocal teaching is also good for nonreaders. Reciprocal teaching seems to help good and poor students alike. Good students benefit from constructing elaborate questions, while poor students learn effective strategies for improving their own comprehension. Again, the interactive nature of reciprocal teaching seems to keep more students involved.

When incorporating the instructional strategy of reciprocal teaching in a lesson, the teacher will have to incorporate slightly modified strategies for assessment. In the main, teachers will have to rely on their listening skills to determine which students are learning the strategies. Teachers should be especially looking for students who make the transition from decoding to sophisticated comprehension. In some cases, the teacher may require students to write out questions and summaries. Some students may require additional scaffolding before they can successfully

execute the strategies of reciprocal teaching. Over time, the teacher should try to eliminate his direct influence as much as possible. The nature of reciprocal teaching is similar to modeling in that teachers will demonstrate a method of self-instruction that students will learn to execute on their own.

Questioning

The questioning component of reciprocal teaching involves developing questions based on the content of the passage. Students will have to determine the essential information in the passage and then construct questions to test their own knowledge. Essentially, students are learning a self-assessment strategy for reading comprehension. In the clarifying stage, students will be asked to add detail to their summaries of the text. This component of reciprocal teaching is especially important with low-comprehension students, who may read automatically without much understanding. Usually, the clarifying process helps students to refocus their attention on the meaning rather than the sound of the text. In the final stage, predicting, students will speculate about what will happen next in the text. The ability to make a reasonable prediction depends on accurate comprehension.

Challenges of ESL content-area instruction

Many of the difficulties that English language learners have in reading literature in English have to do with differences of culture. If students do not have background knowledge of indigenous literary genres, they may have a hard time orienting themselves within the text. Students may also have a hard time with the abundance of idiomatic expressions in literature, as well as with the use of regional dialects. Some students will express confusion if a piece of writing does not follow a clear and organized structure. Students may have a difficult time with figurative language and unorthodox sentence structures. Students may be unfamiliar with the language of literary analysis, and may have a tendency to literal-mindedness in their consideration of imagery and symbolism. Finally, English language learners may have a difficult time expressing their opinions or reactions to a story, especially when the setting or context is unfamiliar.

Mathematics

Often, students from other cultures emphasize getting the right answer to a mathematics problem at the expense of performing the right process. Students from other cultures may print their numbers differently and may have learned a different way to use the comma and decimal point. Many students will not have worked with manipulatives and may not understand the point of such activities. Many students will have never encountered a word problem and will be temporarily flummoxed by the process. Perhaps most important, many students will not be familiar with the jargon of mathematics. In many cultures, students are encouraged to perform mental math and so may not be used to demonstrating their calculations on paper. Similarly, many students will have learned math through memorization and will be inclined to repetition in their learning. Finally, many cultures do not teach math in a "spiral" fashion, so many students will not have any experience with geometry or algebra.

Science

In the United States, science classes tend to be much more interactive than in other countries. English language learners may not be comfortable thinking independently and drawing their own conclusions. They will also have to learn a tremendous amount of new vocabulary in order to understand scientific texts. Learning all of this new jargon, and being asked to learn new concepts as well, may be overwhelming for many students. Students may also be unfamiliar with basic scientific visual presentations and laboratory equipment. They may not have a firm background in the scientific method, and so may need explicit direction more often than other students do. Students may not be familiar with cooperating with another student in academic work. Finally, students may have a hard time with scientific texts, in which sentence structure is often complex and the passive voice is used frequently.

Social studies

Many ESL teachers claim that their students have the hardest time with social studies. This is usually because students who have arrived from other cultures have very little background knowledge to draw on in this content area. Students may be able to memorize information in preparation for a test, but without a real foundation of knowledge, this information is quickly lost. Students may also struggle to incorporate higher-level thinking skills on unfamiliar subjects. Students may be ignorant of social studies vocabulary. Students may not be used to expressing their personal opinions, and indeed may not have strong opinions on subjects covered in social studies. Some concepts that appear in American social studies classes are wholly foreign to incoming students. For instance, some students will struggle to understand democratic rights, privacy, and social mobility. Finally, the sheer amount of text covered in a social studies class may be overwhelming for many incoming students.

Reading guides

Creating a reading guide will help students organize and consider the material in an English textbook. It can be especially helpful when students want to compare their notes to the content of the course text. The first step in creating a basic reading guide is to have students look at the table of contents. Students should identify the basic structure of the book, including subtopics and sections within each major unit. Once they begin looking at the text, students should try to identify the thesis of each chapter and all the supporting arguments. Students should make a note of any unfamiliar vocabulary. It can be especially helpful to have students focus on an individual paragraph, to examine how it works. This exercise will often help students develop their ability to read quickly and understand academic language in English. Students can then write their own summary of the chapter, at whatever proficiency level they are capable. It is important that the construction of a reading guide be challenging but not impossibly frustrating for students.

Evaluation of concepts

When students are learning to read academic works in English, it is essential for the teacher to work through abstract concepts with them. When starting out, the teacher might want to isolate one important concept or idea from a content-area lesson. It is a good idea to choose an idea that allows for significant analysis. The teacher should then ask students to describe the characteristics of a concept. Some concepts are concrete, meaning that they can be directly experienced in the external world, while others are abstract. Teachers can ask students whether the concept has a broad application or whether it can only be applied to the narrow terms of the content-area lesson. The teacher can help students draw up a short list of ways in which this concept manifests itself in the world. Students often have a difficult time dealing with concepts in English because of the preponderance of figurative language;

teachers should be prepared to help students understand the linguistic expressions used to describe the concept.

Vocabulary acquisition vs. development of cognitive-academic language

When teaching students to read academic texts in English, the teacher will have to address the matter of unfamiliar vocabulary on a regular basis. One way to do this is to teach word analysis skills, whereby the students will learn common prefixes, suffixes, and root words. A large portion of academic language in English is taken from Latin and has a set of regular prefixes and suffixes that can be learned easily and profitably. Another way to help students work through large amounts of unfamiliar vocabulary is by establishing cognate relationships. Teaching cognates gives students a way to relate new words in English to words they know in their native language. In many cases, uncommon English words will appear in slightly modified form in other languages (especially Spanish) much more often. It is important, however, to avoid setting up a habit of one-for-one translation that ignores the English idiom.

Independent reading

Once they have achieved a modicum of linguistic skill, children should read independently for increasing amounts of time. Teachers should maintain a special collection of books at various reading levels, so that students can find literature that is appropriate to their proficiency. It is hoped that children will develop an interest and ability to read in a variety of texts and genres. There are a number of benefits to independent reading. If it is successful, it builds confidence and increases fluency. It helps readers make personal connections with literature. It may start a lifelong habit of reading. In any case, independent reading forces students to apply reading strategies for a sustained amount of time.

Reading aloud

Reading aloud to children serves a number of purposes. When a teacher reads aloud, he is modeling fluent reading by emphasizing punctuation and features of the text. An expressive oral rendition of a text can go a long way to helping students learn basic linguistic patterns. The teacher can also ask students questions about what is then read, to stimulate critical thinking and reading comprehension skills. By providing some background knowledge before reading aloud, a teacher can help students to learn anticipatory and predictive skills. Research has shown that reading aloud develops knowledge of written language syntax and text structure. It also helps develop oral language and vocabulary. Reading aloud helps create a community of readers and introduces students to a variety of texts and genres which they may decide to explore on their own.

Shared reading

One of the activities that teachers often use to increase linguistic ability is called shared reading. In shared reading, members of the class take turns reading the same text aloud. Students who are not reading follow along in their own copy of the text. It is important that the text being read be comprehensible to students at all levels of proficiency. Shared reading explicitly demonstrates basic reading strategies like matching words with an oral rendition. It also helps students develop predictive skills and enhances their sense of narrative structure. Perhaps most important, shared reading provides social support during early reading attempts. As long as the teacher maintains a positive and supportive environment in the classroom,

shared reading can be a great opportunity for students to help one another achieve greater understanding.

Guided reading

Guided reading can be one of the most useful activities for students with limited proficiency in academic language. In this activity, the teacher works with small groups of students with similar reading processes and needs. The teacher will select and introduce new books to each group, and then the group members will take turns reading the text out loud. As this is going on, the teacher will circulate throughout the room offering advice and support to the various groups. Guided reading gives students a chance to experience a wide variety of texts, and gives students a nice mixture of reading aloud and following along. The process of guided reading encourages students to develop their comprehension and analysis skills. Also, research suggests that when positive social communities are formed, students are more likely to strive for increased linguistic proficiency.

Informal reading

Reading instruction in the various content areas may require some modification of the textbook and materials. The teacher will likely have to select key vocabulary and concepts and cover these explicitly with students prior to the lesson. To be successful, students will need to learn the common organizational patterns and outlines used in academic prose. The teacher should help students to spot common textbook cues that indicate meaning and structure. Many teachers perform informal reading inventories to determine each student's skill at decoding and comprehending. This system places students into one of three categories: independent, instructional, or frustration. Students at the independent level recognize words with 97 percent accuracy, understand at least 80 percent of what they read, and can read aloud smoothly. Students at the instructional level can recognize words with 92-96 percent accuracy, understand 60-70 percent of what they read, and read aloud in a halting fashion. Students at the frustration level recognize less than 91 percent of the words in the text, understand less than half of what they read, and read aloud poorly.

Patterns of exposition

The sets of reading skills required to master academic texts will vary according to content area. All academic texts will require logic and critical thinking skills, but certain disciplines are notable for the presence of characteristic types of thought. For instance, social studies texts often emphasize cause-and-effect relationships and chronological sequence of events. These texts frequently ask the reader to compare and contrast events or people. In science texts, on the other hand, there is a great deal of classification and problem-solving rhetoric. Science texts also frequently deal with cause-and-effect relationships. In mathematics, the text often makes an assertion and then supplies evidence and supporting arguments at great length. Mathematical texts are riddled with symbolic relationships and operations. There is a great deal of jargon in mathematical texts. In literary texts, the language is often figurative or lyrical, which may be difficult for more literal-minded beginning students. Also, in order to adequately express their opinions about literary texts, readers will need to master the terminology of literature, such as plot, setting, character, etc.

Matthew effect

The development of vocabulary is more complicated than simply learning the definitions of obscure words. Teachers must understand all of the factors related to the development of vocabulary, academic language, and background knowledge, because the development of vocabulary at an early age, specifically from prekindergarten through second grade, is essential to students' future achievement in vocabulary and reading. When it comes to vocabulary learning, there is a tendency for more advanced students to make more progress than struggling students, thus widening the performance gap even further. This phenomenon is known as the Matthew effect, after a Bible verse that begins, "For to all those who have, more will be given." Teachers should be aware of the Matthew effect and understand how it affects the development of vocabulary, academic language, and background knowledge. Effective instruction and intervention can minimize the damage related to the Matthew effect.

Vocabulary and content knowledge

Vocabulary knowledge and concept learning are intertwined, and it is impossible for one of these factors to improve without corresponding improvement in the other. For instance, the acquisition of vocabulary requires the learning of concepts, and the learning of concepts provides a framework for the development of vocabulary. In a sense, sophisticated words are a form of shorthand for difficult concepts. Also, effective vocabulary instruction is a major boon to the growth of background knowledge. As students develop the language of a new content area, they are likely to begin fitting these words together conceptually. It is futile to teach students vocabulary they are conceptually unequipped to handle.

Reading and building vocabulary

In general, written language contains a larger and more sophisticated vocabulary

- 58 -

and more complicated language structures than speech. For this reason, text is more important in the development of vocabulary, academic language, and background knowledge. A reader has time to go back and look at an unfamiliar word, while it may not be appropriate for a listener to ask the speaker to repeat or clarify. Independent reading, then, is essential in the development of vocabulary, academic language, and background knowledge. For instance, research has consistently shown that daily reading volume is directly correlated to academic achievement. Independent reading material does not need to be advanced or complicated; in fact, the most important criterion is that it interests the student. It is important to encourage independent reading at appropriate levels, because this will improve students' vocabulary, academic language, and background knowledge. Teachers should provide daily opportunities for sustained silent reading.

Vocabulary instruction

There are a number of factors to consider when developing vocabulary, academic language, and background knowledge. To begin with, not all words should be given equal emphasis. Some words occur much more frequently and should therefore be of greater importance in instruction. This is yet another reason why the context of vocabulary and academic language is so important. It is a bad idea to find a list of difficult words and proceed through it alphabetically, because the students will have very little context for the words they are learning. Instead, teachers should approach vocabulary thematically. For instance, a teacher might spend one week teaching vocabulary words related to government, and the next teaching words related to legislation. It is a good idea to link new vocabulary to the lesson being covered in other content areas. The most

important thing is to ensure that students have a context for new words, so that they will be able to incorporate them in their speaking and writing as soon as possible.

Homophones

Students must be able to accurately recognize and incorporate common homophones. Homophones are words that sound the same but have different spellings. Two of the most common homophones in English are *sail/sale* and *bare/bear*. Students are likely to confuse these words unless they receive relevant and explicit instruction. Teachers should begin by presenting these words in isolation and ensuring that students are familiar with both spellings. Then, teachers should help students differentiate these homophones by linking the written version of the word with a picture or example of its meaning. Finally, the words should be presented in context.

Semantic and syntactic approaches

Word analysis instruction should be balanced and comprehensive. It is a good idea to let students approach unfamiliar words from both the semantic and syntactic perspectives. A semantic approach emphasizes the meaning of words. A child is using the semantic approach when he thinks about context and about what type of word would make sense in a given sentence. A teacher can guide the student towards an appreciation of semantics by asking questions about the meaning of the sentence and the likely meaning of an unfamiliar word. The syntactic approach, on the other hand, emphasizes the order of the words in a sentence. English has fairly regular syntax, so the reader can often predict what type of word (e.g., noun, verb) will appear next in a sentence. A teacher can stimulate students to think about syntax by asking the student to read a sentence and determine whether it makes sense. A teacher can ask the student whether the words in a sentence appear to be in the right order.

Activities that reinforce

Students should read a number of texts containing words with the affixes, syllable patterns, and orthographic patterns and rules that have been discussed in class. It is important for students to encounter these words in different contexts, including expository, literary, and reference works. In addition, students should be given plenty of writing opportunities to apply their knowledge of multisyllabic spelling and complex orthographic patterns. Descriptive writing exercises are a great way to elicit the use of just-learned words, as students will search for the right words to express their thoughts. Also, reading and personal journals can be a good venue for students to use the more complicated words they have recently learned.

Differentiation of word analysis instruction

Word analysis can be a challenge for many students, and so there is likely to be a great range of performance in the same class. Teachers must be able to address the strong and weak students in the class. In particular, teachers need to provide differentiated instruction for students who are struggling or have reading difficulties or disabilities. For instance, a teacher needs to be able to go back and focus on key skills and knowledge, like syllable patterns and morphemes that occur frequently. Some students need to have the same material approached from different perspectives before they fully master it. The teacher should be able to outline a number of real-world examples for an abstract concept. The use of songs and poems to illustrate syllabification is

one helpful way to bring struggling students up to speed. Finally, a teacher should be able to provide differentiated practice situations for the skills that have been taught.

Instruction related to word analysis should be differentiated for English language learners. Most of the time, these students require extra training in the common English roots, prefixes, and suffixes. Many foreign languages do not include these morphemes, and so students may not have heard them in conversation throughout their lives. Moreover, many languages do not include affix systems, and so students may need some basic training in how these word parts can alter meaning. For this reason, it may be necessary to provide these students with more exposure to morphemes that are second nature to native English speakers. Some students benefit from the use of flashcards that cover common English morphemes.

Improving reading rate

There are some excellent strategies for building reading rate. For instance, when decoding is not automatic, the student should be asked to whisper read while being monitored. Whisper reading is essentially just reading aloud to oneself. Because the student is reading aloud, he is forced to read each word. Whisper reading allows the entire class to get the benefits of reading aloud without distracting one another. Once decoding has become automatic, students should be asked to read silently by themselves and should be held accountable for their comprehension. In other words, the teacher should at the very least ask the student some questions that test whether the student has obtained the literal message of the text.

Modeling, phrase-cued reading, and intentional, teacher-directed instruction

Some strategies for improving fluency with respect to prosody include modeling, phrase-cued reading, and intentional, teacher-directed instruction in a specific subject area in order to build content knowledge and academic language. Modeling is the demonstration of the task to be learned. Repeated reading and choral reading are examples of modeling. Phrase-cued reading, which is similar to modeling, is a system in which the teacher reads a text in phrase-sized chunks. The text being read by the teacher needs to be visible to the class; this can be accomplished either by holding up a book or by projecting the text on a screen. In any case, the students need to be able to follow along with the teacher, who will be pointing at each successive phrase with a finger or pen. The idea is for students to begin looking at sentences as collections of phrases rather than as discrete words or groups of letters. When students begin to organize their oral production by phrases rather than letters or words, they will have obtained some degree of fluency. Finally, in some cases, prosody may be improved by explicit instruction in the content area to be discussed. Some priming with respect to vocabulary and subject matter will help students anticipate the content of the text and will enable the emergence of prosody.

Synonyms and antonyms

To begin with, instruction should include definitions that can easily be understood by students. Much of the vocabulary in content areas is difficult necessarily because it is representative of difficult concepts. In order to understand the words, students must understand the concepts. It is important, then, that instruction include meaningful examples in context. Words should not be presented simply in list format without any explanation as to how they are used. The teacher should describe the sorts of text in which a word is used, and should demonstrate its use in a sentence. Students especially need these examples when dealing with new concepts, lest they become disoriented. Whenever appropriate, guided discussions should include the identification of synonyms and antonyms. A synonym is a word that means the same thing, while an antonym is a word that means the opposite. So, for instance, *arid* is a synonym for *dry*, while *moist* is an antonym for *dry*. Students should be encouraged to come up with examples of synonyms and antonyms for new vocabulary words.

Concept maps

Teachers should incorporate explicit oral and written strategies to promote the integration of word knowledge. It is important for students to take several different approaches to a new word, so that they develop a little dexterity in handling it. The teacher should help the students work out the relationships between words, and, if it is useful, should depict these relationships graphically. A concept map, in which lines representing relationships are drawn between the words, is one way to illustrate relationships of vocabulary. In an even more sophisticated concept map, students write verbs on the connecting lines to describe the relationship between the words: for example, in a concept map about Congress, the word *passes* might be written on the line connecting *Senate* to *legislation*.

Cluing

Another popular technique for teaching new vocabulary is cluing. In this method, the teacher writes four sentences on the board for each new word. The first sentence uses the target word in a

- 61 -

sentence: "Larry's *celerity* made it possible for the job to be done by 5." At this point, the students will not have been taught the definition of the target word. The second sentence describes the target word in some way: "Rabbits, runners, and racecars are all known for their *celerity*." The third sentence defines the target word: "*Celerity* means swiftness or speed." Finally, the fourth sentence asks a question with the target word: "Can you name something that moves with *celerity*?" The cluing technique may seem over-simple, but it effectively slows down the introduction of new words so that students can develop a context almost immediately. Through cluing, the student is shown how the word is used, given some examples, told the definition, and encouraged to use the word to answer a question. Rather quickly, the student has made four approaches to mastery of the word.

Word logs

Another method of vocabulary instruction is the creation of word banks and word logs. These are lists of new vocabulary words, either those explicitly taught by the teacher or those the student comes across in his own academic work. This list is referred to frequently, so that the student has multiple exposures to each new word. At the same time, the student should be asked to perform some tasks with the new words, such as using them in a sentence or looking up the definition in the dictionary. The creation and maintenance of a word bank or log helps personalize vocabulary instruction and allows the student to focus exclusively on the words he needs to learn.

Challenges of teaching vocabulary

A teacher must be able to provide differentiated instruction for English language learners. This may require reactivating prior knowledge by creating explicit connections between prior and new knowledge. Often, students will have mastered the concepts associated with vocabulary and academic content, but will not yet have the words in English. As much as possible, the teacher should capitalize on the transfer of cognates. The teacher should build on the students' current language skills and reinforce their knowledge of basic, functional grammar to make reading comprehension easier. When necessary, this may include some instruction in the student's native language. The teacher should emphasize reading instruction that encourages the development of academic language. This will likely include the explicit instruction of more complex language structures and the key vocabulary in the relevant text. Also, a teacher needs to contextualize new vocabulary and concepts. This can be done with visual aids, like pictures, charts, word organizers, and graphic organizers. Many teachers find success with a sequence of preteach-reteach-practice-review. Teachers should work to build morphological knowledge, including the meanings of the common root words used in academic language.

Assessing vocabulary

As with other forms of assessment, vocabulary assessment should take place before, during, and after instruction. One of the most common methods of formal or informal assessment is to ask students to use new vocabulary words in a sentence. If a student knows the definition of a word but cannot incorporate it in real linguistic production, he has not yet fully acquired it. Other, slightly more sophisticated vocabulary assessments ask students to identify synonyms, antonyms, or analogies for new vocabulary words. When constructing these sorts of assessments, the teacher should be sure that there are acceptable answers (for instance, not all words have a ready antonym). With vocabulary instruction, it is essential to use this sort of assessment as a point of departure for further exploration and instruction. It requires detailed analysis to determine exactly where a student is falling short of his potential. Instruction should be responsive to the results of assessment and should incorporate as much informal assessment as possible.

Differentiating assignments

When an informal or formal assessment indicates a significant discrepancy between students, teachers can modify assignments so that they become suitable for a broad spectrum of abilities. For students functioning at a low level, the objectives of the assignments can be simplified, either by reducing the number of required parts or by making the required parts easier. Students may be asked to compose a drawing instead of a written response. The teacher may find that it is appropriate to divide students into small groups based on ability level, and then allow students to conduct discussions in lieu of individual written responses. The teacher may also find it is appropriate to adjust the length and difficulty of assignments; for reading comprehension exercises, for instance, the teacher may determine that it is appropriate to diminish the overall length of the reading assignment.

Grouping

In many cases, a teacher will determine that it is appropriate to separate students into small groups by ability level. This can be done a number of ways. One is by pairing high-functioning students with low-functioning students in a peer assistance program. It is often beneficial for both the superior and inferior student to examine material in a partnership of this kind. The teacher may also separate students into cooperative groups in which all the students are at roughly the same level. When doing this, teachers should

ensure that content material is comprehensible to some degree to every member of every group. In some cases, teachers may divide students into small groups and then provide direct instruction to these groups individually. This is usually necessary in cases in which the discrepancy between the highest-functioning group and the lowest-functioning group is extreme.

Small-group instruction

There are a number of advantages to dividing students into small groups by ability level. For one thing, the teacher will be able to monitor student progress closely. In a larger group, it can be difficult to monitor the progress of individual students at the same time. When students are broken into small groups in which each member has specific responsibilities, it becomes much easier for teachers to assess the contributions of each member. Small-group instruction for this reason enables teachers to provide immediate feedback. By circulating throughout the room while students are working, teachers will be able to provide immediate responses to questions and concerns raised by the groups. The teacher will also be able to provide data-driven differentiated instruction. This is again because assessment becomes much easier when students are broken into small groups. When each individual in the class has a clear performance record, the teacher can collect data that is helpful in making future instructional decisions.

Alternative assessments

It is essential that ESL teachers utilize alternative assessments to provide students with opportunities to demonstrate mastery of knowledge and skills. Alternative assessments are anything distinct from formal tests or examinations. These assessments often incorporate authentic classroom tasks in order to collect information about student achievement. Alternative assessments will allow the teacher to consider the performance of the student from a number of different perspectives, and will focus on the process performed as much as the results produced. Alternative assessments, because of their informal and improvisatory nature, can be developed to assess a broad range of knowledge and skills. Teachers who incorporate alternative assessments in their daily lesson are able to accumulate more data with which to make decisions about future instructional strategies.

Assessment

Clarifying table

A clarifying table is a tool to help students separate a topic into smaller, more manageable parts. The purpose is retention and comprehension by taking notes in a systematic way. The core concept is captured, supporting ideas are recognized, clarifying details are reported and connections to previously learned material are made. The steps to teach the clarifying table:

- I Do It: The teacher prepares a completed example and explains the components. It is usually necessary to do this step at least twice.
- We Do It: The teacher, acting as a guide, and the class construct a table together. This step is repeated until the students grasp the concept.
- You all Do It: The students are divided into pairs or small groups to create their own tables. Support comes from each other rather than the teacher.
- You Do It: Each student creates a table by himself for his particular topic.

A clarifying table is a visual device created to capture and organize information.

- Section 1: a definition of the word or term or a summary of the topic.
- Section 2: details that clarify the meaning of the word or term or facts related to the topic.
- Section 3: the major meaning of the word or term, or the core idea of the topic.
- Section 4: the knowledge connections to information already known.
- Section 5: a statement explaining the word or term or an example of the topic.
- Section 6: a statement explaining the incorrect use of a word or term or an example of what the topic is not about.
- Section 7: a sentence using the word or term correctly or a topic sentence that can be used as a basis for a paper.

Using a clarifying table

Because it is a powerful elaboration tool, a clarifying table can be used to identify core concepts in any subject; develop reading skills; improve note-taking ability during lectures, while researching topics, and in preparation for potential pop quizzes, unit tests, and final exams. The device can be used in many ways in most classrooms. Some ideas:

- Paraphrasing Tool: Students read assigned passages on a particular subject and use the table to take notes for later class discussions and to review when preparing for tests.
- Note-Taking Tool: The students write down key ideas and interesting details during a lecture, which can be reviewed in preparation for pop quizzes, unit tests, and final exams.
- Outline Tool: The students use the table to gather information, organize ideas, and plan the structure of any written assignment including one-page essays, book reports, and research papers.

Sample clarifying table
Word, Term, Topic

Core Idea or Concept: _____

Clarifiers	Knowledge Connections
1.	1.
2.	2.
3.	3.
4.	4.
5.	5.
6.	6.
Don't Confuse With	**Not An Example Of**
1.	1.
2.	2.
3.	3.
Sample Sentence Or Topic Sentence	

Note: can be modified depending upon the subject and specific assignment.

Motivating secondary students

By the time students reach secondary school, many feel as though they were failures because they cannot read well, dislike reading for any number of reasons or have a negative view of reading in general. Some had bad experiences in middle school and thus turned away from reading, especially in an academic setting. An effective way to motivate these students is to create a classroom atmosphere of recognition and respect for cultural and language differences (which may account for certain reading issues). Keeping these differences in mind when selecting reading material sends a positive message and encourages the students to read the assignment. Another motivating strategy is to assign reading tasks from sources other than textbooks, such as newspapers, magazines, and trade books. The content is current, reflects the real world, and students can make connections relevant to their lives. Public praise and positive feedback are huge motivators for students struggling to improve their reading skills.

Linguistic knowledge

Linguistic knowledge is defined as understanding the system: how the language works, what the words mean, and how to use the words properly. The system is composed of several parts. The definitions cited are from The American Heritage College Dictionary.

- Phonology: the sounds of the words and their proper pronunciation.
- Semantics: the meaning of the signs and symbols used to form the words.
  - Morphology: the structure and form of the words including inflection (changing pitch or tone of voice), derivation (adding prefixes and suffixes to change the meaning), and compounds (combining two or more words to form a different word).
  - Word Meaning: the idea or thought conveyed.
- Syntax (grammatical structure): the rules governing the formation of sentences.

In order for students to learn, integrate, and use the language system correctly, they must be given opportunities to read in many genres and from a variety of source material.

Literature

The American Heritage College Dictionary defines literature as "the body of written works of a language, period, or culture." This is the commonly accepted definition; however, literature can mean different things to different people. Some only consider serious literary works to be literature and would ridicule and refuse to consider any composition that did not meet a strict set of arbitrary criteria. But according to the dictionary definition, any written work is part of a nation's literature and reflects its culture and diversity.

Throughout the centuries, different genres have been explored. Early history was preserved in oral literature, by the older generation telling the next generation stories and traditions. The earliest written documents had a religious and/or didactic purpose. The Age of Reason produced nationalistic epics and philosophical treatises. Romanticism focused on popular folk tales. Early nineteenth century literature embraced realism and naturalism, and the twentieth century spawned symbolism and character development.

Literary criticism

It is impossible for the reader to separate his background knowledge, morality and ethics and overall philosophy of life from the material which he reads. His understanding of and response to the written word is predicated on his history; he integrates what he reads with who he is and what he knows. Any literary theory or approach that discusses how the reader feels, how he perceives the author's world, how the content affects society's morals or ethics, and what the literature is trying to convey is by definition based on reader response. Literature is a partnership; the author's ideas must be read, understood and integrated by the reader or the work has no meaning. A good literary critic recognizes and acknowledges his biases and preconceived notions and ensures that his audience is aware of them, as they will affect his feelings about and his interpretation of the work.

Late nineteenth and early twentieth century literary criticism

In the late nineteenth century, literature was studied in fragments for its wit or humor rather than its serious ideas and observations. During this time, some authors like Matthew Arnold became known more for the critical study of other people's writing than for their own literary work.

Early in the twentieth century, a movement that came to be known as Russian Formalism came to have a far reaching impact on the study of literature. Its focus was on literary devices and technique rather than content. This critical approach held that the words themselves and how they are used can and should be studied. The author's background, biography, and philosophy were considered taboo and should be ignored. In the United States and England the movement was known as The New Criticism. Both schools ignored the content, the author's intent, and the reader's response; only form and technique were considered important.

Current state of literary criticism

Literary criticism in today's educational institutions is a combination of parts of earlier approaches plus recognition of the importance and inevitability of reader response. In the late 1980s, literary criticism once again began considering the author's intent, his history, and his philosophy, as well as reader response when studying literature. There are many areas for research and study. Some critics only study traditional literature, others focus on theoretical texts. Other critics only study minority and women's literature. Some interested in cultural studies read and critique popular genres like comic books and pulp fiction. Other cultural studies critics view literature through a social history lens. Some are film and music critics. There is room for all approaches and viewpoints as well as official recognition of various non-traditional forms of literary expression.

Schools of literary criticism

- Cultural Studies: focused on the role literature plays in daily life; critics include Raymond Williams, Dick Hebdige, Stuart Hall, Theodore Adorno, Paul Gilroy, and John Guillory.
- Comparative Literature: compared and contrasted literature from different languages, countries and cultures; critics include Susan Bassnett, Charles Bernheimer, Terry Eagleton, and Edward Said.
- Deconstruction: determined what can be interpreted in the text that is not explicitly stated; critics include Jacques Derrida, Paul de Man, J. Hills Miller, and Gayatri Spivak.
- Feminism: researched and emphasized relationships between females and males; critics include Luce Irigaray, Helene Cixous, and Elaine Showalter.
- Marxism: focused on themes of class differences and class conflicts; critics include Georg Lukacs, Valentin Voloshinov, Raymond Williams, Terry Eagleton, Fredric Jameson, and Walter Benjamin.
- New Criticism: studied what is written, not the goals of the writer; critics include W.K. Wimsatt, F.R. Leavis, John Crowe Ransom, and Robert Penn Warren.

Refuting objections

Traditional text-only critics believe that reader response criticism gives the reader permission to interpret the text as he sees fit, without consideration for form and function. In other words, understanding and interpretation is subjective rather than objective. Text only critics expect the reader to divorce himself from his culture, educational level, socio-economic status, personal history, and background knowledge so that he can read objectively.

Reader response criticism recognizes and admits this criterion is impossible to achieve. Reading is both subjective and objective. A fluent reader must be aware of the various components of the literary work; if he is not, he cannot appreciate and study its form and function. Therefore the composition itself is central to the process. However, a fluent reader brings his personal history to the process and can thus understand and integrate the information into his background knowledge, which completes the writing/reading partnership process.

Types of reader response criticism

The individualist approach focuses on highly personal responses to the work. These reactions can generate provocative class discussions. Keeping a journal that explores how the literary piece affected the student or reminded him of a personal experience makes it relevant to his life and will help him integrate the information.

Experimenters suspend their values as they read and are able to accept the improbable as possible and fantasy as real. When they are finished reading the work, they leave the improbable world and reenter the real world. This is called a "willing suspension of disbelief" and can be used to generate lively discussions of interesting and intriguing possibilities.

Uniformists are confined by the limits of the literary work itself, e.g., characters, setting, stated or implied meaning, et cetera. Broad or general concepts are considered inappropriate for discussion. Interpretation is limited to specific activities contained in the work.

Technical quality of assessments

One issue that must be considered when developing academic assessments is the technical quality of the examination. The National Center for Research on Evaluation, Standards and Student Testing (CRESST) developed the following criteria to evaluate technical quality:

- Cognitive Complexity: requires problem-solving, critical thinking and reasoning ability.
- Content Quality: correct responses demonstrate knowledge of critical subject matter.
- Meaningfulness: students understand the value of the assessment and the tasks involved.
- Language Appropriateness: clear to the students and appropriate to the requested task.
- Transfer and Generalization: indicates ability to complete similar tasks and the results permit valid generalization about learning capabilities.
- Fairness: performance measurements and scoring avoid factors irrelevant to school learning.
- Reliability: consistently represents data added to students' background knowledge.
- Consequences: it results in the desired effect on students,

instructors and the educational system.

Content standards

Content standards define the specific areas of knowledge every student needs to learn. These areas are usually the traditional subjects of English (or language arts), mathematics, science, social studies, music, art, and drama; some also include general concepts and interdisciplinary studies. Some reflect one grade level and specific academic content, while others combine grade levels and integrate the content across academic disciplines. Standards should not be so broad they cannot be used as instructional guidelines or to evaluate students effectively.

Specific standards are created by individual states and various national educational organizations; ideally, the groups work in tandem. The content standards should be a result of community meetings that include academic and business representatives so that the requirements of both are recognized and met. These meetings should be moderated by state leaders and open to the public so that everyone helps define what needs to be taught and the methods used to teach it.

Performance standards

Evaluating students' progress using performance standards is tricky because there is no clear definition of the term. Are the standards based upon test performance? If so, do they take into account test grading practices? Do they mean the method of reporting test scores, e.g., basic equates to unacceptable, proficient to adequate, and advanced to excellent? How good is good enough? The Goals 2000: Educate America Act says "performance standards means concrete examples and explicit definitions of what students have to know and be able to do to demonstrate that such students are proficient in the skills and knowledge framed by content standards." Performance standards must also be appropriate for the age, feasible to administer, and useful for evaluating progress. According to this definition, content and performance should be evaluated together in order to obtain a clear picture of the student's progress or lack thereof.

Articulation matrix and Bloom's taxonomy

An articulation matrix is the relationship between activities and outcomes. It is a defined set of goals and the methods used to reach them. For example in a graduation matrix, completing the required courses is the outcome, and the lectures, homework assignments, projects, papers, tests, and evaluations are the activities.

Bloom's Taxonomy, which is a hierarchical classification system, is an articulation matrix that outlines six levels of cognitive learning. At each step, students reach a predictable level of mastery:

- Knowledge Level: ability to define terms.
- Comprehension Level: finish problems and explain answers.
- Application Level: recognizes problems and uses methods to solve them.
- Analysis Level: ability to explain why the process works.
- Synthesis Level: can use the process or part of it in new ways.
- Evaluation Level: can create different ways to solve problems and use designated criteria and can select the best method to obtain the correct solution.

Credibility and feasibility

For any assessment method to be successful, it must be introduced to the community in a way that builds support rather than causing confusion, resentment, and skepticism. Parents, teachers, students, and the public need to understand the purpose of the assessment, what it is intended to accomplish, why it is necessary and how it will logically integrate with methods already in place. Allowing the community to review the test and try to answer some of the questions will usually help generate acceptance of the new tool.

Development, scoring and reporting costs, and teacher expectations should be considered before a new assessment is introduced and implemented. Sometimes the cost is prohibitive. Teachers may not be qualified to prepare students or to administer the test and training may not be available or affordable. These potential stumbling blocks need to be addressed before a new assessment is added to the existing requirements.

Assessment station

An assessment station is a designated area, inside or outside of the classroom, used for the specific purpose of evaluating students' progress performing a task. Individuals or groups can be assigned to complete a task, use a piece of lab equipment or work with some technological device. The purpose is to assess the knowledge acquired, processes used, skills displayed, and general attitude about the task, and if working in a group, how each student interacts with the other members of the team.

The assessment station should function the same way every time it is used. This builds consistency and reduces the time needed for explanations and demonstrations before and during future assessments. Instructions should be clear, concise and specific and explain exactly how the area should be left for the next student. Activities performed in the assessment station should be simple, straightforward and relate to the material being studied.

Using an assessment station

Because the assessment station is an interactive tool, the area needs to be equipped with the appropriate equipment necessary to complete the task. If the activity is an experiment, the area needs to be ventilated and appropriate safety precautions taken, e.g., having water available and a fire extinguisher at hand. The students need to understand how to operate the instruments in a safe manner and therefore instructions should be provided both in writing and verbally. Questions should be asked and answered before any activity is started. If it is a group activity, each student needs to contribute to the assigned task.

The work submitted by each student is evaluated using a rating/grading scale or a checklist. For example if the task required the use of a microscope, the checklist should have points related to its use. If it was a group project, cooperation, helpfulness and leadership skills should be noted.

Individual assessments

Individual assessments focus on the progress each student made during a defined period of time (e.g., every six weeks, at the end of the semester) rather than in a team collaboration. A variety of activities such as written assignments, oral presentations, and class participation should be incorporated into the assessment in order to obtain a broader, more realistic view of the student's

understanding of the material. The assessment process should be fully explained so that the student knows what is expected. He is evaluated using one or all of the following standards:

- self-referenced —based on his previous level of progress
- criterion-referenced — a defined, school or district-wide standard
- norm-referenced — based on the progress of groups of students the same age or grade level

Using a combination of standards instead of relying on one method presents a clearer, more accurate picture of the student's growth.

Group assessments

Group assessments focus on how students cooperate and collaborate in completing a project assigned to the group rather than to a single student. The same activities used in individual assessments are used, such as written assignments, oral presentations, and group participation, but they are used to evaluate social and interactive skills as well as the work produced. The students' willingness to accept being evaluated for a group project is based on if and how long they have been exposed to this type of cooperative collaboration and if they feel the grading system is applied fairly. If this project is the first time students in a competitive environment are expected to work together, there may be some misunderstandings and objections about what is expected, how it works, and how each student will be evaluated. It is critical the teacher explains the evaluation process clearly, answers questions, addresses reservations, and closely monitors individual contributions as well as the progress of the project.

Advantages and disadvantages of assessments

Individual assessments are easily understood by students and parents and mesh with most school districts' systems. Because each student is evaluated based on criteria established by state performance and/or content standards, it is easy to measure the success of department curricula. Self-referenced standards provide feedback about the student's strengths and weaknesses. They can help motivate the student to work harder and take more responsibility for his learning. Students sometimes set personal goals and expectations. Individual assessments help them measure their success. These evaluations provide the teacher insight into any special help the student might need.

Individual assessment can create and encourage a very competitive environment in which some students are unable to compete effectively. It makes it difficult to evaluate students' ability to work with a team and judge their interaction with others both of which are important to the educational experience. They can also be also very time consuming for the teacher to complete fairly and accurately.

There are three ways to evaluate a group project: group grade only, individual grade only, or a combination of both. The reason for group projects is to teach cooperation in a team environment. Giving everyone the same grade can foster some degree of esprit de corps. It also frees the teacher from having to decide who was responsible for what part of the project. A group grade, however, can cause resentment, especially if students are not used to working in a group and are used to earning grades based on a competitive scale. Students understand individual grades, but in a group project environment the competitive scale diminishes the spirit of cooperation because everyone is working for himself rather than for the good of the team. Giving a group grade and an individual grade addresses both issues. Basing eighty percent of the grade on cooperation and collaboration and twenty percent on individual production recognizes the importance of working for the group and the necessity of individual contributions.

Performance contracts

A performance contract is a written agreement between an individual student or a group of students and a teacher about a specific activity. The assignment can be a research paper, an oral presentation with props, or some other project. The contract clearly states the goal, explains the activity, establishes a timeline, and describes who will do what and how it will be done. Sometimes the agreement also details the criteria to be used to evaluate the finished product. This tool helps students learn to plan a project by breaking it into manageable parts and shows them how to utilize their time more efficiently. Not only can the completed project be graded, but the performance contract itself can be evaluated. The teacher should assess the student's participation in setting up the contract, his willingness to compromise when necessary and his general attitude about the concept and the process.

Performance contracts can be a great learning experience for students by teaching them how to plan and prioritize and encouraging them to avoid procrastination. However, some students may have trouble understanding the concept, so it may be necessary to review the planning, organizing, and writing steps several times before they are able to grasp the idea. Using contracts can also

- 72 -

help a struggling student in other areas of his life. These agreements can be developed to address attendance requirements and expected behavior standards or to plan weekly or monthly homework schedules.

If a teacher has never used performance contracts, he needs to understand that setting up the system and helping the students write their agreements is very time consuming, especially in the beginning. It can help, as a class project, to create a performance contract based on a completed project. This strategy sometimes reduces the learning curve for all the students.

In order for a performance contract to be a learning experience, the guidelines for writing one should be very general. The teacher can either give the student a written list of suggestions or, preferably, discuss them one-on-one. Some questions that might be used:
- What work items are you planning to include?
- Where you will find the necessary data: Personal reference books, the internet, the library? Do you have additional sources?
- How long will it take to outline a plan, research the topic, and finish the project?
- What criteria should be used to evaluate the finished product?

Questions that might be used to evaluate the completed contract:
- Is the contract realistic relative to required completion date?
- Are the contract questions appropriate to the project objectives?
- Were reliable and appropriate sources chosen?
- How comprehensive is the plan?

- Does the student understand his capabilities and recognize his limitations?

Example of a performance contract

Student's Name: _____
Teacher's Name: _____
Contract Dates: _____to_____
Purpose of Contract: _____
I am planning a study of:
_____
Reason for choosing this topic:
_____
Main focus of the study:
_____
Questions I want to answer (add as many lines as needed):
_____
Sources I plan to use (check at least 5):
Books ___; Interviews ___; Experiments ___; Magazines___; Encyclopedia___; Newspapers___; Museums___; Pictures, Films, Videos___; Other Sources/ My Research___
Explain: _____
The finished product will be in the form of:
_____
The learning skills I will use:
_____
The study will be completed by (different dates may be given for various segments):
_____
The study will be reviewed by:
_____
Evaluated by:
_____
The evaluator will be looking for:
_____
Student's Signature
_____
Teacher's Signature
_____

Portfolio

Once decisions have been made about what will be included, it is important to begin with baseline data for comparison as the portfolio grows. Selected material can be placed in a folder or large envelope with the student's name on the front.

Each addition needs to be dated with an explanation attached stating why the item was included and what features should be noted. Teachers who use portfolios will often create assignments with the intention of including it in the package. As the contents grow, it may become necessary due to space limitations to review the items and remove some daily work, quizzes, or tests. Once the portfolio is complete, the teacher needs to have a method to evaluate the contents and review the student's progress in areas such as creativity, critical thinking, originality, research skills, perseverance, responsibility, and communication effectiveness. A checklist can be useful (see card 192).

Portfolios and student assessment

A portfolio is a collection of the student's work assembled over a period of time (e.g., six week grading period, one semester, the entire year). Various items can be included: contracts, copies of completed activities such as papers; presentations and pictures of props; performance assessments made by the student, his peers, and the teacher; copies of class work and homework; classroom tests; and state-mandated exams. A portfolio is a powerful aide in assessing the student's progress and an excellent format to present to parents so they can review their child's progress. The decision on what to include should be a collaboration between the student and the teacher. What will be included: examples of best work, worst work, typical work, or perhaps some of each? Will the student keep a copy as a reference point? Decisions need to be made and rules established as early as possible in the process so that progress is accurately and fairly recorded.

Student feedback form

Student feedback form
Use the following form when asking for student feedback on a group project:
Rating For Group Project
Student Name: _____
Date of Project _____to _____
Circle the phrase that describes how you feel.
Choosing the members of your group:
I really like it.   It's okay.   I don't like it.
Having the teacher choose group members:
I really like it.   It's okay.   I don't like it.
The group deciding how you are going to complete the project?
I really like it.   It's okay.   I don't like it.
Comments:
_____
_____
_____

Work products, response groups

Work Products are completed assignments that are evaluated on the basis of the topic chosen as well as creativity, originality, organization, understanding of the subject matter, social and academic progress, and success in meeting and/or exceeding predetermined criteria along with any other items deemed important by the individual teacher. Work products can take many different forms, including but not limited to research papers, poems, fiction and non-fiction stories, bulletin boards, video and audio tapes, computer and laboratory demonstrations, dramatic performances, debates and oral presentations, paintings, drawings and sculptures, and musical compositions and performances.

Response Groups are discussions about a particular subject. Frequently, the students themselves start them spontaneously in response to a shared experience. They want to talk about the event because it affected all of them in some way. Teachers can gain insight into the students' critical thinking skills, information and observations shared, willingness to participate in the discussion and behavior within the group.

Self and peer-assessment

Self-assessment allows the student to become involved in the evaluation process. He takes more responsibility for the learning process because he is expected to reflect upon his attitude about and attention to assigned activities and the product produced. To be truly effective, the student should be involved in developing the evaluation criteria. It gives him more control. Instead of the teacher having all of the power and being perceived as such, some power shifts to the student in allowing him to help determine the rating scale used, to participate in evaluating the finished product, and to provide direct input into the grade which he receives.

During peer-assessments, students learn by listening to other students critique their work and make suggestions on ways to improve it. The student doing the evaluation must think analytically about their peer's work product; in doing so, it should help him become more critical about his own work. Teachers need to moderate these discussions and stress consistency, being descriptive and not judgmental, realistic, positive, and reflective.

Book response journal, comparison chart, conferences

The Book Response Journal is a place for students to express their feelings about concepts and ideas discovered in the literature they read whether in a book, magazine, on the internet, or some other source of information. Students are encouraged to use these journals to comment on everything which they read. Teachers can use the journals as a way to ask questions, comment on the student's observations, and suggest additional reading material. Book response journals can and probably should be reviewed in student-teacher conferences.

Comparison Charts are a graphic way to organize ideas, events, characters, plot lines, and the like so that they can be compared and contrasted. They can be used by individual students and are a very effective tool for small groups to use in order to generate lively discussions.

The main purpose of a Conference is to collaborate, assess, and guide. They can be used for setting goals, coaching and mentoring, and evaluating the student's progress.

Graffiti wall, interview, KWL technique

A graffiti wall is a designated area to brainstorm ideas, concepts, observations, questions, and conclusions about a topic. It can be used as an evolving record of the progress made by the group as they begin to understand the subject being researched and discussed. It can develop into a class dictionary and thesaurus used to enrich the students' vocabulary.

An interview is a dialogue between the student and the teacher. Typically one or more questions are asked or problems posed in such a way as to determine the depth of understanding rather than to elicit specific answers.

A KWL is an effective way to assess how well the student grasped the concepts and can be used to judge the effectiveness of the teacher's lesson plan. The acronym stands for "Know," "Want," "Learned," and refers to what student knows and wants to know at the beginning of the lesson and what he has learned at the end of the lesson.

Demonstration, discussion, goal setting, I learned statement

A demonstration turns a concept into a concrete, observable experience using one or more of the five senses. It can be an audio-visual presentation, a piece of art or music, or a personal interpretation using drama or dance. It can be an experiment or an explanation of how something works.

A discussion should be a safe forum for students to explore and explain ideas and concepts. They should be encouraged to speak, listen, and comment on and respond to their own and others' opinions, feelings, and reactions to a specific topic.

Goal Setting is an excellent way to help students learn to plan a project and experience success. It should be a collaborative effort with the teacher and encourage the student to reflect on his performance or lack thereof.

The purpose of an I Learned Statement is to encourage the student to express what he learned from a lecture, class discussion, homework assignment, or some other activity.

Learning logs, oral attitude survey, oral presentation, problem-solving activity

A learning log is similar to a book response journal except that the student records his feelings about and responses to concepts and ideas covered in all of his classes. Keeping a log is a way to encourage critical thinking and improve writing skills.

Oral attitude surveys is a method to encourage students to share their own ideas, learn about the ideas of fellow students and think about topics from different perspectives. They can also evaluate their performance and rate the effectiveness of the discussion.

An oral presentation can be a speech, a dramatic recitation of a story or a poem, a video, or a debate that is evaluated using particular criteria.

A problem-solving activity presents a question to the class. The group is expected to develop a method to find the answer and then solve the problem. Both the method and the solution are evaluated.

Anecdotal record

An anecdotal record is a written description of observed behavior. They are usually kept in an alphabetized book, binder, or folder and should be organized so it is easy to find notes concerning a particular student. There are computer programs available that make retrieving the data simple.

To be effective, observations need to be made frequently and incidents need to be described completely and objectively; the teacher's analysis should be used as a guide for appropriate responses. Both successful situations and unsuccessful attempts need to be recorded in order to present an accurate picture of the student's progress.

The evaluation context is:
- Formative: recalling the incident may raise an alert that something that needs to be addressed.
- Summative: since observations are made over a period of time, they are an effective way to track student attitude, behavior, knowledge acquired, cognitive skills learned, etc.

- Diagnostic: consistent attention to performance may spotlight areas that need special attention.

Methods of data recording

There are three ways to record data about individual student performance. Each provides important information and lends itself to evaluating different aspects of student growth.

Anecdotal Records are observations of day-to-day activities, e.g., how the student interacts in a group, his ability to complete a hands-on assignment, his demeanor while taking tests, and his development of particular cognitive skills. All these offer opportunities for teacher comments.

The criteria on Observation Checklists vary depending on what the teacher wants to evaluate. They can be used to measure the growth of knowledge, a change in attitude, or the understanding of new skills. Checklists can also be used to evaluate written assignments, oral presentations, class participation, completion of individual and/or group work, or any activity that requires assessment.

Rating Scales are similar to observation checklists. The difference between the two is that checklists are used to determine the presence or absence of a skill, while rating scales measure the quality of the performance.

Observation checklist

An observation checklist is a list of specific skills, behaviors, attitudes, and processes that are relevant to a student's development and contribute to his ability to successfully complete learning activities. To be effective, these checklists need to be used frequently and be collected over a period of time. One or two observations can be misleading and will not provide an accurate measurement to reach a fair evaluation. Before a using a checklist, a teacher must decide upon its purpose, how and when it will be used, and what the criteria will be. During the observation period, all occurrences of each item shown on the list need to be recorded. It is helpful for later evaluation if the teacher has a quick reference shorthand system to describe each appearance, e.g., ! equals excellent, @ equals adequate, ? equals iffy, X equals inappropriate. After the session, notes should be added to clarify or elaborate the shorthand ratings.

Sample form for an anecdotal record

Sample anecdotal record for a group discussion
Subject Under Discussion: _____
Students' Names: _____
Date and Time Period of Observations: _____
Characteristics to be evaluated:
Balance between talking and listening: _____
Respect for others: _____
Actively participating in discussion: _____
Stating own opinion: _____
Acted as scribe:_____   *Effectiveness:* _____   Acted as reporter: _____   *Effectiveness:* _____   Acted as participant: _____   *Effectiveness:* _____   Acted as time-keeper: _____   *Effectiveness:* _____
NOTE: form may be modified to fit the observer's particular requirements.

Sample observation checklist			

Subject Being Discussed: _____
Date: _____ Class: _____
Time Elapsed: _____

	Student Names		
Spoke Clearly			
Listened to Other Opinions			
Waited for turn			
Comment was Relevant			
Challenged a Comment			
Stated Reasons for Challenge			
Noticed a Discrepancy			
Stated a Relationship Between Ideas			
Offered a Conclusion			
Inclusive Behavior Shown			

NOTE: can be modified according to teacher requirements.

Developing an observation checklist

Developing an observation checklist takes time. It can be helpful to write down all the skills, behaviors, attitudes, and processes required to acquire mastery of the subject and that are appropriate for the particular age group. The language should be simple and easy to understand, so that the checklists can be used during student and parent conferences. Items needed for the specific task or activity to be evaluated can be chosen from the master list. There should be no more than twelve items on a checklist: any more than that becomes difficult to track, especially when observing several students at the same time. Individual checklists can be developed for specific functions, e.g., participation in a class discussion, proficiency at using a microscope, the mechanics of preparing a term paper. Whatever the rating scale, it must be used consistently, applied fairly, and easy to use during the observation period.

Oral presentations

Oral presentations offer a wealth of possibilities to evaluate student growth and development in several areas, including:

- Understanding of the subject,
- Planning and organizing abilities, and
- Communication skills.

This flexible assessment tool can be assigned to an individual student or as a group project. If given to a group, additional skills can be evaluated including response to other opinions, listening behaviors, active participation in discussions, and contributions to the work product. Teachers need to recognize that some students may have difficulty with or little or no experience conceptualizing, organizing, and delivering a presentation. To address these issues as well as any performance anxieties, it is necessary to establish a classroom atmosphere of acceptance so that students feel confident when giving a presentation. Allowing students some control over the choice of topic also helps alleviate some of the stress involved in standing up in front of the group.

Rating scale

A rating scale is used to evaluate a student against a predetermined continuum. It is particularly useful for rating an oral presentation such as a speech, debate or stage performance, and for students to use as a self-assessment tool. To increase the scale's reliability, when developing the criteria to be evaluated, the activity needs to be broken into specific, manageable parts. Each criterion may need its own rating system. Scale points need to be created.

- Will the evaluation be based upon the one to five number scale with five being the highest, or
- Will the Very Good/Good/Average/Poor/Very Poor standard be used?

- Will another system be developed?

It is helpful for the teacher to decide at the beginning of the semester which units of study will be evaluated using this method and to develop the criteria and rating system ahead of time.

Sample rating scale
Rating Scale
Student Being Rated: _____
Activity: _____
Student Doing The Rating: _____
Date: _____

Presents Argument Clearly		Demonstrates Background Knowledge	
☐	5 Very Logical	☐	5 Very Knowledgeable
☐	4 Logical	☐	4 Knowledgeable
☐	3 Average	☐	3 Average
☐	2 Not Very Logical	☐	2 Not All That Knowledgeable
☐	1 Totally Illogical	☐	1 Not Knowledgeable At All

Answers Relevant Questions		Organization	
☐	5 Very Relevant	☐	5 Very Organized
☐	4 Relevant	☐	4 Organized
☐	3 Average	☐	3 Average
☐	2 Some Relevance	☐	2 Not Always Organized
☐	1 No Relevance	☐	1 Not Organized At All

NOTE: can be modified to address different topics.

Written assignments

Written assignments can take many forms, including essays, reports, term papers, short answers questions, journal and log entries, letters, articles, poetry, solutions to math puzzles, and research, to name a few. It is important that the teacher's expectations and the rating scale are explained with as much detail as possible, especially if students are unfamiliar with the process or are afraid of writing in general. The entire process should be reviewed: choosing a topic, planning, organizing, researching, outlining, writing a first draft, reviewing content, editing, writing a second draft, proofreading, asking someone to read the final draft, and meeting the deadline. Criteria need to be developed for each segment so that when the student and teacher meet for regular consultations during the process, there is a framework for discussion. If it is a group project, it is critical for the teacher to monitor the progress and make sure that every student is contributing to each phase of the process.

Written assignments, presentations, performance assessments, homework

Students are expected to engage in and complete various activities as a normal part of daily classroom participation. Teachers not only rate work products but they can and should use these activities to gauge progress in other goals such as social development, communication skills, and cognitive growth.

- Written Assignments: The ability to plan, organize, and produce a coherent, well-written essay, report, or term paper is just as important as the content of the finished product.
- Presentations: Whether planned or spontaneous, oral presentations need to be organized, logical, and engage the attention of the audience.
- Performance Assessment: Evaluating a student's participation and performance is important for helping him develop social and communicational skills.
- Homework: Homework requires independent study, planning skills, and the ability to prioritize. The student is expected to remember to do the work and turn it in by the required deadline.

Rating scale for oral presentation

Rating Scale For An Oral Presentation	5	4	3	2	1
Student's Name: _____					
Date & Class Period:_____					
Voice is well modulated.					
Presentation is well paced.					
Pauses and emphases are appropriate.					
Can be heard easily by everyone.					
Material is: Organized					
Logical					
Interesting					
Good preparation is evident.					
Information used is on topic.					
Language is appropriate.					
Creativity in preparation and presentation.					
Audience is involved.					

Oral assessments

Oral assessments are used for two reasons: when written assessments are not feasible, and to evaluate a student's mastery of such topics as verbal language proficiency, debating skills, and the ability to think and respond quickly. These types of assessments can be stressful and some students may have trouble responding and become tongue-tied; and therefore it is important to conduct the session in private or in an atmosphere of acceptance. As an interactive form of communication, the teacher needs to avoid filling in the blanks and providing body language clues that might influence the student's response. It is also important to avoid accentuating gender, race, or cultural differences in the content or delivery of the questions and/or tasks. The examination period should be long enough and the tasks required general enough in order to ensure that the student's knowledge and proficiency can be adequately presented and evaluated.

Performance assessments

- Performance assessments are used to evaluate students' progress in specific tasks like demonstrating a skill, solving a complex problem with multiple parts, or participating in a general classroom discussion. The teacher is looking for what the student has learned and retained through what he does and not merely what he says. Information gathered through performance assessments is easy to communicate to students and parents because it describes observable, verifiable actions and offers concrete discussion points to use during conferences. There are four steps to successfully integrate performance assessments into a balanced, comprehensive view of student progress: What is to be observed and assessed.
- Develop the criteria to be used.
- Decide which recording method to use between anecdotal records, an observation checklist, or a rating scale.
- Inform the students that they are being evaluated, on what they are being evaluated, and the criteria being used.

Performance test

A performance test is used to evaluate a particular skill that is one of the primary objectives of the class. Playing a musical instrument, using the backhand stroke in tennis, making a dress, doing a tune-up on a motor vehicle, and conducting a lab experiment are all skills that can be tested using this method. The teacher must ensure that the same criteria are used to evaluate each student and that every student has the same amount of time to demonstrate the skill. If it is an outdoor activity, climate conditions should be considered. Students need to be informed ahead of time on what they will be evaluated and when it will take place. In designing a performance task, teachers should be as specific as possible and consider the objective carefully. Students should be evaluated on both the process and the results. An observation checklist or rating scale is helpful in evaluating a performance test.

Quality tests and quizzes

Tests need to ask the right questions to accurately measure students' knowledge. There are several things to consider:

- Does each item represent an important idea or concept? If students understand the main objectives, their knowledge should be evident in their responses.
- Is each item an appropriate measure of the desired objective? Consider information presented and teaching strategies used.
- Are items presented in easily comprehensible language with clearly defined tasks? Students should not have to decode words or wonder what the item is asking them to do.
- Is the difficulty of the item appropriate? It should not be too difficult or too easy to complete.
- Is each item independent and free from overlap? Completing one item should not lead to completing additional items.
- Is the subject matter covered adequately?
- Is the test free of gender, class, and racial bias? Choose examples that are either familiar or unfamiliar to everyone.

Checklist for written assignment

Sample checklist for written assignment
Student Name: _____
Class: _____
Title of Paper: _____

	Yes	No	Comments
Understood objectives & requirements			
Met the timeline due dates			
Understood criteria for evaluation			
Actively participated in consultations			
Responded appropriately to suggestions			
Used reliable research sources			
Developed & followed a workable outline			
Used examples of prior knowledge			
Used good analytical & reasoning skills			
Developed good questions & answered them			
Worked in a methodical manner			
Used good grammar, sentence structure, spelling			

NOTE: checklist may be modified to reflect teacher's particular requirements.

Homework

Homework should never be assigned as punishment or due to the teacher falling behind as a result of a poorly executed lesson plan or due to outside circumstances. It should be used if students are unable to complete a project during class, to gather information, to practice new skills, or to devise a solution to a complex problem based on a real life situation. Assigned tasks should be interesting and relevant to the students' daily experiences.

Guidelines for assigning homework:

- Provide clear, unambiguous, written instructions. What is

expected and how the results will be evaluated.

- Answer questions and address concerns.
- Make sure the due date is reasonable.
- Consider other academic requirements students may have.
- Be sure resource material is adequate and readily available.
- Collect the assignment on the date specified, grade it, and return it promptly.
- Be consistent with assessment protocol and provide thoughtful, helpful comments.

Test effectiveness

Teachers should have confidence that a test accurately measures students' knowledge: therefore it is important to monitor its effectiveness each time it is used. Before the test is given, all items should be reviewed to ensure that they still meet the criteria established for understanding the material and if one item does not meet the criteria, either rework it or remove it. If most students, including the better ones, miss the same question, perhaps it is too difficult or is not worded properly. If the item is salvageable, rework it, and if not, delete it. Asking for student feedback on one or two items is an effective way to determine if they are still appropriate or if they should be reworked or removed. Veteran teachers usually develop a "feel" for whether a test is an accurate reflection of what students know. If individual items or entire tests are reused, it is imperative to keep them in a secure place to minimize the possibility of cheating.

Checklist for student comprehension

Assessment of Subject Understanding And Ability To Orally Present Concepts

Student Name: _____

Class: _____

Brief Description of Topic:

_____

☐	Obviously read the material/watched the film/listened to the tape of background information.
☐	Able to identify main ideas and concepts.
☐	Information organized and presented logically.
☐	Showed evidence of prior knowledge and/or understanding of the topic.
☐	Creatively linked new data with prior knowledge.
☐	Defended position clearly and logically using good examples and solid reasoning.
☐	Accepted criticism from teacher and peers of reasoning used and position taken.
☐	Able to be heard by everyone.
☐	Spoke clearly with good cadence and used proper English.
☐	Keep audience interested and engaged.

NOTE: may be modified to meet teacher requirements.

Extended open-response items

Using an extended open-response item is a very effective method to determine how well students understand the subject matter. This type of item measures students' ability to evaluate and synthesize information and how effectively they communicate using the written word. Depending upon how the item is worded, it allows students to describe and explain, compare and contrast, and develop and summarize the ideas and concepts learned. Since one item might be easier to answer than another, it is better to give all the students the same information to consider so that the evaluation is based upon the same premise. It is important that students understand beforehand the criteria that will be used to assess the response. Accurate facts and figures; a clear, concise writing style; and persuasive arguments might be the focus of the evaluation or perhaps rather the focus is creative expression, personal opinions, and/or conclusions and critical thinking.

Extended open-response items can be evaluated using either holistic scoring or analytic scoring; there is not much difference in reliability and effectiveness between the two methods. Holistic scoring measures a list of specific elements, e.g., clarity of the objective, choice of ideas explored, persuasiveness of the arguments, effectiveness of vocabulary, sentence structure, and organization of the essay. Each item is recognized and noted and the final grade is based upon the response as a whole. Analytic scoring can evaluate the same elements but the difference is that each one is given a rating and the final grade is a sum of those rating values. For example: clarity earns twenty of twenty-five, choice of ideas earns eighteen of twenty, persuasiveness earns twenty-five of twenty-five, vocabulary and sentence structure earns fifteen of fifteen, and organization earns twelve of fifteen for a final grade of ninety. Analytic scoring evaluates with a little more detail than holistic scoring.

Short-answer items

Short-answer items require a specific answer to a specific question. They can be a one or two word response, a brief definition, or a short paragraph. They are helpful when a teacher wants to know how well students have learned individual facts, figures, dates, definitions, etc. When using a completion or fill in the blank item, the answer should be placed at the end of the statement. This gives the student the opportunity to read all available information before having to answer. For example: Bright, bold,

beautiful is an example of _____. The response (alliteration) is a one-word answer. If the answer requires more information, the instructions need to clearly state how much data is required. For example, "Give three important reasons the United States became involved in World War II." Multiple choice and true/false questions can be turned into short answer questions by requiring a brief explanation justifying the choice.

Multiple choice item lists

A multiple choice item has a direct question or a complete statement called the stem, which is followed by several possible answers of which usually only one is correct (multiple responses can be requested). These items are designed to test recall and recognition of facts as well as the ability to make associations. The stem needs to be stated in such as a way as to require a specific answer. The language needs to be simple, short, and concise but must include enough data and state the information clearly enough that there is no confusion. Avoid using clues that might indicate the correct answer and be wary of using "all of the above" and "none of the above" as possible responses. These too cause confusion. Ensure that the stem of one item does not include the answer to another. Asking for the correct or incorrect answer is common. Asking for the best answer requires using critical thinking skills.

Matching item lists

Matching items are used to test recall of specific facts. This is a quick, effective method to determine how well students have integrated information and made associations. The first step is to group homogeneous facts together and then develop parallel lists of premises and responses. The information needs to be closely related; if it is not, common sense instead of knowledge of the subject will dictate the matches. List items randomly to avoid providing clues as to what premise matches which response, e.g., alphabetically by first word or by length of answer. Keep lists manageable as too many items can be confusing. The entire question needs to be on the same page; dividing it between two wastes time and changes the dynamics. Having the students group related facts and develop premises and responses as a class exercise is a good method to review the material. It also provides data to use on a future test.

True/false item lists

Depending upon how they are worded, true/false items can be used to test content knowledge, recall of facts, ability to define and/or use an idea or concept, and to evaluate information. The most efficient way to develop true/false items is to review textbooks and other resource material and make a list of ideas, concepts, facts, and miscellaneous data. It is important to construct the statement using clear, concise language that is grammatically correct and unambiguous. In order to avoid confusion, use only one idea, concept, or fact in each question. Make the statement positive rather than negative. If using a negative statement, make sure its negativity is clear. The idea is to challenge, not confuse students. Use more false items than true ones because, statistically, guessers tend to check true more often than false. Try to include some plausible false answers but avoid trick questions.

Preparing tests

It is a good idea to use several types of questions when preparing tests. This will prevent the students from getting bored, expose them to a variety of testing formats, and encourage them to recall and respond to information in different ways. Matching and true/false questions are an excellent way to quickly assess how well students remember specific facts, as well as their ability to memorize data. Multiple choice and short-answer questions require a little deeper knowledge of the subject and better reasoning and thinking skills. These four testing options are reasonably quick and easy to grade. Open-response questions can be used to evaluate in depth content knowledge, the use of critical thinking skills, and the ability to communicate thoughts and ideas through the written word. This option requires more time, effort, and concentration to evaluate fairly, and is a more effective tool in some situations and courses than it is in others.

Time management ideas

Effective time management is crucial for every teacher. Accurate, fair assessment of students' academic and social progress is equally important. It is critical to develop ways to accomplish both efficiently. Organization is a key ingredient in the equation; time spent searching for things is time wasted. Collaborating with colleagues to develop assessment tools; sharing instructional methods, testing techniques, and formats that work; and establishing standards and priorities for evaluations take time in the beginning but ultimately save time. Teachers who expect perfection from themselves and/or their students are striving to reach an unrealistic goal. Using evaluation tools with appropriate frequency, assessing their value at regular intervals, constructing and saving good testing items, and using standard formats when possible are all ways to use time efficiently. Preparing lessons, organizing record keeping and evaluating the effectiveness of each on a regular basis will help develop a sensible, workable use of limited time resources.

Culture and Professional Aspects of the Job

Culture

A culture is a comprehensive style of living that is developed in a society and maintained from generation to generation. Culture is manifested in a group's traditions, rituals, language, social norms, technology and economic structures. Broadly speaking, culture is everything which is learned by a member of a particular society, though it may include things that an individual learns but which become assumed and are never made explicit either in the individual's mind or in his social interactions. For this reason, many experts feel it is difficult to properly study one's own culture; they suggest that only the unclouded eyes of a foreign observer can perceive a society's most fundamental values.

Material culture

A society's material culture is the set of all of the physical objects which the people of that society have either created or to which they assign cultural meaning. Material culture may therefore include objects like books, jewelry, buildings, and furniture, to name just a few; but can also include natural areas, if those areas have been considered by the members of the society in a special way. As an example of this latter kind of material culture, a sociologist might point to Native American society, in which the land itself held immense cultural value. Along with verbal culture, material culture makes up the sum total of that which sociologists have at their disposal for study.

Nonmaterial culture

Nonmaterial culture is all of a society's customs, beliefs, political structures, languages, and ways of using material objects. In the United States, for instance, the emphasis placed on religious freedom and individual liberty might be considered an example of material culture. The boundary, however, between material and nonmaterial culture is never altogether clear; how, for instance, should one distinguish between the American flag and that for which it stands—the idea of freedom? The values and norms, as opposed to the physical things that are used to express values and norms, are that which make up a society's nonmaterial culture. Typically, nonmaterial culture is more difficult to change than material culture, though its change may be more difficult to observe. Teachers need to be aware of the material and nonmaterial elements of their ELL students' native cultures.

Cultural cooperation and accommodation

The extent to which an English language learner thrives depends upon the relationship between ones culture and that of the school. Cooperation and accommodation refer to two ways in which the members of different cultures interact with one another. Cooperation is an agreement between two parties to work together towards a common goal; typically, cooperation refers to short-term goals which can be pursued without altering ones beliefs or values. Accommodation, alternatively, is an agreement between two conflicting cultures to acknowledge but ignore their differences and try to work together toward common goals, instead. Countries that have two or more cultural groups within them, such as Israel or Iraq, are always trying to work out some kind of accommodation, so that positive progress can be made for all the citizens of the nation despite their divergent systems of belief.

Cultural assimilation

Assimilation is the process whereby individuals are absorbed into a particular society after having been members of a different one. Assimilation can either be voluntary, as in the case of people fleeing religious persecution to a friendly society, or forced, as in the case of some ethnic groups that have been required to observe national customs contrary to their own. The process generally includes learning a new language and a new set of social values and norms. For English language learners, assimilation is a necessary consequence of attending a new school. Typically, assimilation is easier for the young and for individuals who are educated and well-traveled. Many critics of the process argue that making cultures homogenous through forced assimilation stifles innovation and productive dialogue within a society.

Cultural values

The values of a culture are its highest ideals. In the United States, for example, one might say that freedom and equality are two of our most important values. Values are usually very general concepts and may be complementary; for example, the values of hard work and material success seem to go together. Values are quite fluid and may come into conflict with one another, which can create social conflict and disorganization. An example of this is the conflict in mid-twentieth century America between the value of equal rights and that of segregation; ultimately, it was clear that only one of these values could remain. It is rare for American academic standards to challenge an ELL student's cultural values, but there is likely to be some conflict. Teachers should be sensitive to

this conflict without seeking to avoid it.

Cultural sanctions

Cultural sanctions are any rewards or consequences given to an individual or group to pursue or renounce a certain course of behavior. Sanctions may either be positive, as when a reward is promised for doing something properly, or negative, as when a punishment is promised for doing something wrong. Although the most common use of the word refers to international economic pressures (as in, for instance, the economic restrictions placed on Iraq during the 1990s), all societies place sanctions on their members in order to elicit approved behavior. People who uphold the values and norms of their society are rewarded by preferential treatment from their fellows, while those who transgress can be punished socially, economically, or legally. In a sense, ELL students are sanctioned to the extent that their native language and culture prohibits them from succeeding as students. A teacher's goal is to identify and eliminate these cultural sanctions.

Cultural norms

Norms are specific rules regulating behavior in a culture. Norms may or may not be directly codified in the law of a society, but they are intended to encourage behavior which promotes the society's values. Taking again the example of the United States, one might say that treating men and women equally is a social norm, insofar as equality between the sexes is a value to which our culture aspires. This is not a norm in many other cultures, though, and some ELL students may display surprising behavior because of their familiarity with different norms. Norms depend on values for their justification, and values depend on norms for their enactment. Norms may vary greatly from society to society, such that the same behavior may be approved or condemned depending on where it is performed. Most of the time, norms are so customary for the members of a society that they are performed automatically.

Formal and informal norms

Norms may be considered formal or informal depending on whether they are codified in the laws of the society in which they apply. Formal norms are written law; for example, the prohibition of murder, the forced payment of taxes, and the sanctity of the institution of marriage. Informal norms, on the other hand, are unwritten codes of conduct. Examples of informal norms might include the prohibition of spitting in public or the encouragement of deference to women. Typically, a society formalizes the norms which are most important, and for which violators should be punished. Formal norms tend to be much more consistent among various societies than informal norms.

Social markers, laws, and folkways

A social marker is any part of behavior that indicates the identity, character, or way of understanding of a particular group of people. Social markers can be laws, folkways, traditions, or other patterns of behavior. A teacher should be on the lookout for the social markers displayed by ELL students. Laws are simply social norms that have been made explicit and are enforced by the government. There are plenty of norms, however, which are encoded in law but are also internalized-- the prohibition of murder, for instance. Folkways are social norms that have become habitual or traditional in a society. In the United States, for instance, we are accustomed to tipping a waiter or waitress for their service. Because this practice is so

ingrained in our daily life, it is an American folkway.

Cultural pluralism, subcultures, and reference groups

Cultural pluralism exists when multiple distinct cultures exist within the same society after a process of accommodation. These self-contained cultures should not be confused with subcultures, which are smaller cultures within a large culture. Subcultures usually have a set of norms and values that are different from those held by the larger society to which they are a member. In the United States, we might consider punk rockers or hippies as subcultures, because they have different values than Americans on the whole, but do not really have a self-sustaining or separate society of their own, either. Reference groups are those groups to which individuals aspire and compare themselves, and against which one evaluates one's own qualities. For example, a man who considers himself to be wealthy might purchase a yacht or an expensive sports car because of a desire to resemble those whom he aspires to imitate, rather than necessarily desiring said objects.

Dominant culture and ethnocentrism

In any society, the dominant culture is the group whose norms, values, and behavior patterns are forced on the rest of the society. Many nations, including the United States, have laws that are designed to restrain the dominant culture from extinguishing minority cultures. In the United States, for example, the English-speaking culture is the dominant culture. Ethnocentrism describes the tendency to view one's own cultural patterns as superior and to judge all others only as they relate to one's own. This philosophy has been at the root of some of humanity's worst atrocities, including the Holocaust, which was perpetrated by Germans who believed they must maintain the purity of their superior race, and colonial conquests, in which Western nations brutally imposed their customs on various indigenous peoples. Obviously, a teacher of ELL students must strive to promote assimilation without ethnocentrism.

Cultural relativism

Cultural relativism is the idea that any particular part of a given culture can only be understood in relation to the rest of the culture, and as a product of its context. In large part, cultural relativism is a reaction to Western ethnocentrism, or the belief that Western culture is superior to all others. Some critics argue that cultural relativism inevitably leads to the absence of any standards at all, and makes judgment (and hence constructive criticism and progress) impossible. Its proponents counter that the general similarity in moral code between various cultures implies that there is a set of innately human values, and that cultural relativism offers the only approach wherein the sociologist can explore the nature of his own assumptions.

Progress, cultural lag, and diffusion

The idea of progress is the idea that social and technological progress is inevitable. A cultural lag is created when a change in one part of society is not immediately answered by corresponding changes in the other parts. A typical example of this is when new technology brings rapid progress to the day-to-day lives of the citizens, and the religious institutions do not adjust their practices to incorporate it. This typically produces a period of relative inactivity in the society. Diffusion is the process by which technological, political, and social innovations spread from one society to another. The process of diffusion is usually accelerated in pluralist societies that are accustomed to

a healthy internal debate.

Acculturation

Acculturation is an extensive borrowing by one group of cultural traits from another group. Acculturation can also describe the exchange of cultural traits between two cultures that are in close contact for a long period of time. Acculturation may occur such that the recipient culture incorporates new traits without significantly altering its own culture; an example of this is the acquisition of Chinese linguistic characters into Korean and Japanese society. Of course, acculturation may also have a devastating effect on one of the cultures, as in the savagely unequal exchange between Europeans and Native Americans. Many groups are currently trying to resist the acculturation encouraged by globalization. In the ELL classroom, a certain amount of acculturation is inevitable, but the teacher should be sure to affirm the worth of both English-speaking culture and the native cultures of the students.

Syncretism

Syncretism is the conscious adopting of the cultural elements of a dominant group by a subordinate group. One classic example of this kind of syncretism is the economic transformation of Japan after World War Two. The Japanese, with help from the Western powers, rapidly developed an industrial base and market economy modeled after that of the United States. Syncretism has often been used to describe the interplay of religions within a society; for example, it is invoked hopefully by those who would like to see reconciliation between the Protestant and Catholic churches. There is a danger in syncretism of losing elements of culture that are unique to the subordinate culture, and thus discouraging debate and innovation. In the classroom, some argue

- 88 -

that syncretism should be avoided, as it can be perceived to devalue the native culture of the ELL student.

Culture shock

Culture shock is the feeling of disorientation that a person may feel when they encounter cultural values, norms, or practices that are contrary to their own. Culture shock may occur when an individual goes to another country, moves to a different environment, or simply encounters something with which he is unfamiliar in his own culture. Culture shock typically has four phases: the honeymoon, in which the new thing is perceived as good; the shock, in which the individual becomes disoriented; the negotiation, in which the individual labors to make the new thing acceptable to him or herself; and acceptance, in which the positives and negatives of the new culture have been absorbed and reconciled. It may be assumed that ELL students will have already passed through the honeymoon and shock periods, and will need assistance with negotiation and acceptance.

Convergent cultural evolution

When different cultures develop similar cultural traits because they live in similar environments, it is known as convergent cultural evolution. For example, societies that developed in tropical environments have been shown to have arrived at similar agricultural practices independently. Similarly, cultures that develop in densely-populated areas tend to be different from those that arise in rural areas. For one thing, rural cultures tend to place more emphasis on the strength of the family unit, because there are fewer people readily available to care for the young. In urban culture, there may be more emphasis placed on specialization and division of labor, as the size of the population allows for a diverse market economy. For teachers of English language learners, the manifestation of convergent cultural evolution may at first be surprising. Often, students from distant regions will have more in common with their new classmates than one would expect. The danger for a teacher is to assume that the presence of some convergent cultural evolution obviates the need for further assimilation.

Cultural determinism

Cultural determinism is the assertion that the potential for variation in human societies is unlimited, and that cultural forces can shape human nature into almost any form. This idea has manifested itself in a number of different societies, typically as a source of the culture's sense of uniqueness. For example, the ancient Greeks attributed their self-proclaimed superiority to their language, and actually coined the term "barbarian" to describe foreigners (literally, those who, to the Greeks, made gibberish sounds like "bar-bar"). Even today, many Americans feel that the democratic system has somehow made them unique in history. A teacher of English language learners should be aware of the deterministic effect of language, but should avoid attributing superiority to any linguistic culture.

Cultural gatekeepers

The cultural gatekeepers of a society are the people who permit or forbid the introduction of new elements of culture into their society. Specifically, cultural gatekeepers are people who have control over the means by which ideas are distributed in a society, and therefore decide which ideas are distributed. For example, radio executives can decide which new songs will get airtime, and in effect control which songs will become a part of the popular culture. Of course, cultural gatekeepers like movie and radio executives, fashion buyers, and editors are subject to the demands of the market, and therefore cannot always introduce the things which they personally find worthy; instead, cultural gatekeepers often simply mimic elements of the culture that are already present. The idea of the cultural gatekeeper is an interesting one for ELL instruction, because it suggests that some students will be especially instrumental for encouraging their fellows. In other words, some students will have the charisma and acknowledged authority to convince others of the necessity of adopting elements of English-speaking culture.

Cultural universals

Cultural universals are the elements of culture that are found in virtually every society. The anthropologist George Murdock once compiled a list of these universals, and it included sports, cooking, courtship, dancing, family, games, language, music, religion, and restrictions on sexual activity. Although these elements appear in every culture, the particular forms in which they emerge are quite various. Most of them have a clear role in perpetuating the society; it is easy to see, for instance, why cooking, courtship, and language should be universal. Sociologists are still debating, however, why it is that more trivial things like sport and music should be found in every society, and what role these things play in the continuation of the social group.

Cultural pluralism for English language learners

Cultural pluralism exists when several distinct cultures thrive alongside one another. There may be a dominant culture, but it does not seek to eliminate the others, and indeed often looks to absorb useful elements from them. The ELL classroom should aspire to cultural pluralism, because it creates the most value for students. When the various members of the class are eager to learn about and incorporate aspects of each other's culture, efficient and accelerated learning is possible. Cultural pluralism can be explicitly encouraged by teachers by creating an inclusive learning environment in which students feel comfortable sharing their backgrounds and cultural traditions. Cultural pluralism is undermined by instruction that directly or indirectly values one culture over another.

Intra- and intergroup differences

In the ELL classroom, it is useful to distinguish intragroup differences from intergroup differences. Intragroup differences exist within a particular cultural or linguistic community. For instance, within the community of Spanish-speaking people are Argentineans and Mexicans, who may not have a great deal in common besides language. It is important for a teacher to recognize these differences and not simply to lump all the members of a linguistic community together. Intergroup differences exist between the members of distinct cultural and linguistic communities. The differences between students from Haiti and students from Russia, for instance, are intergroup, because these students share neither a culture nor a language.

Instruction for immigrants

In many ELL classrooms, the majority of the students are immigrants, meaning that they have moved to the United States during their lifetime. Teachers can expect that these students will have a more difficult time adjusting to American culture, including but not limited to language issues. Immigrant students are likely to have parents who are also unfamiliar with the United States, and so

- 90 -

it may be necessary for the teacher to spend more time in communication with them. Immigrant students are more likely to have spent time in a distinct educational milieu, so a teacher may have to work on basic American academic skills like punctuality, taking turns, etc.

Instruction for the children of migrants

Migrants are people who leave their home country in search of work. In the United States, there are many migrants from Central and South America who have come to work in agriculture and construction. These workers are often here illegally, and they therefore may be reticent to interact with a teacher. It is important to allay any concerns that these parents might have about dealing with school officials, who are concerned with educating children rather than citizenship. The children of migrants are often far below grade level, because their frequent travel has constantly interrupted their education. They may be unfamiliar with the rituals of school. Also, the children of migrants are likely to have spent the majority of their lives in a relatively small community, and therefore may be more shy about mixing with their peers. Teachers should be sensitive to these issues as they help the children of migrants adjust to the classroom.

Instruction for refugees

Refugees have come to the United States to escape from religious, political, or other persecution. Their passage to the United States is typically orchestrated by the federal government, and, while efforts are made to place refugees in communities near others who share their culture, some may be feeling quite isolated when they enter school. Many refugees are placed in regions with a vastly different climate and topography than that to which they are accustomed,

and this may be disorienting at first. Also, many refugees were traumatized by the events that drove them from their homeland, and may be dealing with psychological issues. In all, refugees can be among the most fragile classes of student for an ELL teacher. These students are typically familiar with formal education, but may need time to adjust to other aspects of life in the United States.

Instruction for ELL students born in the United States

Of all the students in an ELL classroom, those who were born in the United States should be the easiest for a teacher to handle. However, these students often have grown up in communities where no English is spoken, so it should not be assumed that they will be any more fluent than their fellows. Students who were born in the United States should be conversant with the American academic system, and can be relied upon as resources for other students. These students may become bored with some of the remedial elements of ELL instruction, and therefore alternate activities should be established for when the main part of the class is concentrated on learning basic aspects of life and education in the United States.

Teacher's cultural background and instruction

A teacher's cultural background can have an influence upon instruction in a number of ways. To begin with, a teacher may have adopted the assumptions and prejudices common to his culture, and may propagate these in the classroom. Most ELL teachers are aware of this possibility, however, and do a good job of preventing adverse influence. A less noticeable source of cultural influence is the teacher training program. Teachers earn their certification in programs that often have a pronounced bias towards the norms of white culture. Indeed, many critics have charged that the standardized tests required for admission to education programs have an inherent cultural bias. Because there are so few alternatives, many teachers are unaware of the potential for creeping bias. It takes effort to explore other paradigms for instruction.

Too often, discussions of multicultural education focus on the diversity of students, and fail to account for the unique cultural background of the teacher. However, the teacher's treatment of his own background is as important as discussions related to students'. A teacher should be upfront about any potential biases stemming from his background. More importantly, during preparation for instruction, a teacher should consider at length how his background might affect instruction. Of particular use would be any instances from a teacher's personal history in which he realized the assumptions or prejudices associated with his culture, and then used that awareness to develop a more expansive multicultural view.

Nonverbal communication and turn-taking habits

Sometimes, ELL teachers are overly attuned to the linguistic differences between students, and they fail to recognize important nonverbal elements of communication. These include proxemics (the distance between interlocutors), posture, gestures, and eye contact. These nonverbal forms of communication can convey approval or disapproval, express personal identity, or conform to cultural ritual. It is important for a teacher to be aware of the elements of nonverbal communication common to different cultures, so that he can more accurately gauge student behavior and pinpoint potential problems before they occur. A particular area of emphasis is on the cultural norms surrounding turn-taking. In some cultures it is common for people to elbow their way forward rather than wait their turn. Such behavior is not considered rude. A teacher should be aware of this and should gently guide students towards the American norm of turn-taking.

Promoting cooperation between students from different backgrounds

One of the inherent problems of the common pluralistic approach to multiculturalism is that it overemphasizes the distinctions between cultures and thereby tacitly encourages students to self segregate. To combat this problem, teachers should set up activities that require students from different cultures to cooperate. Once students have achieved a certain level of linguistic mastery, they should be able to work in collaboration with students with a different primary language. Another way to promote cooperation is to lead activities that emphasize the similarities between cultures. For instance, students could be asked to describe the traditional holidays in their cultures, and then to identify the common elements. In most cultures, holidays will be celebrated with special foods, dancing, and songs. These general characteristics are true of many cultures.

Multiculturalism

Multiculturalism is the set of values and norms that suggest that different races in a pluralistic society should learn to understand and appreciate the differences between them, rather than seeking to impose one style of life upon another. The multicultural view emphasizes the inherent dignity in all human groups, and seeks to find ways to harmonize relations without compromising any group's beliefs. In the United States, multiculturalism exists in protection for the rights of minority groups to preserve their religious and cultural practices. Some critics of multiculturalism argue that it prevents assimilation and integration, and can thereby lead to disharmony in the society, or an under-performing and economically segregated labor force.

Social role

A role is a person's particular niche within a society. Every role has a set of expectations and norms that define how the person holding it should behave. For example, in the case of the role of the father, most societies expect that a person will provide economic and material support for the rest of his family. It is quite possible to hold multiple roles at the same time, and indeed to acquire and cast off roles as one moves through life. Culturally acknowledged roles help to provide a society with its basic structure. Much of the trouble resulting from an individual's passage from one culture to another comes from the difficulty in discovering and occupying an accepted role in the new society. This transition can be facilitated by a knowledgeable and sensitive ELL instructor.

Role performance, impression management, and studied nonobservance

Role performance is the way people holding a particular role actually behave, as opposed to the way they are expected to behave as holders of that role. Impression management is one's conscious manipulation of one's role performance. Successful role management requires that an individual has an accurate understanding of his role, as well as the expectations society has for him. Studied nonobservance is the sociological term for when members of a society ignore lapses in one another's role performance, in the interest of preserving

harmony within the society.

Role set, role strain, role exit, and role-taking

The role set is the full group of roles associated with any particular status. A college professor, for instance, must by turns be a mentor, expert, friend, and colleague. Role strain is the difficulty an individual may have in meeting the social obligations of a role. Most sociologists would say that every individual experiences role strain to some degree, as no person is perfectly suited to any role. Role exit is the process of leaving a role that formerly had been integral to the individual's personality. Everyone exits roles throughout their life, for example leaving behind the role of son when one's parents die, or leaving the role of student when one graduates. Role-taking is the process whereby an individual imagines himself in the role of another, and tries then to understand the meaning of what the other is expressing. Developing this sense of empathy is an important first step towards enabling students to inhabit roles in both their native culture and English-speaking culture.

Socialization

Socialization is the process through which individuals born into a society gradually become participating members of that society. This involves learning the culture, including the prevailing social values and norms, and learning to assume the behavior appropriate to a specific societal role. Experts usually distinguish between primary socialization (the period in which an infant acquires the rudiments of language), and secondary socialization (in which the individual is trained to join a particular social group). Socialization is impossible without the active participation of the society, especially the family, education, and religious groups. Most experts concur that socialization

Copyright © Mometrix Media. You have been licensed one copy of this document for personal use only. Any other reproduction or redistribution is strictly prohibited. All rights reserved.

continues in some degree throughout an individual's entire life, though it is most crucial in childhood. For ELL students, of course, transition to English-speaking culture is another instance of intense socialization.

Gender socialization

Gender socialization is the process through which an individual learns about the various gender roles in his society and comes to take one. Sociological research has shown that boys and girls are treated quite differently in most societies; parents encourage their children to act in gender-appropriate ways, and are embarrassed or angry when children display traits of another gender. Peer pressure also subtly lets children know what clothing and behavior is appropriate to their gender. Studies of American schools during the 1990s showed that teachers generally assigned different tasks to boys and girls. It has also been observed that most children's books and television programs present stereotyped gender roles.

Class socialization

Sociologists have determined that there are fundamental differences in the ways children are socialized depending on their social class. In fact, research has shown that the specific values stressed by parents vary depending on their class. Middle-class parents tend to emphasize responsibility, self-control, and curiosity about why things happen, whereas working-class parents are more interested in teaching their children manners, neatness, honesty, and obedience. The inference drawn by sociology is that individuals in higher classes tend to place more emphasis on self-direction and obeying internal standards, as opposed to conformity and obeying external standards. There is speculation that this difference is the result of working-class parents being so thoroughly involved in slavish work that they come to identify with the ethics of conformity and obedience. One of the emphases of critical multiculturalism has been to extend the treatment of bias in the ELL classroom beyond race and ethnicity to socioeconomic status.

Primary socialization

Typically, an individual's primary socialization occurs among his family. The family is the first mirror a child develops for himself, and it is the family's reactions to his behavior that forms the behavioral habits he will take into the society at large. Mothers and fathers typically have complementary ways of relating to children, which provides for a more balanced socialization process. The presence of siblings can give the child some experience at conflict, cooperation, and competition. Generally, however, primary socialization in the family means the child is born into a particular social status, and will absorb a particular set of values, attitudes, and beliefs.

Secondary socialization

Secondary socialization is that socialization that the individual undergoes outside of the family unit: from friends, at school, and from the media. An ELL student undergoes a variation of secondary socialization in the classroom. A child's peer group provides him with experience dealing with others of relatively equal status. In this setting, children can take some power in their relationships, and learn about friendship and conflict resolution. Socialization at school is important as well because it places the child in a subordinate relation to someone other than his parent, and prepares him for life among bureaucratic, impersonal organizations. Television is probably the most important socializing agent among the mass media; most research shows that it tends to reinforce stereotypes about social roles and norms.

Anticipatory socialization and desocialization

When an individual begins to alter his beliefs or norms because of an expected socialization process he is about to undergo, it is known as anticipatory socialization. One possible example of anticipatory socialization might be a college graduate who, before actually getting a job, adopts the dress and lifestyle of a member of the business community. Some ELL students will demonstrate this behavior. Desocialization is the process of casting off one version of self and one set of values. Desocialization is followed by resocialization into another set of values and norms. Sociology asserts that as individuals move through life, taking on and casting off various roles, they are constantly altering the set of values and norms that are most in line with their status. Therefore, they are constantly engaged in a process of desocialization and resocialization. To some extent, this process should be expected in the ELL classroom, but it should not be accelerated through the denigration of the student's native culture.

Internalization of norms

The internalization of norms is basically the development of a conscience. It refers to the condition whereby the members of a society accept the norms of that society as correct, to the point that they no longer even need to think of them explicitly. Internalization is crucial because it means that the governing authority does not have to make sure individuals are policed at all times. In the United States, for instance, most citizens simply *feel* that stealing from one's neighbor is wrong; the immorality of theft is a norm that has been fully internalized in American society. Some sociologists have speculated that genetics may be intertwined with the internalization of norms, as many common norms promote survival and successful propagation of the species. An ELL teacher should expect that most students will share norms, regardless of their native culture. However, there may be some small but important differences.

Differential socialization, horizontal socialization, and vertical socialization

Differential socialization is the way in which different members of the same society may develop markedly different traits, depending on what role their society intends for them to assume later in life. This differentiation can occur in one of two ways. When sociologists are referring to a fundamental difference in the socialization, for instance the different requirements that a society has for doctors and teachers, they call it horizontal differentiation. When sociologists are referring to differences in socialization caused by varying social status, for instance the socialization of the wealthy compared to that of the poor, they use the term vertical socialization. Every individual is subject to both kinds of differentiation in his socialization. It is important for an ELL teacher to understand this concept so as to avoid pigeonholing students.

Attachments, investments, involvements, and beliefs

Attachments are the bonds formed between individual members of a society, as for instance the love between family members or friends. Investments are the material and emotional costs that a person expends in order to make his place in a society and, hopefully, secure the future rewards of participation in that society. For students, learning English makes an investment in the English-speaking culture. A person's involvement in his society is the amount of time they spend engaged in nondeviant activities, and a person's beliefs are their ideas about how the members of their society should behave. The development of involvements and beliefs will be a consequence of the formation of attachments and investments by students.

Family

The family is the basic unit of society. The size and configuration of the family varies from culture to culture, but the general functions remain the same. The most obvious and important function of the family is to nurture and socialize the young, but the stability provided by family life is also a benefit to the society at large. In the United States, family structure was extremely rigid and stable during the colonial period, as adverse economic conditions made family members very dependent on one another. As the country became more prosperous, however, family life became more and more improvised and careless, resulting in a rise in crime. In the early-eighteenth century, however, the traditional family roles that survive somewhat today (that is, father as breadwinner, mother as caretaker) appeared, and the family structure became much more stable. The students in an ELL class are likely to emerge from vastly different family structures.

A nuclear family is a family group consisting of one adult couple (one male and one female) and their children. The strong bond among the members of a nuclear family is a consistent feature of almost every society, with one notable exception being the Israeli kibbutz, in which children are raised by the entire community without any particular parents. An extended family consists of more than one adult couple, often the parents, brothers and sisters of a particular heterosexual couple. In many human societies, people live among their extended families, rather than just in a nuclear family unit. This is especially typical in societies where people do not have to move particularly quickly (that is, in agrarian or industrial rather than hunting and gathering societies).

Patrilineality and matrilineality

In a culture operating on the principle of patrilineality, a person inherits his title and property from his father's side of the family. Patrilineal descent is much more common that matrilineal descent, in which things are inherited from the mother's side. In fact, societies that operate on matrilineality often transfer property not to the women themselves, but to the male heirs of a woman. For this reason, even in such a woman-based system, women see little material benefit. In a society operating on a patrilocal rule of residence, married couples will live either with or close to the man's family. In a culture observing a matrilocal rule of residence, married couples will live with or near the woman's family.

Endogamy, exogamy, polygamy, polyandry, and polygyny

There are several distinctions within the institution of marriage, to account for differences in arrangement and configuration. Endogamy is the practice of forcing someone to marry within his own group. The group in question could be the individual's religious, tribal, racial, national, or other group. Exogamy, on the other hand, is the practice of marrying outside the group. Polygamy describes any marital group that consists of one man or woman and his or her multiple spouses. Within polygamy, polyandry is the practice of forming marital groups consisting of one wife and two or more husbands. Polygyny, on the other hand, is the formation of marital groups of one man and two or more wives.

Soliciting cultural information

English language learners come from various and diverse backgrounds, and a teacher cannot be expected to have familiarity with each student's native culture. However, a teacher should know how to go about acquiring some degree of familiarity, particularly with regard to those cultural aspects that will affect the student's progress. The first and best resource for a teacher is the student and the student's family. Even within a general culture or ethnicity, a family is likely to have specific characteristics and idiosyncrasies that relate to education. For instance, a teacher might assume that all students from the Middle East have a patriarchal view of gender relations, only to discover that there are countries in the region with a more westernized attitude about such things than one might expect.

A great deal of useful information can be obtained from the artifacts of a culture: that is, the music, film, and literature produced by its members. Many teachers have found that exploring the art of their students' native culture has a broadening effect on every aspect of their lives, not only their instruction. Insofar as it is possible to incorporate these artifacts into the work of the class, it can be greatly beneficial. Another resource is the Internet: there are scores of English-language websites and chat rooms for every culture, and a teacher can often solicit advice from people who represent or are expert in a particular culture. Finally, a teacher can visit the reference department of a local library. Reference librarians are trained to point out useful books and articles that can help a teacher become oriented to a culture.

Applying cultural knowledge

Having obtained an understanding of the native cultures of his students, a teacher should apply this knowledge to instruction. Perhaps the most important aspect of culture to consider is the concept of education. In some cultures, particularly those in Africa and Asia, it is typical for students to passively receive information. These students will not be used to thinking creatively or offering their opinions in class. A teacher should avoid putting them on the spot in the first weeks of class. Many students will be used to a disorganized school structure, particularly those who come from impoverished or semi-literate backgrounds. Such students may need more instruction on basic elements of being a student, like taking notes, adhering to a schedule, and raising one's hand before talking. For a teacher, it is easier to exercise patience with students who struggle to adjust to American-style education when the reasons for the struggle are understood.

School culture vs. student's native culture

When education experts refer to the degree of cultural congruence, they mean the extent to which the culture of the student overlaps with the culture of the school. It is assumed that high cultural congruence is a positive, but this is not always the case. When a student's native culture is very similar to the predominant culture at the school, the student may be disincentivized from learning about the school culture. The student may have the idea that their current cultural orientation is "good enough," and that there is no reason to attempt to master elements of the school culture. A teacher's role is to underscore the differences between cultures without passing judgment or stigmatizing either side. A teacher should encourage students to explore cultural differences without preference or bias. Of course, a teacher's job is made somewhat easier by a high degree of cultural congruence, because students will need less instruction in the basics of being a student in an American-style program.

Cultural values in the classroom

Bilingual educators need to be especially sensitive to the educational needs of culturally diverse learners. This is because these needs can manifest themselves in ways that are not normal for the culture in which the teacher has been raised. All students need not only cognitive and linguistic education, but psycho-social and affective education. On top of that, students need to be receiving professional and vocational skills so that they can hold a job in the future. Teachers need to be aware of the way in which cultural values are formed. Individuals develop cultural perceptual patterns which determine the stimuli that reach their awareness, and go a long way to determining their judgments of people, objects, and events in their lives. Individuals from different cultures will literally think differently. These differences are the results of environmental adaptations, contact with other cultural groups, historical factors, and socio-economic evolution. Students will also develop their personal values based on their relationships with their family, religious group, and peers.

Promoting cultural diversity

Teachers are responsible for creating an effective learning environment for ELL students by remaining sensitive to the cultural values of all students. Teachers should be aware that many students will have a negative predisposition toward authority figures. At times, a teacher may find that his own values and beliefs are in conflict with the values and beliefs of the student. Regardless, a teacher needs to maintain high expectations for his students. Significant research has indicated that the nature of a teacher's

expectations for students has a direct relation to performance. When students feel that the teacher has low expectations for their performance, it tends to diminish their self-confidence and makes failure more likely. In contrast, when teachers have high expectations for their students, students are more likely to take risks and experiment with new methods of study. Students are also more likely to set clear goals and work hard to achieve them.

Structural considerations related to a multicultural classroom

Teachers need to be aware of how the structural aspects of the learning environment will affect the performance of bilingual students. Often, school systems that are entrenched in traditional methods will be especially resistant to making changes to benefit bilingual students. Some schools use aggressive tracking programs, meaning that students are placed into groups based upon ability. In other schools, students will be mixed seemingly at random. Some schools will rely heavily on standardized testing to categorize students, while others will depend more heavily on future evaluations. Finally, the curriculum mandated by the school will have an effect on the learning environment for ELL students. It is essential that the curriculum be as relevant as possible to the needs, interests, and environment of the students. Too many school systems have ethnocentric curricula that alienate foreign students. Also, it is a common practice for the ELL curriculum to simply be a diluted version of the normal course of study.

Respect for diversity

At all times, teachers need to indicate their respect for the cultural heritage and the values of every student in the class. Teachers should always treat students as individuals, and should make a concerted

- 98 -

effort to learn about their cultural and personal values. At the same time, teachers should strive to identify the idiosyncratic learning styles of students, and should incorporate instructional strategies and materials appropriate for each student. One of the best ways to indicate respect for students' heritage is to foster communication with the student's family; often the best source for information about a student's heritage and cultural values will be his parents. Finally, a teacher should become aware of his own teaching and learning style, so as to be better able to accommodate the diverse learning styles of students. The best teachers are those who recognize their own strengths and weaknesses, and adapt to best meet the needs of their students.

Basics of multicultural education

Multicultural education is a specific program of curricula and instructional techniques designed to be inclusive of all racial, ethnic, religious, and linguistic backgrounds. This program was developed to promote democracy by empowering the members of all demographic groups to become informed and participate in the community. It was motivated by the recognition of the changing population in the United States, with an ever increasing and varying mix of minority groups. Elements of a multicultural educational philosophy have found their way into almost every school in the country. However, the ascendancy of this philosophy has not been without some controversy. Some critics charge that the multicultural education program emphasizes the distinctions between cultures, but pays very little attention to the abundant similarities.

Five dimensions of multicultural education

The intention of multicultural education is to advance democracy by empowering minority groups and explicitly challenging students to become active citizens. To this end, the multicultural educational philosophy works in five dimensions. Firstly, multicultural education emphasizes content integration, meaning that different subject matter is related to underscore similarities and differences between cultures. This pedagogical style also emphasizes the knowledge construction process, which means that teachers focus on the ways that students form ideas and opinions, and try to remove any implicit bias. The third dimension is attention to prejudiced reactions, and the fourth is the so-called equity pedagogy, which is an explicit attempt to create a level playing field for all minority groups. Finally, multicultural education promotes a school culture and social structure that is empowering to all students.

Hidden curriculum

A hidden curriculum is a set of informal and implicit rules that a school teaches children in order to help them succeed both academically and socially. Specifically, the hidden curriculum is that set of rules which a child needs to learn in order to survive outside the family, in a larger social organization. Sociologists frequently cite self-discipline as the foremost element of the hidden curriculum. Students must learn to work quietly, get along well with people they may not like, follow orders from someone else, and tolerate frustration. These skills are essential to becoming productive members of the economic community in later life. When polled, most Americans have supported this idea of the hidden curriculum by asserting that "discipline" should be the primary focus of school.

Conservative multiculturalism

In their seminal work *Changing Multiculturalism*, educational experts Kincheloe and Steinberg made a critical study of the various forms of multicultural education. They explicitly favored critical multiculturalism. They claim that conservative multiculturalism makes assumptions that are detrimental to students; for instance, conservative multiculturalists assume that minorities are impoverished or culturally deprived. They tend to emphasize standardized testing that reinforces Eurocentric norms. IQ tests and the SATs are two such tests. According to Kincheloe and Steinberg, conservative multiculturalists believe that the status quo is basically equitable and should not be changed. In their formulation, white culture is not considered as a particular form of human experience, but is instead the standard by which all others are measured.

Liberal multiculturalism

Kincheloe and Steinberg offered a penetrating critique of liberal multiculturalism, which they characterized as a well-intentioned but ultimately damaging attempt to help minorities. According to this critique, liberal multiculturalists assume that all people are the same, and that whatever racial inequality exists is due to a lack of opportunity. In their view, all people are responsible for themselves, and the playing field is essentially level. Liberal multiculturalists celebrate African-American and Hispanic culture, but critics like Kincheloe and Steinberg complained that this celebration is patronizing "tokenism." Also, they charge that the explicit coverage of discrimination and bias in the liberal multiculturalist curriculum is too divisive, and is ultimately destructive to cultural integration.

Pluralist multiculturalism

In recent decades, pluralist multiculturalism has been one of the predominant forms of diversity education. Kincheloe and Steinberg criticize this approach for making certain assumptions that are damaging to students. According to their critique, pluralist multiculturalism assumes that diversity has an intrinsic value, and that a full curriculum will include coverage of other cultures as well as the prejudices and stereotypes that can be damaging to intercultural relations. According to Kincheloe and Steinberg, one of the main problems with pluralist multiculturalism is that it ignores differences of class, and creates a situation in which students are more likely to self segregate. The emphasis on pluralism necessarily means that the differences between cultures are discussed much more often and in greater depth than the more abundant similarities.

Critical multiculturalism

In *Changing Multiculturalism*, Kincheloe and Steinberg promote the philosophy of critical multiculturalism. In this approach, discussion of cultural similarities and differences is merely one component of instruction related to social, institutional, and economic prejudices. Critical multiculturalists believe that justice is available for all people under the current rules, but it is not always distributed evenly. A critical multiculturalist also believes that different knowledge traditions must be explicitly discussed and approved within a school context. A critical multiculturalist does not entirely criticize white culture, but believes that the predominance of the white male view should be called into question in the classroom. Essentially, in the critical multiculturalist view, students should be encouraged to explore their own basis for knowledge and their constructed way of seeing the world.

Student diversity

Cultural identities are strongly embraced by adolescents but they also want to be recognized and treated as unique individuals. Teachers walk a fine line between respecting cultural differences and avoiding overly emphasizing them or disregarding them altogether. Responding to discriminatory comments immediately, using a wide variety of examples, quoting scholars from many cultures and identifying universal problems needing complex solutions can indirectly communicate appreciation of and respect for all cultures. Teachers must take care never to imply any kind of stereotype or make comments that might indicate a cultural bias. They must refrain from asking a student to respond as a member of a particular culture, class or country. Teachers should learn as much as they can about every racial, ethnic and cultural group represented in their classroom. It is also important that teachers respect students' commitments and obligations away from school, their family responsibilities and job pressures.

Cultural influences

Study after study has shown that a student's culture has a direct impact on learning. Since educational standards are based on white, middle class cultural identification, students who do not fall into that demographic face challenges every day. It's not that these students are incapable of learning; they simply judge that which is important and how they express that importance differently. Sometimes it is difficult for them to understand and relate to curriculum content, teaching methods and social skills required because their culture does things differently, emphasizes different

choices and rewards different behavior. Adolescents identify with their culture; they become what they know. If teachers ignore cultural differences, it causes communication issues, inhibits learning and increases the potential for behavior problems. As long as a child has no physical or mental health issues, he is capable of learning. He simply needs that the information presented and examples used to be relevant to his life experiences; otherwise, it does not seem to make sense to him.

Social environment

The social environment is the set of people and institutions with which one associates and communicates. It has both a direct and indirect influence on behavior by the individuals within the group. It is sometimes defined by specific characteristics such as race, gender, age, culture or behavioral patterns. When defined by behavioral patterns it can lead to unproven assumptions about entire groups of people. In America's diverse society, it is essential that teachers recognize that various social groups exist within a classroom and thus determine the best strategies not only to facilitate the learning of "book" facts, but also to encourage understanding and acceptance between the groups. The learning theory called social cognitivism believes that people learn by observing others, whether they are aware of the process or not. Creating opportunities for students to interact with diverse social groups in a neutral, non-threatening situation can bring about positive interpersonal growth that could have long-term societal impact outside of the educational environment.

Socialization

Socialization is the process of learning the written and unwritten rules, acceptable behavioral patterns, and accumulated knowledge of the community in order to function within its culture. It is a gradual process that starts when a person is born and, in one form or another, continues throughout his life. There are many "communities" within a culture: e.g., family, school, neighborhood, military and country. There are six forms of socialization:

- Reverse Socialization: deviation from acceptable behavior patterns.
- Developmental Socialization: the process of learning social skills.
- Primary Socialization: learning the attitudes, values and actions of a culture.
- Secondary Socialization: learning behavior required in a smaller group within the culture.
- Anticipatory Socialization: practicing behavior in preparation for joining a group.
- Resocialization: discarding old behavior and learning new behavior as part of a life transition; e.g., starting school, moving to a new neighborhood or joining the military.

The agents of socialization are the people, groups and institutions that influence the self-esteem, emotions, attitudes, behavior and acceptance of a person within his environment. The first agents are the immediate family (mother, father, siblings) and extended family (grandparents, aunts, uncles, cousins). They influence religious affiliation, political inclinations, educational choices, career aspirations and other life goals. The school's role is explaining societal values, reinforcing acceptable behavior patterns and teaching necessary skills such as reading, writing, reasoning and critical thinking. Peer groups (people who are about the same age) share certain characteristics (attend the same school, live in the same neighborhood) and

influence values, attitudes and behavior. The media (radio, television, newspapers, magazines, the Internet) have an impact on attitude, values and one's understanding of the activities of society and international events. Other institutions that influence people include religion, the work place, the neighborhood, and city, state and federal governments.

Social ineptitude

Social ineptitude is defined as a lack of social skills; in most societies, this term is considered disrespectful. There are medical conditions that may cause a deficiency in social skills such as autism and Asperger syndrome. Someone who believes himself socially inept may have an avoidant personality disorder. A shy person or an overly bold person may observe societal conventions but still exhibit social incompetence; the behavior is simply manifested in different ways. The criteria for social ineptitude are different in different cultures, which makes it difficult to cite specific examples. People trying to integrate into a new environment may unknowingly commit a social faux pas thereby earning the damaging label unfairly. In a culturally diverse classroom, it is critical to create an atmosphere of acceptance so if a student does something inappropriate, the behavior can be quietly and gently corrected without causing humiliation or embarrassment.

Social skills

Social skills are the tools used to interact and communicate with others. They are learned during the socialization process and are both verbal and non-verbal. These skills are integral to becoming an active and accepted member of any environment. There are general skills needed to complete daily transactions such as being able to ask sensible questions and provide logical answers and knowing how to read and write and understand simple directions. If these skills are missing or poorly executed, it can cause various problems and misunderstandings, some of which could have long-lasting and/or life-changing consequences. In smaller groups, other skills may be needed such as the ability to engage in interesting conversation, present ideas to peers, teach new concepts or actively participate in discussions. Using body language and gestures appropriate to the situation and the message, having the ability to resolve conflicts and being diplomatic when necessary are examples of advanced social skills.

Meeting with parents

Studies have shown that the more parents are involved in their children's education, the better the students learn and the fewer behavior problems one must handle. Teachers are an integral part of the process. It is up to them to keep parents informed about the academic and social progress of the students. Report cards only provide letter or number grades and are not designed to explore and explain how well the student is learning and progressing in the intangible skills like critical thinking, reasoning ability, study habits, attitude, communication with adults and peers and other social and interactive development. Sending home periodic progress reports is an effective way to keep parents abreast of changes. Meeting with parents regularly to discuss their child's particular progress and being available to answer questions are excellent ways to work together as a team to ensure the student benefits the most from his educational experience.

Parent/student/teacher agreement

If a teacher should wish to use a formal parent/student/teacher agreement as a way to involve parents, provide students with a written set of expectations and explain their commitment to a successful educational experience, there are several activities that can be included:

- Parent Priorities:
  - Show respect for and support of the student, teacher and the discipline policy.
  - Monitor homework assignments and projects.
  - Attend teacher conferences.
  - Ask about the student's day.
- Student Priorities:
  - Show respect for parents, teachers, peers and school property.
  - Put forth his best effort both in class and at home.
  - Come to class prepared.
  - Talk to his parents about school.
- Teacher Priorities:
  - Show respect for the student, his family and his culture.
  - Help each student strive to reach his potential.
  - Provide fair progress evaluations to students and parents.
  - Enforce rules fairly and consistently.

Many schools use some sort of parent/student/teacher agreement to ensure everyone understands the rules and agrees to abide by them. It can be as simple as requiring parents, students and teachers to sign a copy of the student handbook or it can be a formal contract drafted with specific activities each pledges to perform. Whichever format is used, it should detail each party's responsibilities. This accomplishes several goals:

- Parents are recognized as an important part of the educational experience. They are also made aware of what is expected of them, their children, the teachers and the administration.
- Students are given written expectations, which prevent an "I didn't know" attitude. It encourages respect for himself, his parents, his teachers, his peers and the rules.
- Teachers make a written commitment to students and parents to provide an environment that encourages learning. They list specific, observable behavior which they pledge to perform.

Levels of parental involvement

Some parents are eager to participate in their child's education, some do so only when required, and others avoid involvement of any kind. All three approaches can be a challenge. Eager parents may bombard the teacher and administration with notes, phone calls, emails and requests for information and meetings. Setting reasonable, well-defined limits may be necessary. Parents who only show up when specifically requested (e.g., semi-annual parent/teacher conferences, meeting with the administration about a behavior problem), might only be going through the motions in order to keep their child enrolled in school. They may be incapable of or don't really care to address any underlying issues; they show up because they are required to do so. Parents who are never available and impossible to contact provide no help or insight and offer no support.

Parent/teacher conferences

Basics

Parent/teacher conferences can be stressful experiences for both parties. But with a positive attitude and much preparation, they can be pleasant, provide a forum for the exchange of information and improve the educational experience for the students. The first step is for the teacher to be rested. Fatigue can cause an inability to concentrate, unfortunate misunderstandings and inappropriate reactions. If a teacher thinks parents might be difficult to handle, it might be wise to ask an administrator to sit in. The teacher needs to have a plan prepared with discussion points and copies of the student's work available to review. He needs to keep in mind that the parents may have items to discuss as well, and therefore the plan needs to be flexible and allow time for questions. The discussion should focus on the positive and present negative information with a "we can fix it" approach.

In order to avoid wasting everyone's time during a parent/teacher conference, there are several things a teacher can do to set the scene for a productive meeting. Make initial contact early by sending a note or newsletter home briefly outlining plans and objectives for the year and providing contact information (e.g., phone number, email address, days and times available). This tells parents the teacher is willing to talk and/or meet when necessary. When a date for a conference is set, the teacher should be certain to invite both parents. It is the best way to gauge how involved they are, yet individual family circumstances need to be considered (one-parent families, parents' work commitments, et cetera). Schedule twenty to thirty minute conferences; if more time becomes necessary, schedule a follow-up meeting. Develop a flexible agenda and gather necessary paperwork. Verify parent and student names just before the meeting.

Encouraging parental involvement
Every teacher needs to develop ways in which to involve parents in the education of their children. Some communication methods may be more effective than others depending upon the age of the students, the educational level and time limitations of the parents, and the administrative support and resources available to the teacher. Some schools encourage a parent orientation program at the beginning of the year, in which the teacher informs parents what his expectations are concerning behavior and outlines classroom rules. He presents a broad picture of the material to be covered, projects that will be assigned and homework requirements. If a meeting isn't possible, the same information can be conveyed in a letter sent home just before school starts or during the first week. Besides regularly scheduled parent/teacher conferences, a periodic newsletter, perhaps when report cards are issued, can be sent to update parents.

Being prepared
Parent/teacher conferences are the best time for candid communication. For the encounter to be productive, both parties need to be prepared to discuss the student's strengths and weaknesses, share any concerns and decide upon the best way to help the student meet required goals and reach his potential. Some topics to consider in preparation for this important meeting:
- The skills and knowledge that should be learned and mastered.
- Required academic standards. Give parents a copy to which to refer during the year, and explain these standards.Projects planned and assignments required to complete academic requirements.The evaluation

method, what data is considered and when progress reports are issued.How parents can help. Suggest concrete activities which they can do at home in order to encourage learning and support the teacher's efforts.Programs available for both fast and slow learners.What programs are available to prepare students for life after high school.

Things to remember
Try to use a table rather than a desk and chairs so that the parents and the teacher meet as equals; this creates a more relaxed environment. Start with a positive statement about the student and then briefly review the objectives of the meeting. The teacher should not do all of the talking; it should be a conversation, not a monologue. Avoid educational jargon. Many parents will not understand it or will interpret it incorrectly. Focus on strengths, give specific examples, provide suggestions for improvement and refer to actions rather than character. For example: "Sam turned in his essay the day after it was due," instead of "Sam is irresponsible." Ask for parents' opinions and listen to their responses. Use body language that shows interest and concern and make eye contact. Do not judge the parents' attitude or behavior, and consider cultural differences. Briefly summarize the discussion and end with a positive comment or observation about the student.

Conclusion
If either the teacher or the parents feel that there is more to discuss or that a follow-up meeting is necessary for an update on progress made, a time can be scheduled before the parents leave. As soon as possible after the conversation while the details are fresh, the teacher should make notes of the general discussion and record any specific actions

that he or the parents agreed to take as well as the parents' attitude and willingness to offer support. Any private information and/or family issues which the parents shared should be kept in the strictest confidence. If a cooperative relationship is to be established, parents need to know that their family business will remain private. It is very important and even required in some states that teachers report any indication of or concerns about possible child abuse or endangerment to the authorities. All teachers and administrators need to be familiar with the pertinent statutes in their state.

Pedagogy of the Oppressed

The most influential text in the development of multicultural education was *Pedagogy of the Oppressed* by Paolo Freire. This book is considered very radical, and has actually been banned in several countries. In it, Freire criticizes the traditional notion of students as empty vessels to be filled with the knowledge of the teacher. He claims that this idea, besides being incorrect insofar as it ignores the inherent knowledge of students, recreates the colonization process in which Eurocentric thinking is assumed to be superior. In Freire's model of education, students are the co-creators: that is, they collaborate with the teacher to explore ways of knowing and the assumptions inherent in each culture. Freire describes his method as "dialogic" (as in dialogue) instruction, meaning that the student and teacher engage in an instructional conversation and inform one another.

Antibias curriculum

In recent years, some educational theorists have developed a pedagogical philosophy called the "antibias curriculum." This is in part a reaction to the multicultural curriculum, which is sometimes criticized for being too wide-ranging and scattershot. The antibias curriculum emphasizes the presence of discrimination in all areas: race, gender, linguistic background, ability and sexual orientation. In this curriculum, the emphasis is on explicit treatment of bias. A teacher who uses the curriculum will try to present each side of an issue in which bias is pervasive. For instance, in a discussion of American history, a teacher would be careful to explore how American and European historians have marginalized and deemphasized the contributions of minorities and Native Americans. The explicit goal of the antibias curriculum is social justice.

The theoretical foundation of the antibias approach is that there are two distinct curricula in education: the formal curriculum and the hidden curriculum. The formal curriculum is the set of explicit materials, books, syllabi, and instructional methods used in the classroom. The elements of a formal curriculum would be evident to any untrained observer. The hidden curriculum, on the other hand, is the set of ideas and prejudices that are indirectly or implicitly delivered to students. For instance, the traditional American school system distinguishes different subjects by organizing a class schedule in which students move from one subject to another. There is nothing bad about the system, but it is not necessarily followed in other parts of the world. In other places, there may be less distinction between subjects. Proponents of the antibias curriculum emphasize that teachers need to explore the elements of the hidden curriculum to ensure that they are not favoring one set of students over another. It is generally thought that there is more inherent bias in the hidden curriculum than in the formal curriculum.

Goals of the antibias curriculum

Although the antibias curriculum has the broad goal of social justice, it also has some specific goals. For example, teachers who use the antibias curriculum want to improve the confidence and enhance the self perception of their students. In other words, the teachers want to help the students see themselves and their culture as they relate to others. Similarly, the antibias curriculum seeks to improve empathy by encouraging students to consider the mental and emotional situations of other people. By explicitly covering issues of bias, the antibias curriculum hopes to encourage students to think critically about the subject. Finally, teachers who employ the antibias curriculum aspire to have students who will stand up for themselves and for others against whom are being discriminated.

Criticisms of the antibias curriculum

Although most educational experts acknowledge the validity of the critique offered by the antibias curriculum, there are some who complain that this curriculum swings the pendulum too far in the other direction. For instance, some critics charge that the antibias curriculum has an implicit bias against European ideas and cultural norms. Because these have long been dominant in the United States, it is natural that the antibias curriculum will spend more time problematizing them than it will spend on a critique of Native American ideology. The result, according to some critics, is an overabundance of identification with minority culture. The antibias curriculum has been called "too Afrocentric" by some. Another criticism of it is that it tends to omit the contributions of smaller minorities, like Eskimos and Native Americans.

Cooperating with colleagues

To be successful, an ELL teacher must be constantly cooperating with and learning from colleagues. There are a number of ways to do this; one is to set up regular meetings with them. Many ELL teachers are part of a team of teachers who instruct the same group of students, and these meetings will therefore already be in place. If this is not the case, however, teachers should try to set up frequent meetings with colleagues who either teach the same students or the same subject. These meetings should not be the equivalent of teacher's lounge gripe sessions, but instead should be forums in which new teaching methods can be discussed, teaching content can be coordinated, and basic plans of behavior management can be established.

Peer review programs for ELL teachers

Another way in which a community of ELL teachers can foster professional improvement is through peer review. In a peer review program, teachers observe one another and offer suggestions for improvement. This is especially helpful when it is done among teachers in the same grade level or subject. Another ELL teacher who is fluent in French, for instance, would be a great resource for a non-French-speaking teacher helping new immigrants from West Africa. Of course, in order for this sort of program to work, there needs to be a spirit of collaboration and constructive criticism among the teachers. Unfortunately, school politics and competitiveness often poison the relationships between colleagues, and make it difficult to offer or accept well-meaning suggestions. The best peer review programs establish a specific protocol for criticism and encouragement.

Mentoring programs for ELL teachers

Mentoring is another professional improvement program that can be extremely valuable to an ELL teacher. In a mentoring program, experienced teachers develop relationships with beginning teachers. The schools that use these programs find that they are able to retain a larger proportion of their beginning teachers. When mentoring programs are not offered, new teachers should ask a veteran ELL teacher to act as a mentor, as a mentor can provide guidance on any aspect of teaching, from classroom management to lesson plans. New teachers get the most out of the relationship if they consciously remain open to constructive criticism. A mentor should observe his or her mentee directly in the teacher's classroom, but the mentee should also keep a list of concerns and questions to bring to private meetings. Teachers who accept advice and are willing to see things from a different perspective will grow immeasurably from the mentoring experience.

Peer tutoring programs

Another way that ELL teachers can join with their colleagues in order to improve the quality of instruction is through peer tutoring. In a basic peer tutoring program, more advanced students work with the younger students on class work. For instance, the members of a second-grade ELL class might be paired with the members of a fifth-grade ELL class. The older children will still be using many of the concepts that they learned in second grade, thus it will be beneficial for them to explain and demonstrate these concepts. The younger children, meanwhile, will enjoy working with older children and may be more receptive to the material when it comes from a source other than the teacher.

Peer tutoring relationships are especially fruitful when they are between students from similar backgrounds. In a modern ELL class, there may be students from several different linguistic backgrounds. Some students may be the sole representative of their native culture in their grade level. If there are other students in the school with the same origin, however, they may be profitably united through peer tutoring. Also, peer tutoring programs are a great chance for students to develop their social skills; the older children will practice being generous and considerate of someone younger, while the younger children will practice being attentive and receptive to counsel. Of course, only those older students who have a good grasp of the content and are well-behaved should be involved in a peer tutoring program.

Field trips with other classes

Another way that ELL teachers can band together is by arranging field trips with other teachers, as it is often easier to handle the logistics of a large field trip in cooperation with another teacher. Also, many field trips will have applications to multiple subject areas. For instance, a trip to a local battlefield could have relevance for American history, English, and Social Studies students. A visit to the local natural science museum could be pertinent to content in math, science, and history. It is always a good idea to encourage students to make associations between content areas. Furthermore, a field trip encourages ELL students to mix with other students, forming social connections that improve investment in the academic setting.

Coordinating subject matter

One of the most positive ways for ELL teachers to work with their fellow teachers is by coordinating subject matter. This strategy is often used in teacher "teams" in elementary and middle school, but it can also be effective in high school. Let us consider a brief example of how teachers can coordinate subject matter with great results. Imagine that you are a sixth-grade ELL teacher. Before the school year begins, you could propose that the sixth grade uses "cities" as a theme. Each teacher can then construct lessons in their instructional domain that connect with this theme. As the ELL teacher, you could look at texts that focus on life in the city. The history teacher could teach students about the rise of the big urban centers during the Industrial Revolution. The math teacher could incorporate some study of the various statistics and charts that are used to describe and learn about cities. If your school is located in or near a large city, you might also take some field trips so students can observe first-hand the things that they have learned.

Coordinating instructional content

The net effect of coordinating content seems to be that ELL students learn more. Educational research suggests that all knowledge is associative, and people therefore tend to remember those things that they can easily fit into their existing store of information. If an ELL teacher and his colleagues can link diverse disciplines together by looking at the same subject from a number of different perspectives, they can help students develop a well-rounded and coherent way of intellectually exploring the world. This is especially true for ELL students, who will be encountering a dizzying amount of new information at school. If this material is disconnected and seemingly random, students will be more likely to forget it. Thematic content in multiple subjects helps avoid this problem.

Communicating with colleagues

An ELL instructor should meet with his colleagues at some point during the year so that he can get a general idea of the structure and content of his colleague's classes. During the year, the ELL teacher should stay abreast of that which students are learning in their other classes, and should note associations between disciplines whenever they arise. A teacher should also know when his fellow teachers are assigning major projects or exams, so that he can avoid giving important assignments on the same day. Many schools assign a certain day of the week for tests in each subject; e.g., math tests on Monday, history tests on Tuesday, and so on. If the school does not do this, the ELL teacher should make sure that major projects and examinations are scheduled such that students are not overwhelmed with a flurry of work.

Relationship with school administration

It is important for the ELL teacher to have a strong relationship with the school administration. The principals and support staff of a school are supposed to be there to make life easier, but they can only do this with cooperation. In order to maintain a happy partnership with the school administration, teachers should remember one guideline of great importance: namely, teachers should always report any significant problems immediately; these problems can include disciplinary matters, personal problems, or conflict with school protocol. In large schools where there is little one-on-one contact between the administration and the faculty, it is common for teachers to let their grievances fester in silence. The result is that what could be a cooperative relationship becomes poisoned by resentment and frustration. Teachers who have complaints or concerns about the way the school is being run, or who need help, should immediately discuss the problem with the principal.

Meeting with the principal

An ELL teacher should try to avoid only visiting the principal when there is something wrong. A principal, like any person, will develop certain assumptions about a teacher whom they only see in times of crisis. Also, many principals will resent those teachers who they feel are constantly passing their problems onto the administration. ELL teachers should be referring problems to the principal only as a last resort. It is appropriate to let the principal know about concerns without necessarily asking for help. A teacher should try to check in with the principal periodically when things are going well in class, so that he or she can get a more balanced appreciation of the class' progress. When a teacher maintains a good relationship with the principal throughout the year, he or she will be much more helpful on those occasions of crisis.

Scheduling an observation by the principal

One great way to cultivate a positive relationship with the principal is to invite him or her to sit in on a class. A teacher should invite the principal on a day when a particularly innovative and exciting lesson is planned. It is a good idea to let the students know ahead of time that the principal will be joining the class, so they need to be on their best behavior. During the observation, the teacher should invite the principal to participate whenever appropriate. Many principals were teachers at one time, and will welcome the opportunity to join in with the activities of the class. After the class, the teacher should ask the principal for his opinion. As in relationships with other teachers, teachers should try to remain

open to criticism and accepting of advice. These kinds of observations can be very useful for beginning teachers, who may be unaware of some fundamental mistakes they are making.

Relationships with teacher aides and assistants

Some teachers are lucky enough to have full- or part-time aides and assistants. When this is the case, the teacher should make sure that the aide is being used appropriately. For the most part, an aide should not be busy doing paperwork during class time. It is certainly useful to have another person to help with grading, but this can be done during the planning period or lunch. While the children are in the classroom, the aide should be another set of eyes and ears. In other words, the aide should circulate around the room while students are working. He can answer any questions students may have about the lesson, and can make sure that students stay on-task. Aides are also useful when some members of the class have fallen behind the others. The aide can assemble those students and give them a brief refresher on the recent material as the teacher instructs the rest of the class.

Introductory note to parents

To ensure that one is able to effectively communicate with parents throughout the year, one should try to establish contact at the beginning of the term. Most teachers send a note to parents at the beginning of the year. In this note, one should introduce oneself and give some background information, such as ones educational background and personal interests. One can then describe the plans for the class as well as ones expectations for student conduct. Of course, an ELL teacher faces a unique challenge in composing such a note, because it is likely that many parents will not be fluent in

English. To mitigate this problem, one should either make a translation into the parent's native language or provide access to a translator.

An introductory note at the beginning of the school year is a good place to inform parents as to how much homework students are likely to have during the course of the year, as well as what steps parents can take to ensure that their students are successful. For instance, one might indicate to parents that one is planning to administer a quiz every Friday, so that they can be sure to review material with their child on Thursday night. This note is also a chance to ask for parental involvement in the class. Parents may be called upon to help with supplies or with transportation on field trips. In an introductory note, one might detail some of the needs that the class will have during the course of the year, and ask parents to contact the teacher if they can help.

Frequent updates to parents

After sending this first letter home, it is also helpful to send home periodic notes letting parents know how the class is proceeding. If one has a small number of students, one may even be able to make personal phone calls to each parent. Another way to stay in contact with many parents is through email; if one finds that all (or even some) of the parents in ones class have internet access, one may send out a short weekly update. Whatever format one chooses, one should try to keep parents informed of upcoming evaluations, field trips, and special events. If possible, one should personalize each message with some specific information about the child; this will convey the impression that one is taking a direct interest in the educational progress of each member of the class. It is important to make an effort to communicate both good news as well as bad. For many

parents, the only contact they ever have with the school is when their child has gotten into trouble. One should occasionally make a call or drop a note to praise a student for improved academic performance. Parents will respond very positively to teachers who take the time to praise their children.

Keeping parents alert to student performance

It is also important to let parents know how their children are faring in class by sending home their grades regularly. Many teachers require students to take home their major tests and have them signed by a parent. Increasingly, teachers are posting student grades on a class website so that parents and students alike can keep track. Whichever method one chooses, one should make sure that one does not wait until the end of the term to let a parent know that their student is in danger of failing. As soon as any student falls behind, it is imperative to alert his parents so that a strategy for improvement can be developed. Do not assume that students will keep their parents informed as to how they are doing in class. Many students will claim to be doing well even if they know that this will be disproved by their final grade. As a teacher, it is ones responsibility to keep parents informed.

Parent-teacher conferences

Another important part of developing a positive rapport with parents is the parent-teacher conference. Most elementary schools schedule these near the beginning of the year, often at the end of the first grading period. In middle and high school, parent-teacher conferences are not always mandatory, though they are recommended. If one is a beginning teacher, one may approach ones first conferences with some anxiety. It is important to remember, however, that both the teacher and the parent both have the student's success as a goal. It is important to accurately communicate a student's standing within the class. It is also important for both parties to agree on a strategy for maintaining or improving the student's performance subsequent to the conference. Conferences are meant to be punishment for neither the instructor, the parent, nor the student.

Discussing poor performance

Sometimes, it will be necessary for the teacher to contact a parent because of a student's disruptive behavior or poor academic performance. In these cases, one should plan ones talking points in advance. This is especially important as an ELL teacher, because it is quite possible that the parents will have only limited fluency in English. Under no circumstances should one call a parent while angry; this will only cause the parent to rally to their child's defense and ignore whatever the teacher has to say. One should be able to tell the parent specifically what the student has been doing wrong, and what he needs to do in order to improve. One should also ask questions, to see if there is something happening at home that would cause the student to act in a certain way.

Teacher-parent phone call

When an ELL student is struggling, contacting his parents should not be a last resort. Rather, it should be done soon so that the student's course can be corrected. Many students act out at school because of problems they are having at home; learning about these motivating factors can not only help one understand the behavior, but can lead to possible solutions. In any case, when one calls a parent to communicate bad news, it is important to always maintain a focus on the steps that should be taken for

improvement. Do not call a parent simply to gripe. At the end of the call, make plans to talk again in the near future, so that everyone can assess how the strategy for improvement is proceeding. Always treat the parent as part of a team whose aim is the success of the student.

Open house

Another traditional means of making contact with parents is the open house. Most schools hold an open house at the beginning of the year so that parents can meet the teachers and see the classrooms. Besides being an opportunity to give information about the class, the open house is a chance for the teacher to present himself in a favorable light. The neatness and organization of the room is very important, as is greeting the parents as they enter. One should try to avoid getting bogged down in discussion with any one parent; discussions of individual students should be handled in another setting. The open house is a chance for one to sell oneself and the class. One should demonstrate the structure of one's class as well as present an appeal for help from parents.

Inviting parents to class

Besides the open house, parents should be invited to school whenever their presence will have a positive impact on learning. For instance, if students are going to be putting on a group or individual presentation, parents should be invited to attend. This is especially important in elementary grades, where the presence of a parent can be extremely comforting and motivating to students. Other instances where parents could be invited to attend school are field days, class parties, and field trips. Too often, ELL students create a rigid separation between their school and home lives. Language differences reinforce this separation. By inviting parents to class, an ELL teacher breaks down the division between the academic and the family life, and encourages the student to incorporate what he is learning into all phases of his life.

Incorporating parents into instruction

An ELL teacher should try to take advantage of parents' special skills or talents, especially as they relate to different content areas. For instance, if one is teaching a science-related unit and one of the students' parents is a botanist, you should invite him to speak to the class. If one is teaching a unit on Social Studies and discovers that one of the parents works for the federal government, it might be useful to invite him to speak. Whenever possible, one should be striving to make course content relevant to the daily lives of the students. There is no better way to do this than by incorporating their family members into the lesson.

Lau v. Nichols

The Supreme Court ruling in Lau v. Nichols had a great influence on the expansion of bilingual education in the United States. A group of Chinese-American students in San Francisco claimed that they were receiving an inferior education because of their limited proficiency in English. Title VI of the Civil Rights Act of 1964 asserts that no individual can be discriminated against on the basis of national origin. The Supreme Court agreed that these students were being denied equal educational opportunities. One of the results of this decision was that language was now considered an inextricable part of ethnicity, and therefore any discrimination on the basis of language difference was considered a violation of the Civil Rights Act.

Meyer v. Nebraska (1923)

In the United States, linguistic rights include the right to education, media, and administrative and judicial communication in a language of the recipient's choosing. The Equal Protection and Due Process clauses of the United States Constitution's Fourteenth Amendment prohibit racial and ethnic discrimination, and this prohibition has consistently been shown to extend to language. Minority groups have used the Constitution to protect their linguistic rights, and the courts have supported them. The landmark case in this regard was *Meyer v. Nebraska* (1923), in which the Supreme Court ruled that states cannot restrict foreign-language instruction. This was after World War I, and anti-German sentiment had led Nebraskan politicians to draft legislation banning the teaching of language other than English in any context. The Supreme Court ruled that this legislation violated the Due Process clause.

Bilingual Education Act of 1968

In 1968, Congress enacted the Bilingual Education Act to provide local school districts with federal money for the establishment of English language programs for students whose primary language is Spanish. This act promoted the idea that non-English speakers should be instructed in English but should be allowed to maintain other distinctive aspects of their heritage. The first sum of money disbursed to schools for this purpose was $7.5 million, and was used for new materials, teacher training, and associations between parents and teachers. The Bilingual Education Act of 1968 declared that successful bilingual education programs would be guaranteed federal funds for at least five years.

Although many people saw the Bilingual Education Act of 1968 as a step towards multiculturalism, critics still charged that its terms were too vague and did not require the participation of all schools. After the Supreme Court case *Lau v. Nichols*, in which it was determined that Chinese students in San Francisco were receiving an inferior education, the federal government amended the Bilingual Education Act to mandate school districts to take definite steps towards English language instruction. Whereas before schools were only required to ensure that books and other educational materials were available for all students, now they were forced to establish specific programs to meet the needs of students of all backgrounds.

Castaneda v. Pickard (1981)

In the case *Castaneda v. Pickard*, the United States Court of Appeals for the Fifth Circuit established three criteria for bilingual education programs in the United States. These criteria must be met in order for the program to align with the Equal Education Opportunities Act of 1974. According to this ruling, bilingual education programs must be "based on sound educational theory," must be "implemented effectively with resources for personnel, instructional materials, and space," and must prove to be effective at overcoming linguistic barriers. This case arose from a Mexican-American man's complaint that his three children were receiving an inferior education in south Texas. The man alleged that his children were being discriminated against because their school did not have sophisticated bilingual education programs, and therefore made it difficult for native Spanish speakers to participate in all school events.

No Child Left Behind

The No Child Left Behind Act was signed into law on January 8, 2002, effectively terminating the Bilingual Education Act. The Bilingual Education Act had mandated the creation of native language programs for all students in public schools, whereas the No Child Left Behind Act did away with these programs and declared that students must be tested in English annually. Students whose first language is not English are not allowed to be tested in their native language. The right and responsibility to establish appropriate programs for students learning English as a second language is left to individual school districts.

Subtractive and additive bilingualism

There has long been a controversy in ELL education over the hierarchical relationship between students' native language and English. Many advocates of English-only instruction believe that students are best served when they abandon their original language and culture. The intent of this idea is not necessarily to condemn the native heritage of the student, but to give him the best set of tools to survive in the American society and economy. Any form of bilingual education that places English above the students' first language in this way is known as subtractive bilingualism. In contrast, additive bilingualism exists in programs that seek to improve skills in both the first language and English, and indeed to use the two languages as reinforcements for one another. Additive bilingualism consciously avoids marginalizing the native language and culture of each student.

Practice Test

Multiple Choice Questions

1. An ARD is an _____ meeting, during which a(n) _____is created for the student by_____.
   a. Additional Resources Development; Individual Education Plan (IEP); teachers, parents, counselors, administrators, and others working with the student
   b. Admissions, Review, and Dismissal; Individual Education Plan (IEP); teachers, parents, counselors, administrators, and others working with the student
   c. Admissions, Review, and Dismissal; Interim Efforts Policy (IEP); teachers, parents, counselors, administrators, and others working with the student
   d. Additional Resources Development; Immediate Emergency Plan (IEP); teachers, parents, counselors, administrators, and others working with the student

2. Scientifically-based, quality classroom instruction involves teaching essential skills, differentiating instruction for the needs of individual students, organizing instruction systematically, and:
   a. Presenting sufficient and meaningful reading and writing experiences for students to practice strategies.
   b. A and C.
   c. Reviewing and re-teaching as required to ensure that students have integrated essential content.
   d. Daily drilling of new material.

3. Is acculturation or assimilation more likely to produce second language learners who are successful at both BICS and CALP thresholds?
   a. Assimilation: when learners feel their own culture is respected, their affective filter will rise, motivating them to learn.
   b. Acculturation: adapting to a new culture, which includes understanding cultural expectations, semiotics, values, and beliefs, is essential to second language acquisition in that it provides appropriate context.
   c. Acculturation: when language learners prioritize the demands of their new culture over their culture of origin, with time they abandon their prior cultural values and expectations and become a tabula rasa upon which the adopted culture can more fully write itself.
   d. Assimilation: when language learners prioritize the demands of their new culture over their culture of origin, with time they abandon their prior cultural values and expectations and become a tabula rasa upon which the adopted culture can more fully write itself.

4. That tiny red car is a <u>Smart car</u>. In this statement, the underlined words are:
  a. A predicate adjective
  b. Predicate adjectives
  c. A predicate nominative
  d. Predicate nominatives

5. My neighbor's pit bull puppy is <u>protective</u>. In this statement, the underlined word is:
  a. A predicate adjective
  b. A predicate nominative
  c. A predictive phrase
  d. The object of a preposition

6. The primary approach to teaching English to non-native speakers prior to 1960 was:
  a. Two-way immersion
  b. Sheltered English
  c. Immersion
  d. ESL

7. Lau v. Nichols (U.S. Supreme Court, 1974) determined that ELLs must be given what right?
  a. To the same educational opportunities as all students
  b. To receive private tutoring until they are working at grade level or above
  c. To instruction that they have the skills to understand
  d. To unbiased, fair grading practices

8. How can a teacher best simplify a text for ELLs at the beginning and intermediate stages?
  a. Substitute one-syllable words for two-syllable words; delete as much text as possible and provide illustrations instead; have students keep reader response journals
  b. Shorten the text by putting more words on each page; delete illustrations that will distract the reader; provide a glossary of terms at the end of the book
  c. Shorten the text; abbreviate sentences; substitute simple, concrete language for more complex language; break complex sentences into two or three simpler, more direct sentences; omit detail that enhances the text but doesn't change or clarify meaning
  d. Clarify the text by offering interpretations at the bottom of each page; provide a Spanish-English glossary of terms at the end of the book; omit illustrations that will distract the reader

9. How are traditional ESL programs and Content-Based ESL Curriculum (CBEC) different?
  a. Traditional programs are immersion programs in which LEPs are taught only in L2, and must "sink or swim." CBEC offers instruction in a two-way immersion format, given in both L2 and L1.
  b. Traditional ESL programs prioritize social language skills. CBEC offers instruction in content areas that are age-appropriate to the LEPs' mainstreamed peers.
  c. Traditional ESL programs focus on grammar; CBEC focuses on phonetics.
  d. Traditional ESL programs prioritize a high level of CALP and do not find BICS to be central to communication.

10. Which takes longer to develop, BICS or CALP?
   a. BICS.
   b. CALP.
   c. They are interrelated and therefore develop at the same pace.
   d. They are not interrelated, but they take approximately the same time to develop.

11. The new ESL teacher is compiling a file of information for each of her students. Her files include level of L1 education and literacy; level of L2 competency in the four modalities of speaking, writing, listening, and reading; the type of depth of English study the student has undertaken; the student's interests and personality type; and the most effective learning styles for the particular student. What does the teacher most likely intend to use these files for?
   a. She will use the information they contain to vary her lessons to meet each student's specific needs.
   b. She will send them home periodically so that parents can read her notes and sign off on them.
   c. She will use them to document evidence of what she has covered in class, so that, in the case of a lawsuit, she has a paper trail.
   d. She will share the students' files with classmates so they can get to know one another on a more intimate, personal level.

12. A class is doing a project about a kitchen they have been in. The project can be based on a grandparent's kitchen or that of a friend; an outdoor "kitchen," such as at a campground or on a deck; a play kitchen that they recall from pre-school; or any other type of kitchen. The students can work individually or in a small group of their choosing. Some students are drawing and painting, while others are creating 3-dimensional models. One group is creating a play that takes place in a kitchen. One child is writing about her grandmother, who cooks tortillas on a hot rock. Another is creating a shoe-box diorama that depicts a fisherman smoking a fish in a temporary smoke-house. The teacher has reviewed vocabulary with the students, but a number of them approach her for help with English words. What has the teacher created this project to do?
   a. Expand the vocabulary of her students. Many of her ESL students lack basic English vocabulary, and the teacher knows that kitchen items, such as knives, saucepans, and cups are very commonly-used words that the students need to know.
   b. Determine each student's preferred learning style.
   c. Encourage students to be curious about and respectful of differences in culture.
   d. Teach students about different cooking methods.

13. Which of the following statements is true?
   a. ELLs typically are better able to express themselves verbally than they are to listen and then interpret what is being said by someone else.
   b. ELLs who are not literate in their first language have a better chance at becoming literate in their second language.
   c. ELLs often understand more in terms of vocabulary and correct syntax than they demonstrate in their own speaking.
   d. Once an ELL has achieved BICS competency, CALP competency will soon follow.

14. What is Krashen's Monitor Hypothesis concerned with?
   a. The importance of frequent assessment and adjustment of teaching methods according to the results
   b. The degree to which an ESL teacher is monitored and advised by a mentor
   c. Monitoring learning by using computer programs specifically designed for ELLs to offer a stable and consistent model of learning achievement
   d. The ways in which language learning influences acquisition

15. An approach to language learning that begins with practical communicative usage and that over time incorporates grammar, vocabulary, phonemic awareness, etc. is known as a(n) _____approach.
   a. Top down
   b. Bottoms up
   c. Left to right
   d. Right to left

16. Second language acquisition research suggests L2s tend to integrate formulaic expressions and then apply them to understand linguistic rules. This statement is:
   a. True
   b. False
   c. Neither true nor false
   d. Ambiguous

17. What is a possible outcome when teachers interpret oral language proficiency assessments, such as the Language Assessment Scales-Oral, the Woodcock-Muñoz Language Survey, and the IDEA Proficiency Test in terms of an ELL's general scholastic performance?
   a. The student is more likely to receive the help she needs, both in terms of language learning and in terms of academic achievement.
   b. The student is more likely to be held back a grade.
   c. The student is more likely to be placed in a special education program.
   d. The student is more likely to be placed at a level higher than her language abilities can support.

18. Cummins' Common Underlying Proficiency theory holds that using one language encourages proficiency in both L1 and L2. What is the opposing theory?
   a. Opposing Underlying Proficiency
   b. Separate Underlying Proficiency
   c. Anti-Underlying Proficiency
   d. Oppositive Underlying Proficiency

19. A teacher has decided to incorporate Total Physical Response strategies into her classroom instruction. She will:
   a. Break from academic instruction every hour for 10 minutes of organized exercise
   b. Involve her students in a series of physical activities in response to her instructions and requests
   c. Break for academic instruction every hour for 5 minutes of independent exercise
   d. Break from academic instruction two times a day (excluding lunch) for guided meditation practice and Brilliant Mind exercises

20. In language acquisition, what is Stage II also called?
   a. Speech Emergence Stage
   b. Receptive Stage
   c. Intermediate Proficiency Stage
   d. Early Production Stage

21. Who is required by law to follow a student's IEP?
   a. The school nurse
   b. The school cafeteria
   c. Teachers who work with the student
   d. No one is strictly required; an IEP is considered a best practice and should be followed, but if a teacher feels it is in the student's best interest to modify or deviate from the plan, she can do so without penalty

22. Basic Interpersonal Communicative Skills (BICS) and Cognitive Academic Language Proficiency (CALP) describe two distinct thresholds of language proficiency attained by a language learner. What are these two thresholds?
   a. BICS skills are necessary for academic communication, require content-specific vocabularies and more sophisticated syntax, and do not rely upon external contextual information, while CALP skills permit social communications that are face-to-face and include contextual information, informal vocabulary, and relatively simple syntax.
   b. BICS skills are limited to single-word responses in oral communication, include a very limited vocabulary in L2, and permit some interface with L1, while CALP skills require external contextual clues in order to be interpreted.
   c. CALP skills are limited to single-word responses in oral communication, include a very limited vocabulary in L2, and permit some interface with L1, while BICS skills depend heavily upon prior knowledge.
   d. BICS skills permit social communications that are face-to-face and include contextual information, informal vocabulary, and relatively simple syntax, while CALP skills are necessary for academic communication, require content-specific vocabularies and more sophisticated syntax, and do not rely upon external contextual information.

23. An SDAIE approach can be problematic for an individual ESL teacher because it requires specialized training, and because it is most effective when the program is adopted system wide. What strategy can such a teacher use to provide CBEC to her students without receiving that specialized training or having system wide support?
   a. Determine the content areas that ESL students will be taught in the following semester and begin preparing them well in advance through a variety of approaches
   b. Teach concepts essential to a core understanding of the material that reach beyond just specialized vocabulary
   c. Organize learning thematically, and teach a series of interrelated, in-depth lessons related to that theme
   d. All the above

24. Because the United States began as a melting pot of people from many different nationalities and ethnic groups, bilingual communities and education were a matter of course. It was essential for business people who served members of a particular culture to know that language, and immigrant children who did not speak English were often taught in their language of origin. By WWI, the United States began to develop a strong sense of itself as a nation, and English emerged as the "national" language. Non-English-speaking children were no longer taught in any language other than English. When did this trend begin to reverse, and why?

    a. After WWII; Americans began to see themselves as part of a "world nation" consisting of a vast and diverse group of individuals with cultural ties worthy of respect.

    b. In the 1960s; Cuban immigrants established a successful bilingual program, and the Civil Rights movement put attention on correcting educational and social agendas that were prejudiced in favor of the white middle class.

    c. The late 1950s; the influence of early hippies and beatniks, who preached the idea of loving one another and living in peace had a strong, immediate impact on the field of education.

    d. The 1990s; with the Clinton administration, which balanced the federal budget in 1998 and had a 236 billion-dollar surplus. Clinton saw bilingual education as an essential step toward leading the nation into the 21st century as a world leader in terms of both economic and social issues.

25. A classroom teacher has a highly diverse classroom, with children from 11 different countries speaking 6 different languages. How can she encourage mutual cultural respect?

    a. Label objects in the room with all six languages; invite speakers from each of the countries to visit the classroom and talk about one or two aspects of their cultures; break the class into culturally diverse smaller groups for class projects and study; invite students to teach the class songs from their cultures.

    b. Organize field trips to local museums to view the works of painters from other lands; show students photographs of types of clothing from the various countries; announce a "language day" once a month, on which only the teacher is allowed to speak English, and everyone but the English speakers are allowed to speak in their native tongue.

    c. Give each child a journal, and ask them to use it to write down memories and information about their countries of origin. They may show their journals to one another, but two rules apply: 1) If you share with one, you must share with all and 2) Anyone you show your journal to must, in turn, show you theirs.

    d. Hang flags representing all the different cultures the classroom contains; teach the class to greet one another in all of the languages and require them to do so before class starts each day; group children by language/cultural group for projects and group study to strengthen their bond.

26. A classroom teacher with several mainstreamed ESL students is frustrated. She has noted that few of their parents come to parent-teacher conferences, and those who do, come inconsistently and have little to say. She is aware that many of them have limited English skills, and also that several have very young children at home. What can she do to encourage the parents to increase their participation in their children's education?

    a. Drop in unexpectedly at their homes with a gift of freshly baked bread or cookies.

    b. Send home an announcement about a Foreign Parents' night, in which foods from many lands will be featured and for which they will be the featured speakers.

    c. Invite several parents from the same or similar cultures to work with their children, a translator if one is available, and herself to create a classroom presentation on some cultural aspect that will be of interest to the students. For example, Mexican and other Central American parents might present a slideshow on the Day of the Dead, followed by a show-and-tell of objects used in that celebration.

    d. Nothing. They have made it clear to her that they have priorities that do not include the needs of her student, their child. It's best if she simply expects less of them and takes it upon herself to provide additional academic and emotional support to the poor child, who is clearly being neglected.

27. Two young women are at a coffee shop. They are having an animated conversation about three young men sitting at a table across the room. Much of their conversation seems cryptic, either because they do not want others to understand, or because most of what they are talking about is fully present in the room, allowing them to use a verbal shorthand—or both. They don't realize a linguist in sitting at the next table, observing them and noting the relationship between orally manifested meaning (language) and contextual information conveyed through gesture, facial expression, inference, etc. In what area of linguistic study is the eavesdropper engaging?

    a. Pragmatics

    b. Contextual linguistics

    c. Social linguistics

    d. Etiquette orality

28. Communicative competence consists of both organizational competence (requiring competence with grammar and discourse) and pragmatic competence (which involves sociolinguistic and speech acts) and is currently the objective of many language education programs. To whom can the spread of its ideas best be attributed?

    a. Canale and Swain

    b. Chomsky

    c. Hull

    d. Krashen

29. Which answer best describes the stages of language acquisition?

    a. Letter recognition stage; vocabulary development stage; listening stage; contextually predictive stage

    b. Recognition of primary syntactical patterning stage; articulation stage; contextual referencing stage; BICS stage; CALPS stage

    c. Pre-production stage; early production stage; speech emergence stage; intermediate fluency stage

    d. Listening stage; copying stage; single-word response stage; multiple-word response stage; confidence stage

30. How are language acquisition and language learning distinct?
    a. They are not distinct; the terms are interchangeable.
    b. Language acquisition develops unconsciously through use, while language learning requires instruction.
    c. Language learning precedes and is required for language acquisition.
    d. All the above.

31. Realia means:
    a. Real-world experiences
    b. Reliable and, therefore, trustworthy methods of instruction
    c. Concrete objects used in demonstrations to develop vocabulary and encourage discourse
    d. Manifested, or "realized," concepts.

32. Current research suggests that employing a student's L1 in support of his or her L2 is likely to:
    a. Increase comprehensibility
    b. Decrease comprehensibility
    c. Increase cultural load
    d. Decrease that student's willingness to learn a new language

33. Canale and Swain find communicative competence in the relationship of what four elements?
    a. Competence in grammar, vocabulary, semantics, and phonetics
    b. Reading, writing, listening, and speaking
    c. Reading, writing, math, and science
    d. Competence in grammar, sociolinguistics, discourse, and communication strategies

34. An ESL teacher offers her students the following question to test their understanding of proper English grammar. Which of the following sentences is correct?
    a. Both my dog and my husband thinks I am a servant.
    b. Both my dogs and my husbands think I am a servant.
    c. Both my dogs and my husband thinks I am a servant.
    d. Both my dog and my husband think I am a servant.

35. Ms. Perez wants to raise her students' competency in CALP. Her strategies include "thinking aloud" to demonstrate cognitive process, differentiating instruction by teaching explicitly, and
    a. Asking "what if" questions
    b. Expecting maximum performance from students
    c. Teaching test-taking and study skills
    d. All the above

36. In the Early Production Stage of language acquisition, an L2 learner typically:
    a. Understands 1,000 words and can respond to instructions involving up to three requests
    b. Begins to speak in sentences of one-to-two clauses
    c. Understands up to 5,000 words, but uses only a handful
    d. Understands and uses roughly 1,000 words

37. The parents of a first-grade LEP student do not want her placed in a special education classroom; they feel that she is better off in a regular classroom at her grade level. The classroom teacher, ESL teacher, school counselor, and diagnostician are all certain that she has several interrelated learning disabilities, as well as some emotional issues. Given that she is unlikely to thrive in a regular classroom, will cause an extra burden of work to the teacher, and will without doubt be disruptive and cause problems for other students, can she placed in special education classes?
    a. No; parental permission is required.
    b. Yes; parental permission is required, but in its absence a building can, with requests from four or more professionals, be overridden.
    c. Possibly; the school must refer the case to Children's Protective Services, which will make the final decision.
    d. Temporarily, while the district takes the parents to court to force the issue. If the court rules in favor of the parents, the district must place the student in a regular classroom, pay the parents' legal costs, and pay a fine if the judge so orders. If the court rules in favor of the district, the parents must pay all court costs, but no fine can be assigned.

38. TPR stands for:
    a. Teaching-Productive Resources
    b. Total Physical Response
    c. Tagged Populations Records
    d. Theory of Psychological Reference

39. Which of the following are traditional methods of teaching English?
    a. Drills
    b. Teaching frequently-used phrases
    c. Immersion
    d. All of the above

40. What is the Language Experience Approach also known as?
    a. LEA
    b. Me, Myself, and Eye
    c. Dictated Stories
    d. Directed Stories

41. Who described the Acquisition-Learning, Monitor, Natural Order, Input, and Affective Filter hypotheses?
    a. Swain
    b. Cummins
    c. Gregory
    d. Krashen

42. In 1981 the United States Court of Appeals for the Fifth Circuit overturned a 1978 federal ruling in the case of Castaneda v. Pickard. As a result, a three-pronged assessment was established to ensure that bilingual programs met requirements established by what act?
    a. No Child Left Behind (2001)
    b. Equal Educational Opportunities Act (1974)
    c. The Bilingual Language Act (1968)
    d. The Civil Rights Act (1964)

43. What criteria would be assessed in the previous question?
    a. Students must be taught by bilingual teachers; BICS must be strictly enforced; and textbooks must be bilingual.
    b. The program must be based on current education theory; there must be a 1:5 teacher/student ratio; and it must serve only Stage I and II language learners.
    c. The program must be based on sound educational theory; must be put into service with sufficient personnel, materials, and space; and must effectively overcome language barriers and handicaps.
    d. The program must "teach to the test"; must serve the needs of the community as a whole; and must offer alternatives for home-school families.

44. A kindergarten student new to the United States speaks almost no English. His teacher, who is a fluent Spanish speaker, has noted that both his vocabulary and mastery of underlying grammatical rules in Spanish are also weak. The student depends upon a shared external context to convey a disproportionate amount of his intended meaning in oral communication, or he withdraws entirely. What should the teacher expect from this student in terms of his relative ability to learn English?
    a. Because his first language is not developed, he will most likely obtain English vocabulary and skills more rapidly, both because he is hungry for language and because there are fewer prior linguistic assumptions that could impede L2 development.
    b. Because his first language is not developed, he will most likely obtain English vocabulary and skills much more slowly; the speed with which L2 learners develop proficiency can be anticipated by the degree of richness L1 exhibits.
    c. It is too early to anticipate; each child is a unique being and to base assumptions of future learning on evidence of past learning is a fallacy.
    d. It is too early to anticipate; because the child is so young, is new to the United States, and must therefore be experiencing culture shock and because at this point little is known about his family/social situation, the teacher must remain open and curious about the student's ability to absorb L2, or the teacher will risk doing him an injustice by labeling him and teaching him accordingly.

45. The Cognitive Academic Language Learning Approach and Specially Designed Academic English are examples of:
    a. Sheltered English programs.
    b. Content-based ESL models.
    c. Nothing; both terms are invented.
    d. Both A and B.

46. According to many researchers, a student's mastery of English is a(n)_____ indicator of that student's cognitive abilities.
   a. Clear
   b. Accurate
   c. Inaccurate
   d. Partial

47. An ESL student at the intermediate level depends upon which skills to improve understanding and verbal ability?
   a. Reading and writing
   b. Writing and speaking
   c. Reading and listening
   d. Listening and speaking

48. Ricardo is in fourth grade and new to the school. His English vocabulary is quite strong, both in terms of social communication and in the sciences content area. He also has a solid basic understanding of grammatical structure, which is apparent in his writing skills. However, he is very shy and does not like to communicate verbally. On the rare occasion he does speak, it is either laborious as he reviews and practices mentally to make sure that what he's about to say will be correct, or he becomes anxious and his speech is peppered with errors in grammar and pronunciation. Several members of the class have begun to tease him. He reacts to teasing by blushing, exhibiting confused movements, and on occasion, by crying. How can this teacher support Ricardo's oral communication skills?
   a. Shame the bullies by making them stand in corners and miss recess until they apologize to Ricardo in front of the entire class.
   b. Assign an oral report to each member of the class. Encourage Ricardo, but do not baby him; he needs to develop a backbone.
   c. Give Ricardo many opportunities during the day by inviting him to answer a question even if he hasn't volunteered by raising his hand; pairing him with one of the bullies, so they can begin to bond; and asking him to act as "teacher's helper" and co-teach a topic he enjoys.
   d. Privately meet with the bullies and explain that it's important to welcome Ricardo; ask for their help in doing so. Pair Ricardo with class members who have a gentle, accepting nature to do projects that do not need to be orally presented. Do not force Ricardo to speak publicly, but do find opportunities for private, relaxed conversations about topics of interest to him. Do not correct errors; instead, model correct usage (lower his affective filter).

49. What is the BSM, and what is it designed to establish?
   a. The Bilingual Strategies Method establishes effective instructional methods for mainstreamed bilingual students.
   b. The Bilingual Syntax Measure is a tool designed to assess bilingual students for both native and L2 (English) proficiency.
   c. The Burke-Stanley Milestone establishes points along the continuum from little English to full fluency.
   d. The Babcock Statistical Model establishes a measurable baseline for bilingual educators.

50. In terms of models, which bilingual approach does research indicate is least effective?
    a. Two-way immersion
    b. Sheltered English
    c. Mainstreamed classes
    d. Pull-out ESL classes

51. ESL requires students "to listen attentively and engage actively in a variety of oral language experiences." Specifically, second language learners are, at the appropriate English proficiency level, expected to know whether to listen for information, understanding, or enjoyment; respond to questions and directions; participate in classroom discussions, songs, rhymes, and other language play; and:
    a. Apply critical listening skills to deduce and evaluate ideas that may not be directly stated
    b. Be willing to risk shame or embarrassment caused by errors in speaking, in order to learn
    c. Listen closely and imitate precisely in order to absorb proper pronunciation
    d. Learn the cultural values and expectations of their adopted country

52. A teacher is having fun with her students. She has created numerous sentences that are ridiculous in their "meaning." She has asked her students to tell her which of the sentences are possible in English, regardless of how odd the meaning is, and which sentences cannot make any sense whatsoever. An example of one of these possible sentences is: The grandfather clock and my grandmother are secretly in love. An impossible sentence might be: The shy giggling would not choo-choo the quickly goose. What is the teacher using the assignment to evaluate?
    a. Students' semantic understanding
    b. Students' syntactic understanding
    c. Students' phonemic understanding
    d. Students' morphemic understanding

53. According to Cummins' Threshold Hypothesis, cognitive and academic growth in L2 is largely dependent upon:
    a. Development of CALP in L1
    b. Research-based, high quality instruction
    c. Development of BICS
    d. L2 immersion

54. When does special education law apply to LEPs?
    a. Never; the two are distinct and share no overlap.
    b. Only when an LEP student also has learning, emotional, or physical handicaps as well.
    c. Always.
    d. It has not been definitively decided. The Supreme Court will hear Chin v. Battleridge District later this year.

55. Research indicates that the Silent/Receptive stage of second language acquisition typically lasts up to _____, during which time a learner understands and can respond to roughly _____ words.
    a. Two years; 1,000
    b. Six months; 500
    c. One month; 100
    d. 18 months; 1,000

56. CBEC stands for:
    a. Collaborative Bilingual Education Center
    b. Cooperative Basic English Continuum
    c. Content-Based ESL Curriculum
    d. Cognitive Bilingual Effort Council

57. A student at the Speech Emergence Stage of language acquisition is considered fluent. This statement is:
    a. False
    b. True
    c. Partially true; the student is fluent in BICS
    d. All the above

58. Which of the following presents effective ways a third-grade teacher can help students expand their vocabularies?
    a. Give them a word-a-day to memorize. They must use the word five times in conversation and once in writing. Then at the end of the week, give them the opportunity to write a creative story or poem using all five of the week's words.
    b. Play a game in which one student selects a word from the dictionary that is complex and unknown. Next, singly or in groups, have students take a risk and try to guess the definition.
    c. Teach a unit on prefixes and suffixes. Offer some examples of each. Next, group the students into teams and see which team comes up with the most words that use prefixes and suffixes. Challenge them by asking for a word with both a prefix and a suffix.
    d. Have students find words in newspapers, magazines, and elsewhere that they do not understand. Give them the definitions, and have them write them down in a word book or put them on the word wall.

59. Krashen's Affective Filter Hypothesis theorizes that L2 acquisition can be supported or harmed by:
    a. The effects of overwhelming media exposure
    b. Classroom instruction that immerses the student in effective L2 instruction
    c. The learner's family and community
    d. The learner's positive or negative level of emotional comfort in L2

60. Two teachers are discussing a student with whom they both work. The term "communicative competence" comes up. What aspect of the student's development are the teachers discussing?

    a. Her willingness to listen to another speaker's message and respond kindly and appropriately.

    b. Her ability to use the elements of language (syntax, phonology, morphology, semantics) together with an understanding of social expectations and to use spoken messages that are appropriate in terms of how they are manifested and when, in the course of conversation, they are used.

    c. Communicative competence is transparently interchangeable with CALP; the teachers are discussing her social language skills.

    d. Communicative competence is transparently interchangeable with BICS; the teachers are discussing her academic language skills.

61. The ESL teacher has several students with little knowledge of English. How can she develop competency?

    a. Drill verb cases; build vocabulary with a word wall; read the same books repeatedly to build their semantic understanding

    b. Incorporate extra-linguistic materials into instruction, such as realia, gestures, and enactments (increased comprehensibility, contextual clues)

    c. Have them listen and repeat exercises from a language CD; teach them a "word of the day" and ask them to use it five times in oral or written communication; praise them when they are successful

    d. Invite members of a mainstreamed age-appropriate class to visit, and assign each child to a mainstreamed "mentor" to share conversations on topics the ESL children offer

62. The students in the above example have learned well; both they and their teacher are pleased with their increased competency. Which strategies should the teacher now employ?

    a. Employ vocabulary the students understand and use it to teach new vocabulary; offer hands-on instruction; invite members of a mainstreamed class for peer tutoring

    b. Incorporate extra-linguistic materials into instruction, such as realia, gestures, and enactments (increased comprehensibility, contextual clues)

    c. Have them listen and repeat exercises from a language CD; teach them a "word of the day," and ask them to use it five times in oral or written communication; praise them when they are successful

    d. Drill vocabulary and grammar daily; post new words on a word wall; assign independent reading and oral reports

63. A teacher asks her students to consider the following subject/verb and pronoun/antecedent relationships. Which of the following is correct?

    a. Neither Eric nor Tim admits he made a mistake.

    b. Neither Eric nor Tim admit they made a mistake.

    c. Neither Eric nor Tim admits they made a mistake.

    d. Neither Eric nor Tim admit he made a mistake.

64. An ESL teacher is using dialogue journals with her students. The students write in the journals three times a week on any subject they choose. What is the purpose of such journals?

a. The teacher will discover what is important to her students and can modify her instruction accordingly.

b. To give students ample time to practice writing dialogue, including grammatical practice, such as use of quotation marks, and content practice, such as writing dialogue that is dynamic, interesting, and characterizes the speakers.

c. The teacher will use these journals to correct student misconceptions about rules of grammar and semantics. Because the students are invested in their own words, they will be more open to such correction than in highly-systematized classroom instruction.

d. The teacher will write comments and questions in response, modeling correct English usage.

65. A teacher is having difficulty with her fifth grade ESL students. She pre-teaches lessons by giving students specialized vocabulary they will need, reminds them of prior knowledge, and writes important information on the board in her clearest cursive handwriting. She asks the ESL students if they understand; the students nearly always nod and smile in agreement. She speaks very slowly and loudly and is careful to use a few of the most current slang expressions to make the students feel that she "speaks their language." Nonetheless, the students demonstrate little understanding of the material when tested in an essay format. They do only a little better when asked to choose the correct answer on tests. What is the teacher doing wrong?

a. Some ESL students may not be able to interpret cursive handwriting.

b. When asked a question directly, many students will agree whether or not they understand what is being asked. Moreover, students may agree in order to avoid the embarrassment of admitting in public that they do not understand.

c. The teacher's use of slang that has not been taught as idiom is more likely to confuse the students than to clarify their English.

d. All the above.

66. In order to develop CALP, which of the following methods is most likely to succeed?

a. Give students a variety of communication experiences. Informal conversation with a peer, formal presentation before a class, personal journal writing, and reports will all contribute to the development of a student's CALP.

b. Group students homogeneously so that they can work on projects with a variety of different individuals and learn flexibility in learning styles.

c. Building literacy skills in all content areas will improve CALP and increase language and abstract thinking skills across the board.

d. No methods will work; CALP is a subconscious, natural process that develops in its own time and at its own speed. Attempting to streamline the process is likely to backfire, producing a speaker who is hesitant and insecure.

67. What criticism has been leveled at oral proficiency assessments, such as the Language Assessment Scales-Oral, the Woodcock-Muñoz Language Survey, and the IDEA Proficiency Test?

a. They are biased toward native English speakers.

b. They are biased toward non-native English speakers.

c. They do not accurately reflect native speakers' academic performance and therefore cannot accurately reflect non-native speakers' performance.

d. They do not accurately reflect native speakers' proficiency and therefore cannot accurately reflect non-native speakers' proficiency.

68. The degree to which an L1 learner is successful in acquiring a second language is determined by numerous aspects. Contributing factors include the learner's age, degree of instruction, opportunities to practice, willingness to practice, working and long-term memory, ability to process information, and:

a. Socioeconomic level

b. Degree of L1 development

c. Psychological health

d. Motivation

69. The Reading Proficiency Tests in English (RPTE) is used for _____ students in grades_____

a. All students; 1st-4th

b. LEP students; 3rd-12th

c. LEP students; all grades

d. All students; all grades.

70. A teacher's third grade class includes students from Costa Rica, Chile, Peru, Mexico, Korea, Vietnam, India, Iraq, and the United States. Over the course of several months, the class has explored the cultures of each country. The teacher has been careful to include lessons that demonstrate how different cultures have different values and beliefs about behavior, relationships, religion, and education. She has placed each of her students in small, homogeneous groups and asked them to create some kind of presentation that will teach the class about different cultural expectations and the emotions that can arise when there is cultural confusion. Of the following presentations, which is most likely to be the most effective?

a. A game the group creates that explores the foods of various cultures

b. Oral reports given by group members on how they celebrate Christmas.

c. A play in which a Korean student, a Hispanic student, and an American-born student perform a series of skits demonstrating how different cultures greet acquaintances and the confusion that can arise when people from two distinct cultures meet

d. A fairy tale orally presented in English, Spanish, and Korean

71. Developing a student's capacity for independent academic study and task completion through an approach known as _____ is achieved through the combined efforts of strategies, such as hands-on activities, accessing prior knowledge, pre-teaching content-area vocabulary, and putting the lesson into context with visual aids and modeling.

a. Native Language Support

b. ESL

c. Scaffolding

d. Direct Experience

72. The ESL teacher is fit to be tied. At the first parent-teacher conference, she clearly informed Hector's mother that her son lacked manners and was lazy and self-centered. She gave his mother the assignment of reviewing all school work to make certain it had been done—and done correctly. She conducted the conference in Spanish, because she wanted to be certain Hector's mother, who is Brazilian, understood her. Hector continues to arrive at school with an empty book bag or with homework that has been incorrectly and hastily done. Furthermore, Hector's mother failed to show up at the last conference, calling to say she had to take an extra shift at work. What should the teacher do about this frustrating situation?

a. Separate Hector from the rest of the students by placing his desk in the hall. He needs to learn to be responsible for himself.

b. Ask that Hector be mainstreamed. He isn't doing the work, so ESL can't help him.

c. Try to reestablish positive communication with his family, stressing the importance of the teacher and parents working as a team to find real-life solutions that can be consistently implemented at home and at school.

d. Give up; Hector must remain in her class, but if no one else is trying, it's hopeless. Hector should be given only the time and energy the teacher has left after tending to the needs of other, more cooperative students in her class.

73. A teacher wants to encourage her first graders to have compassion for people from other cultures. She is writing and illustrating a story book about fictional children from all of the countries her students are from. Some of the characters come from wealthy countries and own many things. Others come from poor countries, wear cast-offs, and often go hungry. The story ends as one of the poor children dies of starvation, following which the narrator explains that had she not died, her family would have come to the United States, and she would be a member of this very classroom. The teacher believes this story will effectively portray the concept of compassion and the importance of taking care of one another. Is sharing this book with her students a good idea?

a. No. The students may believe that the character that dies was literally real rather than figuratively symbolic. Children from the countries the teacher has depicted as poor may feel shamed by their apparent poverty or frightened that they, too, might starve to death. Children from countries depicted as wealthy might either feel cheated, not being themselves wealthy, or entitled to the biggest and best of everything.

b. Yes. Children are innocent and open; they will be very moved by the idea of a friend they never got to know. It will encourage a great deal of loving compassion for others.

c. Yes. The students will likely have many questions, especially so because their teacher is the author. After the book has been read, the teacher can address some of these questions, being careful to call on students from all cultures.

d. No. It's likely that the students in the class who identify with the book characters from poor countries will become resentful of the U.S. citizens and try to harm them by forming a gang and waiting in the bathrooms to beat them up.

74. An ESL teacher has asked a group of high school students to visit her classroom and work individually with her students. The teacher has given the high school volunteers tape recorders, paper, and pencils and asked them to begin with a brief conversation with their respective L2s that will lead the L2s to a memory of a personal experience. The volunteers then take dictation, writing down exactly what the non-native speakers say. Next, the volunteers read their stories back to the authors. Following that, the authors read their own stories silently or aloud. This method is designed to simultaneously model encoding, develop sight word vocabulary, and motivate the ESL students to work toward fluency. This approach is known as:
  a. Two-way immersion
  b. Language Experience Approach
  c. B and D
  d. Dictated stories

75. An age equivalent score is used to tell whether a student is:
  a. Working at an appropriate grade level in a particular content area
  b. Working at the same level as others her age
  c. Working at a level that is below or above others her age
  d. B and C

76. An ESL teacher has several students who have attained BICS fluency. What must she do to help the students achieve CALP?
  a. Develop tier 2 vocabulary; teach specialized vocabulary essential to a particular subject area; teach, offer ample practice opportunities, monitor, and re-teach more complex syntactical structures; offer instruction and practice in organizing ideas in terms of text.
  b. Nothing; by definition, a student who is in control of BICS has already mastered CALP.
  c. Nothing; there is no relationship between the two.
  d. Continue instruction as she has been doing; BICS is the first milestone on the way to CALP. The teacher should continue to differentiate learning, provide ample opportunity for classroom face-to-face communication, provide meaningful texts, monitor students' progress, and adjust her instruction accordingly.

77. What 1982 Supreme Court case established for undocumented immigrant children the right to a free education?
  a. Plyer v. Doe; 14th amendment
  b. Lau v. Nichols
  c. Meyer v. Nebraska
  d. Castaneda v. Pickard

78. According to Krashen, people who overuse the monitor are typically:
  a. Introverts who lack confidence
  b. People with poor vision who require enlarged computer monitors
  c. First-year teachers with less ESL experience
  d. Extroverts with a high degree of confidence

79. Tea/tee, stair/stare, and shoe/shoo are:
   a. Homophones
   b. Synonyms
   c. Antonyms
   d. Siblings

80. What should a teacher working with an ESL student who is at the preproduction stage do?
   a. Devise role-playing games and activities
   b. Offer ample opportunity for face-to-face dialogue
   c. Encourage silent students to speak; this is especially important for introverted students
   d. Incorporate gesture, pictures, manipulatives, and other extra-verbal tools into her teaching

81. What are the characteristics of an additive educational program?
   a. It works with students who come from families with a history of drug or alcohol abuse. By starting therapy at a young age, the hope is that these children won't grow up to become addicts as well.
   b. It is a math and social studies program that focuses exclusively on the positive. In math, that means everything is described in terms of addition; for example, subtraction is negative addition. In social studies, it means that only those characteristics of a social group that are joyful, exuberant, or peace-loving will be taught.
   c. It is a program that uses a student's culture of origin as a scaffold to teach her about her new culture.
   d. It is a program that explores all the ways advertisements exploit cultures by furthering stereotypes and prejudices.

82. L2 development can be hindered by which of the following?
   a. Idiomatic expressions
   b. Vocabulary words that have multiple meanings
   c. A, B, and D
   d. Carrying grammatical rules, vocabulary, and pronunciation from L1 and applying them to L2.

83. The teacher is working with a group of ESL students who are at the Speech Emergence stage. She is careful to speak slowly and repeat essential vocabulary, uses gesture to reinforce her instruction, and gives students questions to use when interviewing one another for a writing project. The likely outcome is:
   a. The students will respond well to the variety of strategies as their language skills continue to grow.
   b. The students will become bored.
   c. The students will become anxious and insecure.
   d. The students' decoding skills will be enhanced.

84. A student who is new to the United States understands some English, but his vocabulary is limited, and his grasp of syntax is weak. Although he is 11, his previous education was very limited, so he has been placed in a 4th grade classroom. For the first few weeks, he was very quiet and kept to himself. In an effort to bring him out of his shell, his teacher put him into a pod with several highly social students whose first language is English. The students tried to draw him in, talking loudly and gesturing to make him understand. When he ignored them, they left him alone. To her dismay, the teacher's previously quiet student grew sullen and very angry. He hit a child during recess one day and stormed out of class in the middle of a lesson the next day. What is most likely the problem with the boy?

 a. Since he started out quiet and rapidly became angry, it's probable that he is undergoing some kind of trauma at home.

 b. He is experiencing a high affective filter due possibly to culture shock, which is heightened by being placed with younger students, as well as by his inability to freely communicate. He may feel shame, insecurity, embarrassment, frustration, or a combination of these, which he compensates for and covers up with anger.

 c. He is simply undisciplined. Because he has spent little time in a school, he doesn't clearly understand the dynamics, rules, and regulations, and he must be treated with firm kindness.

 d. He is simply undisciplined. He has probably gotten away with this type of behavior before, and he likely feels that it is a normal way to express pent-up frustration. The teacher must move swiftly to punish him for outbursts or striking others, as such behavior cannot be allowed.

85. What ESL model is a One Teacher Approach?

 a. Resource Model

 b. Transitional Model

 c. Self-Contained Model (a single teacher has students in a self-contained classroom and is responsible for language and academic performance)

 d. Two-Way Enrichment Model

86. A previously happy and affectionate ELL has suddenly become tearful and withdrawn. She reacts very strongly to any kind of unexpected touch, and she has abruptly stopped giving hugs to the teacher or to her friends. She will not tell the teacher what is causing her sadness or hurt, but the teacher is aware that the girl's mother has a new boyfriend who has recently moved in with the family. The student, who used to love writing in her journal both in Spanish and in English, now uses it only for drawings. The teacher has not violated the student's privacy by looking at the journal without permission, but she has noticed that during journal time the girl angrily scribbles what appear to be pictures of a man (or someone wearing a hat and pants) being shot, stabbed, or otherwise tortured. What should the teacher do?

 a. Read the journal without permission; the girl is obviously disturbed, and if she is being abused in some way, the teacher has the responsibility to find out in any way possible.

 b. Nothing at the moment; she should continue to observe the student and offer her an ear. Until the girl asks for help, she can legally do nothing.

 c. Refer the student to the school counselor, who is trained to help in situations such as this.

 d. Get the mother's permission to refer the student to the school counselor. She cannot be referred without parental permission.

87. A student whose L1 is Basque is displaying certain problems. The ESL teacher is uncertain whether he has one or more learning disabilities or if it could be a problem with his language development. She is uncertain what to do. She knows that if she refers him for assessment, he might be inaccurately labeled as learning impaired and placed in a special education class. If his problems are language-based, such a move could be detrimental. She knows that there are no assessments available in Basque in her district, and she feels strongly that he needs to be presented with certain questions and allowed to answer in his own words before a decision is made. The boy's adult aunt, a fluent English speaker and the teacher's neighbor and friend, has offered to help as an informal translator. Is this a suitable fix?

    a. No. The friendship between the teacher and aunt precludes using her as a translator. Both her friendship with the teacher and her familial relationship with the student could affect her objectivity.

    b. No. She is not a trained translator, and, for this reason alone, the aunt is not suitable for this task. The school is legally responsible for providing a trained translator or materials in Basque, if they are available. The teacher must advocate on behalf of the student and try to find a trained translator or the materials in Basque.

    c. Yes. The student needs to be assessed one way or another to determine whether he has learning disabilities or whether his problem is in the area of language development. It is unreasonable for the school to expect the teacher to devote hours to tracking down a translator, and the aunt will do the job for free. There's really no reason not to take her up on it!

    d. Yes. The student will likely feel very comfortable with his aunt translating. There is the added bonus that if he doesn't understand a question or wants to ask what the purpose of it is, they can privately share a conversation about the test out loud, while simultaneously protecting the student's privacy.

88. Cooperative Learning is a teaching approach that combines students at varying scholastic levels and with various learning styles into small groups for learning activities that encourage interaction. All students have ample opportunity to speak, and groups foster a sense of mutual respect. Additionally, students at different levels and with different learning styles observe one another and expand their learning skills and strategies. This approach is most effective when:

    a. The small groups are observed and monitored.

    b. The groups are organized homogeneously.

    c. Students work with the same classmates over the course of an entire school year.

    d. Learning tasks are authentic, challenging, and meaningful.

89. The ESL teacher has a goal of increasing interaction among her students. She has studied Swain's theory of comprehensible output, and is basing her instruction accordingly. Which of the following would be an appropriate strategy for her to employ?

    a. Project-based learning

    b. Manipulatives

    c. Rubrics

    d. All the above

90. What is one difference between ESL and bilingual models?
   a. ESL models are pull-out or push-in. Bilingual models are self-contained.
   b. ESL models are English-only and employ a specific methodology to teach English and continue to develop L1. Bilingual models introduce instruction concepts first in L1 and over time transfer them into English
   c. Bilingual models are pull-out or push-in; ESL models are self-contained.
   d. Bilingual models are English-only and employ specific methodology to teach English and continue to develop L1. ESL models introduce instruction concepts first in L1 and over time transfer them into English

91. Which is more abstract, BICS or CALP?
   a. Neither; both are concrete, hands-on teaching methods.
   b. BICS; academic language requires abstract thinking.
   c. CALP; social language requires abstract thinking.
   d. CALP; academic language requires abstract thinking.

92. Which of the following is NOT required for an LEP's permanent record?
   a. The student's level of language proficiency designated
   b. A writing sample
   c. Parental approval
   d. Program entry and exit dates and notification of same to parents

93. Many times, ESL teachers must simplify a text so that students will be able to understand the ideas. Why is it important that the language be simplified by substituting common words for more abstract ones, by shortening sentences or turning a long sentence into two or three simple ones, or by deleting unnecessary information while modifying the concepts and ideas as little as possible?
   a. ESL students generally are not at the same grade level as their English-speaking peers; therefore, they cannot understand texts that are too difficult.
   b. Grade level content is essential. Simplifying language without simplifying content will help ESL students remain at grade level.
   c. The statement is incorrect. It is essential to modify both language and ideas by stripping them of detail, clarifying language, and making ideas as simple as possible.
   d. It's important to simplify texts by reducing and eliminating content to make it more understandable and, at the same time, retaining as much of the original language as possible. This is to challenge LEPs to reach the highest linguistic goal they can achieve; if language is stripped of meaning, it is more transparent and carries less cultural weight.

94. Many linguistics subscribe to the theory that a second language is both acquired and learned. Describe the distinctions between the two:
   a. Acquiring simply requires exposure and is required for learning. When an aspect of a second language is "learned," it is fully absorbed and understood.
   b. Acquisitioned language is specific to a particular field of study; learned language is general and required for all types of discourse.
   c. Language acquisition is natural, subconscious, and concerned with message content. Language learning is formal, concerned with grammatical rules, and conscious.
   d. Acquired language is that which is mimicked first, prior to understanding. With use comes comprehension of meaning. Learned language is the result of directed instruction and intervention.

Answers and Explanations

1. B: Admissions, Review, and Dismissal; Individual Education Plan (IEP); teachers, parents, counselors, administrators, and others working with the student. The Individuals with Disabilities Education Act (IDEA) is a federal act that protects students with disabilities, including those with limited English, by entitling them to the same quality of education as non-disabled students. The ARD committee is composed of teachers, parents (or guardians), school administrators, and other appropriate persons. One of their tasks is to create an IEP for each student, which must be followed by all teachers involved in that student's education.

2. B: A and C. Presenting sufficient and meaningful reading and writing experiences for students to practice strategies and reviewing and re-teaching as required to ensure that students have integrated essential content are part of scientifically-based, quality classroom instruction.

3. B: Acculturation; adapting to a new culture, which includes understanding cultural expectations, semiotics, values, and beliefs, is essential to second language acquisition in that it provides appropriate context. Acculturation permits ELLs to adapt to new cultural expectations without the loss of the culture of origin. Success with BICS and CALP in L2 is dependent on a degree of success in L1.

4. C: A predicate nominative. A predicate nominative is a noun phrase which defines or clarifies the subject, but is not interchangeable with it. Multiple words do not make multiple predicate nominatives, however; together they create a predicate nominative. It is not correct in English to state "A Smart car is that tiny red car," because Smart cars are multiple and not singular, and because Smart cars come in many colors besides red.

5. A: A predicate adjective. A predicate adjective is an adjective that comes after a linking verb (such as the verb "to be") and modifies or describes the subject. In this example, "puppy" is the subject, "is" is the linking verb, and "protective" is the adjective.

6. C: Immersion. Until the late 1960s, immersion was the primary language instruction model. Typically, immigrant students—many of whom had little or no English—were mainstreamed into a classroom where they received language and content instruction in English only. Immersion is also called the "sink or swim" approach. Research has shown that this method is not efficient or effective.

7. C: To instruction that they have the skills to understand. The 1974 Supreme Court decision as a result of Lau v. Nichols established that school districts must provide ELL students the tools necessary to understand instruction.

8. C: Shorten the text; abbreviate sentences; substitute simple, concrete language for more complex language; break complex sentences into two or three simpler, more direct sentences; omit detail that enhances the text but doesn't change or clarify meaning. Beginning/intermediate stage ELLs will be able to understand ideas, theories, and other forms of meaning when they are offered in the context of a language the ELL can understand.

9. B: Traditional ESL programs prioritize social language skills. CBEC offers instruction in content areas that are age-appropriate to the LEPs' mainstreamed peers. Traditional ESL programs make the rapid absorption of social language skills a priority and, to that end, teach streamlined, socially necessary vocabulary and simple syntactical structures that enable students to communicate their basic needs. CBEC instruction is more deeply grounded in the same content that non-ESL students receive in order to prepare them for mainstreaming.

10. B: CALP. On average, research shows that it takes five years or more from first exposure to gain grade-level Cognitive Academic Language Proficiency (CALP). Basic Interpersonal Communication Skills (BICS) can be achieved within two years of first exposure.

11. A: She will use the information they contain to vary her lessons to meet each student's specific needs. Because all students are individuals with unique abilities, experiences, and personalities, the most effective teaching methods must allow for modifying lessons to specific, individual needs.

12. C: Encourage students to be curious about and respectful of differences in culture. For many people, the memory of a kitchen is especially evocative and suggests warmth, love, and nurturing. As the place where meals are prepared, kitchens are also very much cultural reflections—from the food chosen to the methods used to prepare it. By encouraging each student to share a memory of a particular kitchen, the teacher is encouraging wide cultural respect.

13. C: ELLs often understand more in terms of vocabulary and correct syntax than they demonstrate in their own speaking. The other statements contain information that is false.

14. D: The ways in which language learning influences acquisition. The Monitor hypothesis examines how language acquisition and language learning are related. Krashen sees acquisition as the utterance initiator, while learning is the monitor/editor. The monitor plans, edits, and corrects language acts when the ELL is not rushed. It also follows the rules of the language and fully integrates the rule under consideration. The monitor role should be a minor one, since it is conscious of itself and, therefore, is not intuitive. Interestingly, research indicates that extroverts tend to be under-users who are much more concerned with the immediacy of communication in the moment; introverts and perfectionists are over-users and are determined to speak correctly or not speak at all. Optimal users apply the monitor in a limited but appropriate way and exhibit a balanced personality that is neither extroverted nor introverted.

15. A: Top down. A Top down approach to language learning begins with practical communicative usage that, over time, incorporates grammar, vocabulary, phonemic awareness, and other essential elements of speech.

16. A: True. Second language acquisition research suggests that L2s tend to integrate formulaic expressions and then apply them to understand linguistic rules. Research shows early second language learners integrate a limited number of formulaic expressions that are perceived less as individual words than as functional phrases. These phrases are memorized as global wholes. Phrases such as "Where is the library?" or "Would you like to go with me?" later become templates for discovering the rules of the language. "Where is the library?" becomes the formula for "Where is the airport (Laundromat, etc.)?" "Would you

like to go with me?" becomes the template for "Would you like to eat dinner with me (like to see a movie with me, etc.)?" Over time, the learner realizes that the subject can change, and that the verb must then change to be in agreement.

17. C: The student is more likely to be placed in a special education program. Oral-language proficiency assessments should not be used as an overall indicator of a student's academic performance, as research has demonstrated that ELLs with little English are very likely to be inappropriately placed in special education classes.

18. B: Separate Underlying Proficiency. According to the Separate Underlying Proficiency theory (SUP), no relationship between L1 and L2 language acquisition exists, because each language is retained by a distinct area of the brain that is in no way connected to an area reserved for another language. Currently this theory is generally disregarded.

19. B: Involve her students in a series of physical activities in response to her instructions and requests. Total Physical Response (TPR) employs physical involvement to make learning more meaningful and easier to retain. A sequence of instructions given by the teacher prompts a succession of detailed actions. Advocates recommend special hands-on training with a trained senior instructor.

20. D: Early Production Stage. In this stage, ELLs begin to use words that they learned in the Pre-production Stage. One word and yes/no responses are common. Conversation is initiated with gesture or one or two words. Children in this stage will verbally respond to an increasingly wider variety of linguistic stimulus.

21. C: Teachers who work with the student. By law, all teachers working with a particular student must follow that student's Individualized Education Plan.

22. D: BICS skills permit social communications that are face-to-face and include contextual information, informal vocabulary, and relatively simple syntax, while CALP skills are necessary for academic communication, require content-specific vocabularies and more sophisticated syntax, and do not rely upon external contextual information.

23. D: All the above. By consulting with mainstream teachers to determine what content the students will be learning in upcoming months, she can choose or modify appropriate and understandable texts. The ESL teacher should only teach the content that she feels confident with, and she should emphasize deeper understanding of limited content over a glancing familiarity with a wider range of content.

24. B: In the 1960s; Cuban immigrants established a successful bilingual program, and the Civil Rights movement put attention on correcting educational and social agendas that were prejudiced in favor of the white middle class.

25. A: Label objects in the room with all six languages; invite speakers from each of the countries to visit the classroom and talk about one or two aspects of their cultures; break the class into culturally-diverse, smaller groups for class projects and study; invite students to teach the class songs from their cultures.

26. C: Invite several parents from the same or similar cultures to work with their children, a translator if one is available, and herself to create a classroom presentation on some

cultural aspect that will be of interest to the students. For example, Mexican and other Central American parents might present a slideshow on the Day of the Dead, followed by a show-and-tell of objects used in that celebration.

27. A: Pragmatics. Pragmatics examines how speakers' linguistic understanding depends upon external context, how meaning can be found in the confluence of the rules of a language—its grammar, vocabulary, idioms, and so forth—and contextual information that is not imbedded in the language itself, such as inferences, spatial relationships, and so forth.

28. A: Canale and Swain. This theory determines that communicative competence consists of both organizational competence (competence with grammar and discourse) and pragmatic competence (sociolinguistic and speech acts) and is currently the objective of many language education programs.

29. C: Pre-production stage; early production stage; speech emergence stage; intermediate fluency stage. During the Pre-production stage, language is being absorbed and its meanings learned, but it is not being verbally produced. The early production stage features a willingness to initiate conversation with gesture or a single word and to answer questions with one or two words. Yes and no become commonly used. The speech emergence stage is characterized by developing comprehension and fewer errors in speech. By the intermediate fluency stage, a speaker exhibits greater comprehension, more complex sentence structures, a richer vocabulary, and more sophisticated errors.

30. B: Language acquisition develops unconsciously through use, while language learning requires instruction. Language acquisition is natural, subconscious, and concerned with message content. Language learning is formal, concerned with grammatical rules, and conscious.

31. C: Realia are concrete objects used in demonstrations, to develop vocabulary and encourage discourse. The use of realia during instruction offers students the chance to involve a range of senses. Objects that can be handled, carefully examined, smelled, tasted, or listened to offer a richer learning experience.

32. A: Increase comprehensibility. There is currently a great deal of research that supports the theory that the degree and types of language learning in L1 are a strong predictor of how well L2 will be absorbed and comprehended.

33. D: Competence in grammar, sociolinguistics, discourse, and communication strategies. Competence in grammar requires mastery of the rules of language; sociolinguistic competence requires an understanding of what is appropriate; competence in discourse requires the ability to organize messages into a coherent and cohesive whole; strategic competence refers to the use of communication strategies in ways that are appropriate.

34. D: Both my dog and my husband think I am a servant. My dogs thinks I am a servant, and my husband also thinks I am a servant. The third person singular form of to think, is "thinks." However, the use of the word "both" links the two singular subjects into a plural subject; hence, the verb form must change to "think" to be in agreement.

35. D: All of the above. "Thinking aloud" to demonstrate cognitive processes, differentiating instruction by teaching explicitly, asking "what if" questions to stimulate abstract thinking,

challenging students by expecting maximum performance, and teaching test-taking and study skills are strategies that, taken together, will result in increased cognitive competency.

36. D: Understands and uses roughly 1,000 words. The early production stage lasts approximately six months beyond the pre-production stage and is characterized by an understanding and use of approximately 1,000 words in one-to-two word phrases or by responding to questions with appropriate action.

37. A: No; parental permission is required. Under no circumstances can a student be placed in a special education classroom without the permission of a parent or a legal guardian.

38. B: Total Physical Response. TPR is an approach pioneered by James J. Asher in the late 1960s, which emphasizes physical activity as a means to increase language retention. It involves a set of detailed instructions or commands, which then require appropriate physical actions.

39. D: All of the above. Traditional methods of teaching English included immersion, also known as "sink or swim," which was used until the late 1960s and involved no instruction in a student's L1 and no instruction to teach L2; drills, in which students memorize and repeat sets of information; and teaching frequently used phrases, which has practical and immediate application, but does not teach a user to truly inhabit a language to the degree necessary to use it to express complex ideas.

40. C: "Dictated Stories" is another name for the Language Experience Approach. This strategy creates texts from students' own words, and uses it in reading lessons. A teacher or peer writes down the story verbatim, then reads the story back to the author. Next, the student reads the story himself, either aloud or silently. Students learn about encoding language by watching their own words being written, develop a bank of sight words, and develop fluency as they read their own words. Because this method permits students to record their own lives, it is particularly useful as a way to celebrate multicultural experiences.

41. D: Krashen. Acquisition-Learning, Monitor, Natural Order, Input, and Affective Filter hypotheses are central to Steven Krashen's highly respected theory of second language acquisition. Language Acquisition is subconscious and requires meaningful communication, while Language Learning is conscious and involves formal instruction; the Monitor is concerned with editing and correcting errors in speaking or writing; Natural Order finds there is a predictable natural order in which grammatical structures are absorbed; Input refers to the hypothesis that language is ultimately acquired and not learned, and the Affective Filter hypothesis explores ways in which positive and negative factors such as motivation, self-esteem, and anxiety help or hurt the acquisition of language.

42. B: Equal Educational Opportunities Act (1974) is a federal law banishing discrimination against all members of an educational community, including students, teachers, and staff. School districts are required to actively work to resolve situations in which students are denied equal participation. The EEOA, together with the Rehabilitation Act (1973), the Individuals with Disabilities Education Act (IDEA), and the Americans with Disabilities Act (ADA) regulate learning institutions.

43. C: The program must be based on sound educational theory; must be put into service with sufficient personnel, materials, and space; and must effectively overcome language barriers and handicaps. These are the three criteria that must be assessed as a result of Castaneda v. Pickard.

44. B: Because his first language is not developed, he will most likely obtain English vocabulary and skills much more slowly; the speed with which L2 learners develop proficiency can be anticipated by the degree of richness L1 exhibits. Research has demonstrated that the degree to which an L2 is obtained is related to the speaker's mastery of L1.

45. B: Content-based ESL models. The Cognitive Academic Language Learning Approach (CALLA) and Specially Designed Academic English (SDAE) and other sheltered-English approaches feature using content-area instruction as a vehicle for language instruction.

46. C: Inaccurate. A substantial number of research studies report that mastery of English (or any second language) should not be taken as an indication of the speaker's cognitive abilities. Learning a language is an ever-changing activity that is actualized at any given moment. Cognitive ability is the potential that is not yet actualized. To look at an ELL's control of English at any given moment of time and base assumptions about that individual's potential to think abstractly, organize knowledge into complex systems, and apply ideas across a wide spectrum would be a disservice.

47. D: Listening and speaking. At the intermediate level, listening and speaking practice enables learners to gain an enhanced comprehension of and insight into the complexity of thought and the means by which to express thoughts.

48. D: Privately meet with the bullies and explain that it's important to welcome Ricardo; ask for their help in doing so. Pair Ricardo with class members who have a gentle, accepting nature to do projects that do not need to be orally presented. Do not force Ricardo to speak publicly, but find opportunities for private, relaxed conversations about topics of interest to him. Do not correct errors; instead, model correct usage. It is important to lower his affective filter so that he will, with time, gain the confidence necessary to trust his ability to express himself using a second language.

49. B: The Bilingual Syntax Measure is a tool designed to assess bilingual students for both native and L2 (English) proficiency. As a result of Lau v. Nichols, schools have been issued a federal mandate to determine whether a child is an English Language Learner. Title III of the English Language Acquisition, Language Enhancement, and Academic Achievement Act additionally requires schools to assess bilingual students for both native language and English proficiency, and states must employ assessment measures that provide valid information gathered in a consistent and dependable manner. However, recent research indicates that a greater number of proficiency assessment tools fail to measure a student's true proficiency level, and that these tools generally do not give the same results.

50. D: Pull-out ESL classes. Of the program choices given, pull-out models consistently prove to be less effective.

51. A: Apply critical listening skills to deduce and evaluate ideas that may not be directly stated. The Texas Essential Knowledge and Skills for English as a Second Language requires

K–3 ELL students "to listen attentively and engage actively in a variety of oral language experiences" and expects students to differentiate between listening for information, for understanding or for pleasure; to respond to questions and directions; to contribute to classroom discussions, songs, rhymes, and other language play; and to listen attentively.

52. B: Students' syntactic understanding. The teacher wants her students to understand the types of syntactical arrangements (grammatical structures) that are not allowed. For example, a sentence like "The quickly telephone and lonely" would not be possible because "quickly," an adverb, is modifying "telephone," a noun. In addition, "lonely" is an adjective, but has no noun to modify. Finally, the sentence has no verb. However, a silly sentence like "The quick telephone and forlorn toothbrush waltzed to the music of the moon" is grammatically possible, albeit absurd.

53. A: Development of CALP in L1. The Threshold Hypothesis (Cummins & Swain, 1986) finds that a higher proficiency threshold in the first language is a core contributor to the learner's acquisition of a second language. A speaker who did not achieve Cognitive Academic Language Proficiency in L1 will have more difficulty doing so in L2.

54. C: Always. Students with learning or communication challenges, emotional and/or behavioral disabilities, physical disabilities, and developmental disabilities are eligible for special services. LEP students experience challenges in communication.

55. B: Six months; 500. The Silent/Receptive (Pre-Production Stage) is a brief stage lasting only a few months, in which language learners develop a bank of approximately 500 words they understand but do not use verbally. Newly introduced words that are explained so that the student can understand them are readily added to this bank. It is important that teachers not force or push a student in this stage to speak. They may communicate by pointing or gesturing, can follow commands, and may answer questions with a nod or a single word.

56. C: Content-Based ESL Curriculum. The approach encourages ESL instruction to reach beyond a simply serviceable program of study in order to offer instruction that focuses on content rather than the rules of a language so that ELLs are becoming simultaneously more linguistically proficient and academically proficient.

57. A: False. The Speech Emergence Stage is Stage III of language acquisition, and typically it is arrived at within 1 to 3 years of first exposure. In this stage, learners comprehend well, willingly initiate dialogue and answer questions with relatively simple sentences, and may not understand joke or idioms. The learner is moving toward fluency, but has not yet achieved it.

58. C: Teach a unit on prefixes and suffixes. Offer some examples of each. Next, group the students into teams and see which team comes up with the most words that use prefixes and suffixes. Challenge them by asking for a word with both a prefix and a suffix.

59. D: The learner's positive or negative level of emotional comfort in L2. According to Krashen, because learning a new language involves public practice, a language learner is more emotionally vulnerable. Negative emotions, such as shame, anxiety, or frustration, can obstruct the successful processing of unfamiliar words or grammatical constructions. Classrooms that foster positive feelings of self-esteem and success will encourage taking

risks that are necessary to learning, thereby lowering a student's affective filter and encouraging a high degree of motivation.

60. B: Her ability to use the elements of language (syntax, phonology, morphology, semantics) together with an understanding of social expectations and to use spoken messages that are appropriate in terms of how they are manifested and when, in the course of conversation, they are used.

61. B: Incorporate extra-linguistic materials into instruction, such as realia, gestures, and enactments. Comprehensibility will be increased by direct, hands-on involvement and clues to meaning that exist in the physical context of the classroom.

62. A: Employ vocabulary the students understand and use it to teach new vocabulary; offer hands-on instruction; invite members of a mainstreamed class for peer tutoring. New vocabulary built on previous knowledge will be more readily understood and retained. Hands-on instruction allows non-linguistic experiences that can contribute to understanding. Peer tutoring challenges learners to reach for a higher level of communicative skills.

63. A: Neither Eric nor Tim admits he made a mistake. Eric and Tim are treated as a single subject in this sentence, so the verb must be in agreement. The pronoun "he" refers to either Eric or Tim, but not both. Hence, "he" is correct, and "they" is incorrect.

64. D: The teacher will write comments and questions in response, modeling correct English usage. Dialogue or Interactive Journals offer teachers the opportunity to engage students in the writing process. The teacher responds to a student's entry with questions or comments about the topic introduced by the students. The teacher doesn't correct errors, but instead models correct usage.

65. D: All the above. Some ESL students may not be able to interpret cursive handwriting. When asked a question directly, many students will agree, whether or not they understand what is being asked. Moreover, students may agree in order to avoid the embarrassment of admitting in public that they do not understand. The teacher's use of slang that has not been taught as idiom is more likely to confuse the students than clarify meaning for them.

66. C: Building literacy skills in all content areas will improve CALP and increase language and abstract thinking skills across the board. Cognitive Academic Language Proficiency requires specialized vocabularies for specific content areas and the ability to apply abstract concepts to areas that are not transparently related.

67. D: They do not accurately reflect native speakers' proficiency and therefore cannot accurately reflect non-native speakers' proficiency. A study examined the efficacy of the Language Assessment Scales-Oral, the Woodcock-Muñoz Language Survey, and the IDEA Proficiency Test by giving all three to both native English-speaking non-Hispanic Caucasian and Hispanic students from all socioeconomic levels. Interestingly, these L1 English speakers did not receive similar results from the three tests, which ostensibly assessed for the same information. In fact, none of the native English speakers who were given the Woodcock-Muñoz Language Survey were assigned fluent status. On the other hand, all students scored as fluent in the Language Assessment Scales-Oral, while 87% were described by IDEA Proficiency Test results as being fluent. L1 English speakers who do not

uniformly score in the fluent range throw into doubt the assessment's ability to accurately reflect an L2's proficiency.

68. B: Degree of L1 development. The degree to which an L1 learner is successful in acquiring a second language is determined in part by the learner's motivation, age, previous instruction, opportunities to practice, willingness to practice, working and long-term memory, ability to process information, and the level of L1 proficiency.

69. B: LEP students: 3rd-12th use the RPTE.

70. C: A play in which a Korean student, a Hispanic student, and an American-born student perform a series of skits demonstrating how different cultures greet acquaintances and the confusion that can arise when people from two distinct cultures meet will best demonstrate the types of misinterpretation and confusion that can arise when two cultures bring different expectations to the same experience.

71. C: Scaffolding. Scaffolding provides a student with a combination of strategies to support independent learning, including hands-on activities; accessing prior knowledge; pre-teaching content-area vocabulary; and putting the lesson into context with visual aids and modeling.

72. C: Try to reestablish positive communication with his family, stressing the importance of the teacher and parents working as a team to find real-life solutions that can be consistently implemented at home and at school. The teacher in this example has violated nearly every principal of productive teacher-parent interaction. Rather than enlisting the mother's help in furthering her son's education, the teacher passes harsh judgment on the boy's behavior, implying fault is found at home. She neglects to realize that perhaps the mother isn't a Spanish speaker, but she is a Portuguese speaker. While his home environment might not be optimal, the teacher needs to do everything in her power to establish positive communication.

73. A: No. The students may believe that the character who dies was literally real rather than figuratively symbolic. Children from the countries the teacher has depicted as poor may feel shamed by their apparent poverty or frightened that they, too, might starve to death. Children from countries depicted as wealthy might either feel cheated, not being themselves wealthy, or entitled to the biggest and best of everything.

74. C: B and D. The Language Experience Approach, also called Dictated Stories, enlists the aid of volunteers who take down a story being dictated by a student verbatim. The stories are next read to the authors, and then each author reads her story silently or aloud. This approach utilizes several essential elements of literacy; encoding is modeled, sight word vocabulary developed, and the ownership a young author feels produces motivation.

75. D: B and C. An age equivalent score is used in a norm-referenced assessment to determine whether a student is working at, above, or below a level similar to her peers by studying the average age of others who got the same score as she did.

76. A: Develop tier 2 vocabulary; teach specialized vocabulary essential to a particular subject area; teach, offer ample practice opportunities, monitor, and re-teach more complex syntactical structures; offer instruction and practice in organizing ideas in terms of text.

These are the necessary next steps once Basic Interpersonal Communication Skills have been gained.

77. A: Plyer v. Doe; 14th amendment. In 1975, Texas laws were revised, permitting districts to refuse to enroll illegal alien children. The Supreme Court used this case to strike down the Texas law, finding it in violation of the 14th Amendment, which gives equal rights to all people.

78. A: Introverts who lack confidence. Krashen's Monitor hypothesis places the role of editor in language learning, as opposed to language acquisition, which is intuitive and lacks the desire to revise and correct. The monitor plans, edits, and corrects language acts when the ELL is not rushed, is attending to the language's rules, and has fully integrated the rule under consideration. The monitor role should be a minor one since it is conscious of itself and therefore not intuitive.

79. A: Homophones. Homophones sound alike but are spelled differently and have different meanings.

80. D: Incorporate gesture, pictures, manipulatives, and other extra-verbal tools into her teaching. The preproduction, or silent/receptive, stage of language acquisition is the first stage in which a learner must break into unfamiliar language that offers no easy entry. Visual images, coupled with the appropriate name, gestures indicating type or quality of movement, and other extra-verbal tools, will allow learners to begin to piece together the meanings that their first words carry.

81. C: It is a program that uses a student's culture of origin as a scaffold to teach her about her new culture. An Additive Educational Program is one that supports and celebrates bicultural identity and encourages acculturation, rather than assimilation.

82. C: A, B, and D. Hearing idiomatic expressions that have not been explained and aren't transparent will cause confusion in an L2 learner. English is particularly rich in words with multiple, frequently unrelated meanings; encountering a familiar word used in an unfamiliar way or having to decide in the course of a conversation which meaning out of several possibilities is the correct one can snarl understanding. Transporting syntax, vocabulary, and pronunciation from L1 and misapplying it in L2 (which is called negative transfer) will further render the language opaque.

83. B: The students will become bored. Students at Stage III: Speech Emergence are eager to practice their new skills and learn rapidly. The approaches the teacher is using are better suited to learners at Stage I (preproduction) or II (early production). Stage III learners will be challenged by entertaining and practical language practice, such as performing skits, participating in a mock trial, completing a job application form, writing alternate lyrics to a popular song, and so on.

84. B: He is experiencing a high affective filter due possibly to culture shock, which is heightened by being placed with younger students, as well as by his inability to freely communicate. He may feel shame, insecurity, embarrassment, frustration, or a combination of these, which he compensates for and covers up with anger.

85. C: Self-Contained Model. The One Teacher Approach is one in which a single teacher working in a self-contained classroom carries the responsibility for her students' linguistic and academic achievement.

86. C: Refer the student to the school counselor, who is trained to help in situations such as this. It is essential that the teacher not violate the child's trust by reading the journal or showing it to anyone else. Such a violation of trust at this time could be very damaging. While the teacher should certainly monitor the situation and give close attention to the student's moods and behavior, she should not delay bringing the situation to the attention of the counselor.

87. B: No. She is not a trained translator, and, for this reason alone, is not suitable for this task. The school is legally responsible for providing a trained translator or materials in Basque, if they are available. The teacher must advocate on behalf of the student and try to find a trained translator or the materials in Basque. The fact that the volunteer translator is both the boy's aunt and the teacher's friend compounds the problem, in that her objectivity could be affected by her feelings and desire to help.

88. D: Learning tasks are authentic, challenging, and meaningful. Shared learning activities give students the opportunity to absorb learning strategies employed by other students. Students involved in a shared learning activity will speak, discuss, argue, and consider quite naturally. The opportunity for authentic dialogue is especially useful for ELLs. The more meaningful the task, the more involved and motivated the students—and the more authentic their dialogue—will be.

89. A: Project-based learning. Swain's theory of comprehensible output has resulted in practitioners who have developed strategies that are designed to create opportunities for face-to-face communication that requires authentic negotiation to arrive at shared meanings. In addition to project-based learning, other suggested strategies include cooperative learning, student-teacher individualized communications, and working with a partner to study selected materials.

90. B: ESL models are English-only and employ a specific methodology to teach English and continue to develop L1. Bilingual models introduce instruction concepts first in L1 and over time transfer them into English.

91. D: CALP: academic language requires abstract thinking. Cognitive Academic Language Proficiency is necessary for academic communication, requires content-specific vocabularies and more sophisticated syntax, and does not rely upon external contextual information, thereby requiring users to be able to think abstractly.

92. B: A writing sample. The permanent record must contain parental approval; program entry dates, exit dates, and notifications; designation of language proficiency level; recommendation for placement; LEP identification; criterion-referenced test exemption dates, as well as all pertaining documents; and ongoing monitoring results.

93. B: Grade level content is essential. Simplifying language without simplifying content will help ESL students remain at grade level. Language is the vehicle for meaning. It matters less how a student arrives at a relatively full understanding of the intended meaning, as long as she arrives at it at roughly the same time as her peers.

94. C: Language acquisition is natural, subconscious, and concerned with message content. Language learning is formal, concerned with grammatical rules, and conscious. This describes the Acquisition/Learning hypothesis of Krashen's extremely influential theory of second language acquisition. Of the two, acquisition is the more important, as it imitates the subconscious absorption of language that mimics similar processes young children experience when learning a first language, and because it requires authentic use of the language. Learning is the result of formal instruction about a language and is useful in support of subconscious acquisition.

Secret Key #1 - Time is Your Greatest Enemy

Pace Yourself

Wear a watch. At the beginning of the test, check the time (or start a chronometer on your watch to count the minutes), and check the time after every few questions to make sure you are "on schedule."

If you are forced to speed up, do it efficiently. Usually one or more answer choices can be eliminated without too much difficulty. Above all, don't panic. Don't speed up and just begin guessing at random choices. By pacing yourself, and continually monitoring your progress against your watch, you will always know exactly how far ahead or behind you are with your available time. If you find that you are one minute behind on the test, don't skip one question without spending any time on it, just to catch back up. Take 15 fewer seconds on the next four questions, and after four questions you'll have caught back up. Once you catch back up, you can continue working each problem at your normal pace.

Furthermore, don't dwell on the problems that you were rushed on. If a problem was taking up too much time and you made a hurried guess, it must be difficult. The difficult questions are the ones you are most likely to miss anyway, so it isn't a big loss. It is better to end with more time than you need than to run out of time.

Lastly, sometimes it is beneficial to slow down if you are constantly getting ahead of time. You are always more likely to catch a careless mistake by working more slowly than quickly, and among very high-scoring test takers (those who are likely to have lots of time left over), careless errors affect the score more than mastery of material.

Secret Key #2 - Guessing is not Guesswork

You probably know that guessing is a good idea - unlike other standardized tests, there is no penalty for getting a wrong answer. Even if you have no idea about a question, you still have a 20-25% chance of getting it right.

Most test takers do not understand the impact that proper guessing can have on their score. Unless you score extremely high, guessing will significantly contribute to your final score.

Monkeys Take the Test

What most test takers don't realize is that to insure that 20-25% chance, you have to guess randomly. If you put 20 monkeys in a room to take this test, assuming they answered once per question and behaved themselves, on average they would get 20-25% of the questions correct. Put 20 test takers in the room, and the average will be much lower among guessed questions. Why?

    1. The test writers intentionally write deceptive answer choices that "look" right. A test taker has no idea about a question, so picks the "best looking" answer, which is often wrong. The monkey has no idea what looks good and what doesn't, so will

consistently be lucky about 20-25% of the time.

2. Test takers will eliminate answer choices from the guessing pool based on a hunch or intuition. Simple but correct answers often get excluded, leaving a 0% chance of being correct. The monkey has no clue, and often gets lucky with the best choice.

This is why the process of elimination endorsed by most test courses is flawed and detrimental to your performance- test takers don't guess, they make an ignorant stab in the dark that is usually worse than random.

$5 Challenge

Let me introduce one of the most valuable ideas of this course- the $5 challenge:

You only mark your "best guess" if you are willing to bet $5 on it.
You only eliminate choices from guessing if you are willing to bet $5 on it.

Why $5? Five dollars is an amount of money that is small yet not insignificant, and can really add up fast (20 questions could cost you $100). Likewise, each answer choice on one question of the test will have a small impact on your overall score, but it can really add up to a lot of points in the end.

The process of elimination IS valuable. The following shows your chance of guessing it right:

If you eliminate wrong answer choices until only this many remain:	Chance of getting it correct:
1	100%
2	50%
3	33%

However, if you accidentally eliminate the right answer or go on a hunch for an incorrect answer, your chances drop dramatically: to 0%. By guessing among all the answer choices, you are GUARANTEED to have a shot at the right answer.

That's why the $5 test is so valuable- if you give up the advantage and safety of a pure guess, it had better be worth the risk.

What we still haven't covered is how to be sure that whatever guess you make is truly random. Here's the easiest way:

Always pick the first answer choice among those remaining.

Such a technique means that you have decided, **before you see a single test question**, exactly how you are going to guess- and since the order of choices tells you nothing about which one is correct, this guessing technique is perfectly random.

This section is not meant to scare you away from making educated guesses or eliminating choices- you just need to define when a choice is worth eliminating. The $5 test, along with a pre-defined random guessing strategy, is the best way to make sure you reap all of the benefits of guessing.

Secret Key #3 - Practice Smarter, Not Harder

Many test takers delay the test preparation process because they dread the awful amounts of practice time they think necessary to succeed on the test. We have refined an effective method that will take you only a fraction of the time.

There are a number of "obstacles" in your way to succeed. Among these are answering questions, finishing in time, and mastering test-taking strategies. All must be executed on the day of the test at peak performance, or your score will suffer. The test is a mental marathon that has a large impact on your future.
Just like a marathon runner, it is important to work your way up to the full challenge. So first you just worry about questions, and then time, and finally strategy:

Success Strategy

1. Find a good source for practice tests.
2. If you are willing to make a larger time investment, consider using more than one study guide- often the different approaches of multiple authors will help you "get" difficult concepts.
3. Take a practice test with no time constraints, with all study helps "open book." Take your time with questions and focus on applying strategies.
4. Take a practice test with time constraints, with all guides "open book."
5. Take a final practice test with no open material and time limits

If you have time to take more practice tests, just repeat step 5. By gradually exposing yourself to the full rigors of the test environment, you will condition your mind to the stress of test day and maximize your success.

Secret Key #4 - Prepare, Don't Procrastinate

Let me state an obvious fact: if you take the test three times, you will get three different scores. This is due to the way you feel on test day, the level of preparedness you have, and, despite the test writers' claims to the contrary, some tests WILL be easier for you than others.

Since your future depends so much on your score, you should maximize your chances of success. In order to maximize the likelihood of success, you've got to prepare in advance. This means taking practice tests and spending time learning the information and test taking strategies you will need to succeed.

Never take the test as a "practice" test, expecting that you can just take it again if you need to. Feel free to take sample tests on your own, but when you go to take the official test, be prepared, be focused, and do your best the first time!

Secret Key #5 - Test Yourself

Everyone knows that time is money. There is no need to spend too much of your time or too little of your time preparing for the test. You should only spend as much of your precious time preparing as is necessary for you to get the score you need.

Once you have taken a practice test under real conditions of time constraints, then you will know if you are ready for the test or not.

If you have scored extremely high the first time that you take the practice test, then there is not much point in spending countless hours studying. You are already there.

Benchmark your abilities by retaking practice tests and seeing how much you have improved. Once you score high enough to guarantee success, then you are ready.

If you have scored well below where you need, then knuckle down and begin studying in earnest. Check your improvement regularly through the use of practice tests under real conditions. Above all, don't worry, panic, or give up. The key is perseverance!

Then, when you go to take the test, remain confident and remember how well you did on the practice tests. If you can score high enough on a practice test, then you can do the same on the real thing.

General Strategies

The most important thing you can do is to ignore your fears and jump into the test immediately- do not be overwhelmed by any strange-sounding terms. You have to jump into the test like jumping into a pool- all at once is the easiest way.

Make Predictions
As you read and understand the question, try to guess what the answer will be. Remember that several of the answer choices are wrong, and once you begin reading them, your mind will immediately become cluttered with answer choices designed to throw you off. Your mind is typically the most focused immediately after you have read the question and digested its contents. If you can, try to predict what the correct answer will be. You may be surprised at what you can predict.

Quickly scan the choices and see if your prediction is in the listed answer choices. If it is, then you can be quite confident that you have the right answer. It still won't hurt to check the other answer choices, but most of the time, you've got it!

Answer the Question
It may seem obvious to only pick answer choices that answer the question, but the test writers can create some excellent answer choices that are wrong. Don't pick an answer just because it sounds right, or you believe it to be true. It MUST answer the question. Once you've made your selection, always go back and check it against the question and make sure that you didn't misread the question, and the answer choice does answer the question

posed.

Benchmark

After you read the first answer choice, decide if you think it sounds correct or not. If it doesn't, move on to the next answer choice. If it does, mentally mark that answer choice. This doesn't mean that you've definitely selected it as your answer choice, it just means that it's the best you've seen thus far. Go ahead and read the next choice. If the next choice is worse than the one you've already selected, keep going to the next answer choice. If the next choice is better than the choice you've already selected, mentally mark the new answer choice as your best guess.

The first answer choice that you select becomes your standard. Every other answer choice must be benchmarked against that standard. That choice is correct until proven otherwise by another answer choice beating it out. Once you've decided that no other answer choice seems as good, do one final check to ensure that your answer choice answers the question posed.

Valid Information

Don't discount any of the information provided in the question. Every piece of information may be necessary to determine the correct answer. None of the information in the question is there to throw you off (while the answer choices will certainly have information to throw you off). If two seemingly unrelated topics are discussed, don't ignore either. You can be confident there is a relationship, or it wouldn't be included in the question, and you are probably going to have to determine what is that relationship to find the answer.

Avoid "Fact Traps"

Don't get distracted by a choice that is factually true. Your search is for the answer that answers the question. Stay focused and don't fall for an answer that is true but incorrect. Always go back to the question and make sure you're choosing an answer that actually answers the question and is not just a true statement. An answer can be factually correct, but it MUST answer the question asked. Additionally, two answers can both be seemingly correct, so be sure to read all of the answer choices, and make sure that you get the one that BEST answers the question.

Milk the Question

Some of the questions may throw you completely off. They might deal with a subject you have not been exposed to, or one that you haven't reviewed in years. While your lack of knowledge about the subject will be a hindrance, the question itself can give you many clues that will help you find the correct answer. Read the question carefully and look for clues. Watch particularly for adjectives and nouns describing difficult terms or words that you don't recognize. Regardless of if you completely understand a word or not, replacing it with a synonym either provided or one you more familiar with may help you to understand what the questions are asking. Rather than wracking your mind about specific detailed information concerning a difficult term or word, try to use mental substitutes that are easier to understand.

The Trap of Familiarity

Don't just choose a word because you recognize it. On difficult questions, you may not recognize a number of words in the answer choices. The test writers don't put "make-believe" words on the test; so don't think that just because you only recognize all the words in one answer choice means that answer choice must be correct. If you only recognize words in one answer choice, then focus on that one. Is it correct? Try your best to determine if it is correct. If it is, that is great, but if it doesn't, eliminate it. Each word and answer choice you eliminate increases your chances of getting the question correct, even if you then have to guess among the unfamiliar choices.

Eliminate Answers

Eliminate choices as soon as you realize they are wrong. But be careful! Make sure you consider all of the possible answer choices. Just because one appears right, doesn't mean that the next one won't be even better! The test writers will usually put more than one good answer choice for every question, so read all of them. Don't worry if you are stuck between two that seem right. By getting down to just two remaining possible choices, your odds are now 50/50. Rather than wasting too much time, play the odds. You are guessing, but guessing wisely, because you've been able to knock out some of the answer choices that you know are wrong. If you are eliminating choices and realize that the last answer choice you are left with is also obviously wrong, don't panic. Start over and consider each choice again. There may easily be something that you missed the first time and will realize on the second pass.

Tough Questions

If you are stumped on a problem or it appears too hard or too difficult, don't waste time. Move on! Remember though, if you can quickly check for obviously incorrect answer choices, your chances of guessing correctly are greatly improved. Before you completely give up, at least try to knock out a couple of possible answers. Eliminate what you can and then guess at the remaining answer choices before moving on.

Brainstorm

If you get stuck on a difficult question, spend a few seconds quickly brainstorming. Run through the complete list of possible answer choices. Look at each choice and ask yourself, "Could this answer the question satisfactorily?" Go through each answer choice and consider it independently of the other. By systematically going through all possibilities, you may find something that you would otherwise overlook. Remember that when you get stuck, it's important to try to keep moving.

Read Carefully

Understand the problem. Read the question and answer choices carefully. Don't miss the question because you misread the terms. You have plenty of time to read each question thoroughly and make sure you understand what is being asked. Yet a happy medium must be attained, so don't waste too much time. You must read carefully, but efficiently.

Face Value

When in doubt, use common sense. Always accept the situation in the problem at face value. Don't read too much into it. These problems will not require you to make huge leaps of logic. The test writers aren't trying to throw you off with a cheap trick. If you have to go beyond creativity and make a leap of logic in order to have an answer choice answer the question, then you should look at the other answer choices. Don't overcomplicate the problem by creating theoretical relationships or explanations that will warp time or space. These are normal problems rooted in reality. It's just that the applicable relationship or explanation may not be readily apparent and you have to figure things out. Use your common sense to interpret anything that isn't clear.

Prefixes

If you're having trouble with a word in the question or answer choices, try dissecting it. Take advantage of every clue that the word might include. Prefixes and suffixes can be a huge help. Usually they allow you to determine a basic meaning. Pre- means before, post- means after, pro - is positive, de- is negative. From these prefixes and suffixes, you can get an idea of the general meaning of the word and try to put it into context. Beware though of any traps. Just because con is the opposite of pro, doesn't necessarily mean congress is the opposite of progress!

Hedge Phrases

Watch out for critical "hedge" phrases, such as likely, may, can, will often, sometimes, often, almost, mostly, usually, generally, rarely, sometimes. Question writers insert these hedge phrases to cover every possibility. Often an answer choice will be wrong simply because it leaves no room for exception. Avoid answer choices that have definitive words like "exactly," and "always".

Switchback Words

Stay alert for "switchbacks". These are the words and phrases frequently used to alert you to shifts in thought. The most common switchback word is "but". Others include although, however, nevertheless, on the other hand, even though, while, in spite of, despite, regardless of.

New Information

Correct answer choices will rarely have completely new information included. Answer choices typically are straightforward reflections of the material asked about and will directly relate to the question. If a new piece of information is included in an answer choice that doesn't even seem to relate to the topic being asked about, then that answer choice is likely incorrect. All of the information needed to answer the question is usually provided for you, and so you should not have to make guesses that are unsupported or choose answer choices that require unknown information that cannot be reasoned on its own.

Time Management

On technical questions, don't get lost on the technical terms. Don't spend too much time on any one question. If you don't know what a term means, then since you don't have a dictionary, odds are you aren't going to get much further. You should immediately recognize terms as whether or not you know them. If you don't, work with the other clues that you have, the other answer choices and terms provided, but don't waste too much time trying to figure out a difficult term.

Contextual Clues

Look for contextual clues. An answer can be right but not correct. The contextual clues will help you find the answer that is most right and is correct. Understand the context in which a phrase or statement is made. This will help you make important distinctions.

Don't Panic

Panicking will not answer any questions for you. Therefore, it isn't helpful. When you first see the question, if your mind goes blank, take a deep breath. Force yourself to mechanically go through the steps of solving the problem and using the strategies you've learned.

Pace Yourself

Don't get clock fever. It's easy to be overwhelmed when you're looking at a page full of questions, your mind is full of random thoughts and feeling confused, and the clock is ticking down faster than you would like. Calm down and maintain the pace that you have set for yourself. As long as you are on track by monitoring your pace, you are guaranteed to have enough time for yourself. When you get to the last few minutes of the test, it may seem like you won't have enough time left, but if you only have as many questions as you should have left at that point, then you're right on track!

Answer Selection

The best way to pick an answer choice is to eliminate all of those that are wrong, until only one is left and confirm that is the correct answer. Sometimes though, an answer choice may immediately look right. Be careful! Take a second to make sure that the other choices are not equally obvious. Don't make a hasty mistake. There are only two times that you should stop before checking other answers. First is when you are positive that the answer choice you have selected is correct. Second is when time is almost out and you have to make a quick guess!

Check Your Work

Since you will probably not know every term listed and the answer to every question, it is important that you get credit for the ones that you do know. Don't miss any questions through careless mistakes. If at all possible, try to take a second to look back over your answer selection and make sure you've selected the correct answer choice and haven't made a costly careless mistake (such as marking an answer choice that you didn't mean to mark). This quick double check should more than pay for itself in caught mistakes for the time it costs.

Beware of Directly Quoted Answers

Sometimes an answer choice will repeat word for word a portion of the question or reference section. However, beware of such exact duplication – it may be a trap! More than likely, the correct choice will paraphrase or summarize a point, rather than being exactly the same wording.

Slang

Scientific sounding answers are better than slang ones. An answer choice that begins "To compare the outcomes…" is much more likely to be correct than one that begins "Because some people insisted…"

Extreme Statements

Avoid wild answers that throw out highly controversial ideas that are proclaimed as established fact. An answer choice that states the "process should be used in certain situations, if…" is much more likely to be correct than one that states the "process should be discontinued completely." The first is a calm rational statement and doesn't even make a definitive, uncompromising stance, using a hedge word "if" to provide wiggle room, whereas the second choice is a radical idea and far more extreme.

Answer Choice Families

When you have two or more answer choices that are direct opposites or parallels, one of them is usually the correct answer. For instance, if one answer choice states "x increases" and another answer choice states "x decreases" or "y increases," then those two or three answer choices are very similar in construction and fall into the same family of answer choices. A family of answer choices is when two or three answer choices are very similar in construction, and yet often have a directly opposite meaning. Usually the correct answer choice will be in that family of answer choices. The "odd man out" or answer choice that doesn't seem to fit the parallel construction of the other answer choices is more likely to be incorrect.

Special Report: How to Overcome Test Anxiety

The very nature of tests caters to some level of anxiety, nervousness or tension, just as we feel for any important event that occurs in our lives. A little bit of anxiety or nervousness can be a good thing. It helps us with motivation, and makes achievement just that much sweeter. However, too much anxiety can be a problem; especially if it hinders our ability to function and perform.

"Test anxiety," is the term that refers to the emotional reactions that some test-takers experience when faced with a test or exam. Having a fear of testing and exams is based upon a rational fear, since the test-taker's performance can shape the course of an academic career. Nevertheless, experiencing excessive fear of examinations will only interfere with the test-takers ability to perform, and his/her chances to be successful.

There are a large variety of causes that can contribute to the development and sensation of test anxiety. These include, but are not limited to lack of performance and worrying about issues surrounding the test.

Lack of Preparation

Lack of preparation can be identified by the following behaviors or situations:

Not scheduling enough time to study, and therefore cramming the night before the test or exam
Managing time poorly, to create the sensation that there is not enough time to do everything
Failing to organize the text information in advance, so that the study material consists of the entire text and not simply the pertinent information
Poor overall studying habits

Worrying, on the other hand, can be related to both the test taker, or many other factors around him/her that will be affected by the results of the test. These include worrying about:

Previous performances on similar exams, or exams in general
How friends and other students are achieving
The negative consequences that will result from a poor grade or failure

There are three primary elements to test anxiety. Physical components, which involve the same typical bodily reactions as those to acute anxiety (to be discussed below). Emotional factors have to do with fear or panic. Mental or cognitive issues concerning attention spans and memory abilities.

Physical Signals

There are many different symptoms of test anxiety, and these are not limited to mental and emotional strain. Frequently there are a range of physical signals that will let a test taker know that he/she is suffering from test anxiety. These bodily changes can include the following:

Perspiring
Sweaty palms
Wet, trembling hands
Nausea
Dry mouth
A knot in the stomach
Headache
Faintness
Muscle tension
Aching shoulders, back and neck
Rapid heart beat
Feeling too hot/cold

To recognize the sensation of test anxiety, a test-taker should monitor him/herself for the following sensations:

The physical distress symptoms as listed above
Emotional sensitivity, expressing emotional feelings such as the need to cry or laugh too much, or a sensation of anger or helplessness
A decreased ability to think, causing the test-taker to blank out or have racing thoughts that are hard to organize or control.

Though most students will feel some level of anxiety when faced with a test or exam, the majority can cope with that anxiety and maintain it at a manageable level. However, those who cannot are faced with a very real and very serious condition, which can and should be controlled for the immeasurable benefit of this sufferer.

Naturally, these sensations lead to negative results for the testing experience. The most common effects of test anxiety have to do with nervousness and mental blocking.

Nervousness

Nervousness can appear in several different levels:

The test-taker's difficulty, or even inability to read and understand the questions on the test
The difficulty or inability to organize thoughts to a coherent form
The difficulty or inability to recall key words and concepts relating to the testing questions (especially essays)
The receipt of poor grades on a test, though the test material was well known by the test taker

Conversely, a person may also experience mental blocking, which involves:

Blanking out on test questions

Only remembering the correct answers to the questions when the test has already finished.

Fortunately for test anxiety sufferers, beating these feelings, to a large degree, has to do with proper preparation. When a test taker has a feeling of preparedness, then anxiety will be dramatically lessened.

The first step to resolving anxiety issues is to distinguish which of the two types of anxiety are being suffered. If the anxiety is a direct result of a lack of preparation, this should be considered a normal reaction, and the anxiety level (as opposed to the test results) shouldn't be anything to worry about. However, if, when adequately prepared, the test-taker still panics, blanks out, or seems to overreact, this is not a fully rational reaction. While this can be considered normal too, there are many ways to combat and overcome these effects.

Remember that anxiety cannot be entirely eliminated, however, there are ways to minimize it, to make the anxiety easier to manage. Preparation is one of the best ways to minimize test anxiety. Therefore the following techniques are wise in order to best fight off any anxiety that may want to build.

To begin with, try to avoid cramming before a test, whenever it is possible. By trying to memorize an entire term's worth of information in one day, you'll be shocking your system, and not giving yourself a very good chance to absorb the information. This is an easy path to anxiety, so for those who suffer from test anxiety, cramming should not even be considered an option.

Instead of cramming, work throughout the semester to combine all of the material which is presented throughout the semester, and work on it gradually as the course goes by, making sure to master the main concepts first, leaving minor details for a week or so before the test.

To study for the upcoming exam, be sure to pose questions that may be on the examination, to gauge the ability to answer them by integrating the ideas from your texts, notes and lectures, as well as any supplementary readings.

If it is truly impossible to cover all of the information that was covered in that particular term, concentrate on the most important portions, that can be covered very well. Learn these concepts as best as possible, so that when the test comes, a goal can be made to use these concepts as presentations of your knowledge.

In addition to study habits, changes in attitude are critical to beating a struggle with test anxiety. In fact, an improvement of the perspective over the entire test-taking experience can actually help a test taker to enjoy studying and therefore improve the overall experience. Be certain not to overemphasize the significance of the grade - know that the result of the test is neither a reflection of self worth, nor is it a measure of intelligence; one grade will not predict a person's future success.

To improve an overall testing outlook, the following steps should be tried:

Keeping in mind that the most reasonable expectation for taking a test is to expect to try to demonstrate as much of what you know as you possibly can.

Reminding ourselves that a test is only one test; this is not the only one, and there will be others.

The thought of thinking of oneself in an irrational, all-or-nothing term should be avoided at all costs.

A reward should be designated for after the test, so there's something to look forward to. Whether it be going to a movie, going out to eat, or simply visiting friends, schedule it in advance, and do it no matter what result is expected on the exam.

Test-takers should also keep in mind that the basics are some of the most important things, even beyond anti-anxiety techniques and studying. Never neglect the basic social, emotional and biological needs, in order to try to absorb information. In order to best achieve, these three factors must be held as just as important as the studying itself.

Study Steps

Remember the following important steps for studying:

Maintain healthy nutrition and exercise habits. Continue both your recreational activities and social pass times. These both contribute to your physical and emotional well being.

Be certain to get a good amount of sleep, especially the night before the test, because when you're overtired you are not able to perform to the best of your best ability.

Keep the studying pace to a moderate level by taking breaks when they are needed, and varying the work whenever possible, to keep the mind fresh instead of getting bored. When enough studying has been done that all the material that can be learned has been learned, and the test taker is prepared for the test, stop studying and do something relaxing such as listening to music, watching a movie, or taking a warm bubble bath.

There are also many other techniques to minimize the uneasiness or apprehension that is experienced along with test anxiety before, during, or even after the examination. In fact, there are a great deal of things that can be done to stop anxiety from interfering with lifestyle and performance. Again, remember that anxiety will not be eliminated entirely, and it shouldn't be. Otherwise that "up" feeling for exams would not exist, and most of us depend on that sensation to perform better than usual. However, this anxiety has to be at a level that is manageable.

Of course, as we have just discussed, being prepared for the exam is half the battle right away. Attending all classes, finding out what knowledge will be expected on the exam, and knowing the exam schedules are easy steps to lowering anxiety. Keeping up with work will remove the need to cram, and efficient study habits will eliminate wasted time. Studying should be done in an ideal location for concentration, so that it is simple to become interested in the material and give it complete attention. A method such as SQ3R (Survey, Question, Read, Recite, Review) is a wonderful key to follow to make sure that the study habits are as effective as possible, especially in the case of learning from a textbook. Flashcards are great techniques for memorization. Learning to take good notes will mean that notes will be full of useful information, so that less sifting will need to be done to seek out what is pertinent for studying. Reviewing notes after class and then again on occasion will keep the information fresh in the mind. From notes that have been taken summary sheets and outlines can be made for simpler reviewing.

A study group can also be a very motivational and helpful place to study, as there will be a sharing of ideas, all of the minds can work together, to make sure that everyone understands, and the studying will be made more interesting because it will be a social occasion.

Basically, though, as long as the test-taker remains organized and self confident, with efficient study habits, less time will need to be spent studying, and higher grades will be achieved.

To become self confident, there are many useful steps. The first of these is "self talk." It has been shown through extensive research, that self-talk for students who suffer from test anxiety, should be well monitored, in order to make sure that it contributes to self confidence as opposed to sinking the student. Frequently the self talk of test-anxious students is negative or self-defeating, thinking that everyone else is smarter and faster, that they always mess up, and that if they don't do well, they'll fail the entire course. It is important to decreasing anxiety that awareness is made of self talk. Try writing any negative self thoughts and then disputing them with a positive statement instead. Begin self-encouragement as though it was a friend speaking. Repeat positive statements to help reprogram the mind to believing in successes instead of failures.

Helpful Techniques

Other extremely helpful techniques include:

Self-visualization of doing well and reaching goals
While aiming for an "A" level of understanding, don't try to "overprotect" by setting your expectations lower. This will only convince the mind to stop studying in order to meet the lower expectations.
Don't make comparisons with the results or habits of other students. These are individual factors, and different things work for different people, causing different results.
Strive to become an expert in learning what works well, and what can be done in order to improve. Consider collecting this data in a journal.
Create rewards for after studying instead of doing things before studying that will only turn into avoidance behaviors.
Make a practice of relaxing - by using methods such as progressive relaxation, self-hypnosis, guided imagery, etc - in order to make relaxation an automatic sensation.
Work on creating a state of relaxed concentration so that concentrating will take on the focus of the mind, so that none will be wasted on worrying.
Take good care of the physical self by eating well and getting enough sleep.
Plan in time for exercise and stick to this plan.

Beyond these techniques, there are other methods to be used before, during and after the test that will help the test-taker perform well in addition to overcoming anxiety.

Before the exam comes the academic preparation. This involves establishing a study schedule and beginning at least one week before the actual date of the test. By doing this, the anxiety of not having enough time to study for the test will be automatically eliminated. Moreover, this will make the studying a much more effective experience, ensuring that the learning will be an easier process. This relieves much undue pressure on the test-taker.

Summary sheets, note cards, and flash cards with the main concepts and examples of these main concepts should be prepared in advance of the actual studying time. A topic should never be eliminated from this process. By omitting a topic because it isn't expected to be on the test is only setting up the test-taker for anxiety should it actually appear on the exam. Utilize the course syllabus for laying out the topics that should be studied. Carefully go over the notes that were made in class, paying special attention to any of the issues that the professor took special care to emphasize while lecturing in class. In the textbooks, use the chapter review, or if possible, the chapter tests, to begin your review.

It may even be possible to ask the instructor what information will be covered on the exam, or what the format of the exam will be (for example, multiple choice, essay, free form, true-false). Additionally, see if it is possible to find out how many questions will be on the test. If a review sheet or sample test has been offered by the professor, make good use of it, above anything else, for the preparation for the test. Another great resource for getting to know the examination is reviewing tests from previous semesters. Use these tests to review, and aim to achieve a 100% score on each of the possible topics. With a few exceptions, the goal that you set for yourself is the highest one that you will reach.

Take all of the questions that were assigned as homework, and rework them to any other possible course material. The more problems reworked, the more skill and confidence will form as a result. When forming the solution to a problem, write out each of the steps. Don't simply do head work. By doing as many steps on paper as possible, much clarification and therefore confidence will be formed. Do this with as many homework problems as possible, before checking the answers. By checking the answer after each problem, a reinforcement will exist, that will not be on the exam. Study situations should be as exam-like as possible, to prime the test-taker's system for the experience. By waiting to check the answers at the end, a psychological advantage will be formed, to decrease the stress factor.

Another fantastic reason for not cramming is the avoidance of confusion in concepts, especially when it comes to mathematics. 8-10 hours of study will become one hundred percent more effective if it is spread out over a week or at least several days, instead of doing it all in one sitting. Recognize that the human brain requires time in order to assimilate new material, so frequent breaks and a span of study time over several days will be much more beneficial.

Additionally, don't study right up until the point of the exam. Studying should stop a minimum of one hour before the exam begins. This allows the brain to rest and put things in their proper order. This will also provide the time to become as relaxed as possible when going into the examination room. The test-taker will also have time to eat well and eat sensibly. Know that the brain needs food as much as the rest of the body. With enough food and enough sleep, as well as a relaxed attitude, the body and the mind are primed for success.

Avoid any anxious classmates who are talking about the exam. These students only spread anxiety, and are not worth sharing the anxious sentimentalities.

Before the test also involves creating a positive attitude, so mental preparation should also be a point of concentration. There are many keys to creating a positive attitude. Should fears become rushing in, make a visualization of taking the exam, doing well, and seeing an A written on the paper. Write out a list of affirmations that will bring a feeling of confidence, such as "I am doing well in my English class," "I studied well and know my material," "I enjoy this class." Even if the affirmations aren't believed at first, it sends a positive message to the subconscious which will result in an alteration of the overall belief system, which is the system that creates reality.

If a sensation of panic begins, work with the fear and imagine the very worst! Work through the entire scenario of not passing the test, failing the entire course, and dropping out of school, followed by not getting a job, and pushing a shopping cart through the dark alley where you'll live. This will place things into perspective! Then, practice deep breathing and create a visualization of the opposite situation - achieving an "A" on the exam, passing the entire course, receiving the degree at a graduation ceremony.

On the day of the test, there are many things to be done to ensure the best results, as well as the most calm outlook. The following stages are suggested in order to maximize test-taking potential:

Begin the examination day with a moderate breakfast, and avoid any coffee or beverages with caffeine if the test taker is prone to jitters. Even people who are used to managing caffeine can feel jittery or light-headed when it is taken on a test day.
Attempt to do something that is relaxing before the examination begins. As last minute cramming clouds the mastering of overall concepts, it is better to use this time to create a calming outlook.
Be certain to arrive at the test location well in advance, in order to provide time to select a location that is away from doors, windows and other distractions, as well as giving enough time to relax before the test begins.
Keep away from anxiety generating classmates who will upset the sensation of stability and relaxation that is being attempted before the exam.
Should the waiting period before the exam begins cause anxiety, create a self-distraction by reading a light magazine or something else that is relaxing and simple.

During the exam itself, read the entire exam from beginning to end, and find out how much time should be allotted to each individual problem. Once writing the exam, should more time be taken for a problem, it should be abandoned, in order to begin another problem. If there is time at the end, the unfinished problem can always be returned to and completed.

Read the instructions very carefully - twice - so that unpleasant surprises won't follow during or after the exam has ended.

When writing the exam, pretend that the situation is actually simply the completion of homework within a library, or at home. This will assist in forming a relaxed atmosphere, and will allow the brain extra focus for the complex thinking function.

Begin the exam with all of the questions with which the most confidence is felt. This will build the confidence level regarding the entire exam and will begin a quality momentum. This will also create encouragement for trying the problems where uncertainty resides.

Going with the "gut instinct" is always the way to go when solving a problem. Second guessing should be avoided at all costs. Have confidence in the ability to do well.

For essay questions, create an outline in advance that will keep the mind organized and make certain that all of the points are remembered. For multiple choice, read every answer, even if the correct one has been spotted - a better one may exist.

Continue at a pace that is reasonable and not rushed, in order to be able to work carefully. Provide enough time to go over the answers at the end, to check for small errors that can be corrected.

Should a feeling of panic begin, breathe deeply, and think of the feeling of the body releasing sand through its pores. Visualize a calm, peaceful place, and include all of the sights, sounds and sensations of this image. Continue the deep breathing, and take a few minutes to continue this with closed eyes. When all is well again, return to the test.

If a "blanking" occurs for a certain question, skip it and move on to the next question. There will be time to return to the other question later. Get everything done that can be done, first, to guarantee all the grades that can be compiled, and to build all of the confidence possible. Then return to the weaker questions to build the marks from there.

Remember, one's own reality can be created, so as long as the belief is there, success will follow. And remember: anxiety can happen later, right now, there's an exam to be written!

After the examination is complete, whether there is a feeling for a good grade or a bad grade, don't dwell on the exam, and be certain to follow through on the reward that was promised...and enjoy it! Don't dwell on any mistakes that have been made, as there is nothing that can be done at this point anyway.

Additionally, don't begin to study for the next test right away. Do something relaxing for a while, and let the mind relax and prepare itself to begin absorbing information again.

From the results of the exam - both the grade and the entire experience, be certain to learn from what has gone on. Perfect studying habits and work some more on confidence in order to make the next examination experience even better than the last one.

Learn to avoid places where openings occurred for laziness, procrastination and day dreaming.

Use the time between this exam and the next one to better learn to relax, even learning to relax on cue, so that any anxiety can be controlled during the next exam. Learn how to relax the body. Slouch in your chair if that helps. Tighten and then relax all of the different muscle groups, one group at a time, beginning with the feet and then working all the way up to the neck and face. This will ultimately relax the muscles more than they were to begin with. Learn how to breathe deeply and comfortably, and focus on this breathing going in and out as a relaxing thought. With every exhale, repeat the word "relax."

As common as test anxiety is, it is very possible to overcome it. Make yourself one of the test-takers who overcome this frustrating hindrance.

Special Report: Retaking the Test: What Are Your Chances at Improving Your Score?

After going through the experience of taking a major test, many test takers feel that once is enough. The test usually comes during a period of transition in the test taker's life, and taking the test is only one of a series of important events. With so many distractions and conflicting recommendations, it may be difficult for a test taker to rationally determine whether or not he should retake the test after viewing his scores.

The importance of the test usually only adds to the burden of the retake decision. However, don't be swayed by emotion. There a few simple questions that you can ask yourself to guide you as you try to determine whether a retake would improve your score:

1. What went wrong? Why wasn't your score what you expected?

Can you point to a single factor or problem that you feel caused the low score? Were you sick on test day? Was there an emotional upheaval in your life that caused a distraction? Were you late for the test or not able to use the full time allotment? If you can point to any of these specific, individual problems, then a retake should definitely be considered.

2. Is there enough time to improve?

Many problems that may show up in your score report may take a lot of time for improvement. A deficiency in a particular math skill may require weeks or months of tutoring and studying to improve. If you have enough time to improve an identified weakness, then a retake should definitely be considered.

3. How will additional scores be used? Will a score average, highest score, or most recent score be used?

Different test scores may be handled completely differently. If you've taken the test multiple times, sometimes your highest score is used, sometimes your average score is computed and used, and sometimes your most recent score is used. Make sure you understand what method will be used to evaluate your scores, and use that to help you determine whether a retake should be considered.

4. Are my practice test scores significantly higher than my actual test score?

If you have taken a lot of practice tests and are consistently scoring at a much higher level than your actual test score, then you should consider a retake. However, if you've taken five practice tests and only one of your scores was higher than your actual test score, or if your practice test scores were only slightly higher than your actual test score, then it is unlikely that you will significantly increase your score.

5. Do I need perfect scores or will I be able to live with this score? Will this score still allow me to follow my dreams?

What kind of score is acceptable to you? Is your current score "good enough?" Do you have to have a certain score in order to pursue the future of your dreams? If you won't be happy with your current score, and there's no way that you could live with it, then you should consider a retake. However, don't get your hopes up. If you are looking for significant improvement, that may or may not be possible. But if you won't be happy otherwise, it is at least worth the effort.
Remember that there are other considerations. To achieve your dream, it is likely that your grades may also be taken into account. A great test score is usually not the only thing necessary to succeed. Make sure that you aren't overemphasizing the importance of a high test score.

Furthermore, a retake does not always result in a higher score. Some test takers will score lower on a retake, rather than higher. One study shows that one-fourth of test takers will achieve a significant improvement in test score, while one-sixth of test takers will actually show a decrease. While this shows that most test takers will improve, the majority will only improve their scores a little and a retake may not be worth the test taker's effort.

Finally, if a test is taken only once and is considered in the added context of good grades on the part of a test taker, the person reviewing the grades and scores may be tempted to assume that the test taker just had a bad day while taking the test, and may discount the low test score in favor of the high grades. But if the test is retaken and the scores are approximately the same, then the validity of the low scores are only confirmed. Therefore, a retake could actually hurt a test taker by definitely bracketing a test taker's score ability to a limited range.

Special Report: Additional Bonus Material

Due to our efforts to try to keep this book to a manageable length, we've created a link that will give you access to all of your additional bonus material.

Please visit http://www.mometrix.com/bonus948/priiengspotlan to access the information.